1

WOMAN ALONE AROUND AFRICA

A tale of courage and overcoming the seemingly impossible

JO RUST

Publishing Resources

First published by the author, Jo Rust, 2018.

Postnet Suite 421, Private Bag X1, Jukskei Park, 2153, Gauteng, South Africa

www.jorustadventures.com

ISBN 978-0-620-81398-3

e-ISBN 978-0-620-81377-8

Text design and typesetting by Alison Shepherd, Publishing Resources.
Cover design by Matthew du Preez, Publishing Resources.

Front cover photograph of Jo Rust by Jo Rust.
Back cover photograph of Jo Rust by Jo Rust.

CONTENTS

PROLOGUE

What is the earliest memory of your life? If you took a moment right now and thought back to what you think may be your very first memory, what does it look like? Some people can recall memories from a very young age, while others can't. I have a friend who claims that she can vividly recall the moment she was born. She describes it as a moment where she went from feeling warm, comfortable and happily ignorant to a moment of being exposed to a severe light that hurt her eyes, sounds that felt like they were going to burst her eardrums, moments of disorientation and an onslaught to her senses. I personally think she's confusing this memory of being born with one of waking up with a bad hangover.

One of my earliest memories is of when I embarked on my very first solo adventure! I remember it like it was yesterday. My mother was sitting on the couch at the front door, wearing a brown summer dress with white polka dots (this was the early eighties after all), feeding my baby brother. It was the day after my birthday and I had received a little pink tea set from my grandparents as a gift for my birthday. My Godparents happened to live fairly close by and I somehow got it into my head that I wanted to go and show my God parents, of whom I was very fond, this little pink tea set I had received for my birthday.

At this point, I feel the need to mention that, since I can remember (and to this day still), I have a very active imagination. I have always lived in a very colourful world and used to - not so much today anymore - converse with imaginary friends and mythical creatures and live in my own wonderland. So it comes as little surprise that when I told my mother I was going off to my Godparents' to show them the tea set I had received for my birthday, she thought little of it. She looked at me with caring eyes and a soft smile and told me to have fun and be careful.

With that, I packed a little vintage suitcase that my father had given me - a cute, little school case that a child at primary school in the 1960's might have used. I packed my tea set in the case and off I went, along with my ever faithful dog, Sweetheart. The one detail of this story that I cannot recall is: who named the dog?

My Godparents, Sheila and Peter, lived about three kilometers from where we lived. I'd been there numerous times and had no doubt in my little, imaginative, overconfident mind that I would have no trouble finding it. A few hours later, wandering around the neighbourhood, I realized that I had no idea where I was and started doubting whether I was actually heading in the right direction. Sweetheart had abandoned me by now, I figured she had probably gone back home. I hoped she had found her way home as I didn't know how I would begin to explain later on that I'd lost our dog.

Then, a police vehicle pulled up next to me and my mother, who seemed strangely frantic to me, jumped out of the car, ran over to where I was standing on the grass on the verge, kneeled in front of me, pulled me into her arms and with tears in her eyes, kept repeating "Never ever do that to me again!"

I was no more than four years old when I embarked on my first ever solo adventure. I figure they should have known then...

CHAPTER 1

I don't always know how I get myself into these types of situations, but what I do know is that this is exactly where I'm supposed to be. I'm taped to a chair, my mouth is taped shut and a man, obviously high on some drug, wearing a Kentucky Fried Chicken beanie, is standing in front of me, pointing a loaded gun at my head. The one question that keeps flashing through my head is,

"Are you willing to die for your dream?" The answer is simply and resolutely, with every cell of my being... yes. I have no choice really... I made myself that promise.

The day I decided I wanted to be the first woman to travel around the African continent alone wasn't exactly a moment of elation, but rather an idea born out of a moment of desperation. The first question I am always asked by people who have heard of or read about my solo journey around the notorious 'dark continent' is, "Why?" Why would any person who is sane of mind want to travel alone around and through, what is considered to be, one of the most dangerous and hostile environments on this planet? Well maybe it wasn't a moment of sanity, but rather one of not knowing what else to do.

You see, in my mind, on that fateful day back in October of 2007, I only had two choices. Either take my own life or fight back and do epic shit. I figured back then that destroying myself wouldn't really serve any justifiable purpose, plus I didn't actually have the guts to go through with it and so I opted for doing something epic. The question was just: What?

I am no stranger to depression and debilitating anxiety, what it feels like, the God-awful stench of it and how it can nearly destroy you. How it can smother you and push you down into the deepest, darkest of pits. It's a horrible thing to have to fight against and yet, over 300 million people on this planet face that battle every single day. On the fateful day that I contemplated taking my own life, I experienced the deepest, darkest pit that I don't want to ever visit again in this or any other lifetime.

I grew up a 'gentle old soul'. I have lost count of how many people told me I was an old soul and a gentle child while growing up. A soft-spoken, gentle-hearted, sensitive child from Johannesburg, South Africa. What would cause such a human being to end up in a place where she would feel trapped, helpless and broken - and considering taking her own life? Well... life really. Life can be pretty cruel at times, as I'm sure most of you have experienced. Without going into too much detail, I'll give it to you in a nutshell. It's a few pages of 'not-so-nice' stuff and then we'll get into the good stuff.

I am the eldest of two children, my younger brother and I. My parents married young, as most people did back in the 70's and 80's. They had us two children shortly after they got married and were thrown right into enjoying the responsibilities of taking care of a family, I'm sure a lot of new parents will agree, this can be quite stressful. We lived in a house along with my paternal grandparents. At first, life was great and we were a happy, middle-class family who laughed a lot, had more than we needed and loved one another. As we got older and started going to school, things started changing and we went from four people in the house who worked and provided for the household to three, then two and then only one person who could hold down a job - my father.

I remember the day when, before going to school, my father sat my brother and I down, to explain to us that he wouldn't be able to give us lunch money every day anymore, that we were struggling with money and that he needed our help in understanding that we won't have as much as we used to have before. I looked at my father and felt my tiny, soft heart breaking as I could see the heartache in his eyes. I opened his hand and placed in it the lunch money he had given me and told him that I didn't need it.

As a young, pre-teen child, I suffered incestuous sexual molestation by a female relative. Needless to say, this has caused many issues on various levels. The stage was set, I was broken.

Alcohol abuse became the means by which the adults around me chose to deal with their woes and sorrows. It became worse and worse over the years, to the point where I left home at the age of 17 while I was still in high school. I moved into a commune with a group of male friends who worked at the same restaurant where I was working at weekends to earn some pocket money. On my 18th birthday, I was raped by one of the boys in the house. I dropped out of high school in the final year, but later, went back to finish with Distinctions.

In my final year at school, I had met my first great love. A really handsome boy with a lot going for him, I fell head over heels for the very first time in my life. After school, I secured a job as a Legal Aid at a law firm in the local town. We decided that we wanted to travel the world together and so I quit my job at the legal firm after about six months and we flew to Israel, where we worked on a Kibbutz for a couple of months.

It was my first big adventure traveling through a foreign country and, although I felt scared and unsure at first in a new and strange environment, I absolutely loved the adventure of seeing new places, learning about new cultures and having new experiences. We bought two bicycles six months into our stay in the country and decided that we wanted to cycle from north to south, heading to Eilat. We were based on a kibbutz called Yizra'el, just north of Afula and south of Nazareth. The locals told us that we were crazy to cycle through the country in the summer but, despite the heat, we set out on our adventure and loved every second of it! We ran out of money soon after we completed our adventure through Israel and decided to head home.

I found it very difficult to integrate back into 'normal life'. You know, working in a permanent job with a steady salary, getting married and having 2.5 children, a white picket fence and a Labrador. I had tasted true adventure and struggled with having to settle back into a 'normal' life again. We were flat broke, which made finding a job our top priority. For the next three years, we moved in and out of jobs and struggled to make ends meet. We both found jobs at the same firm working in IT. Sitting in that office, day in and day out, I could feel myself dying from the inside out. My soul was crying out to me, saying,

"You know this is not what you're supposed to be doing." We wanted different things in life and slowly started drifting apart until we made one another just miserable. I loved him a great deal but knew that we were not meant to be together for the rest of our lives. It took me a while to pluck up the courage to finally sit down together and bring an end to our relationship. It was the hardest thing I'd ever had to do in my life... and a few weeks later after I had moved out, he passed away.

My father called me to give me the news. I remember it like yesterday. I answered the phone and my father just said,

"You have to be brave now". At that very point in my life, my whole world came crashing down in tiny pieces. It was like all the pain and suffering and hurt over the years of dealing with abuse, an alcoholic family, being molested as a child, being raped on my eighteenth birthday, the emotional turmoil - it all came to a big, ugly boiling point and I finally broke down. It was the worst day of my entire life.

Shortly after the funeral, I found myself in the deepest, darkest pit of depression I have ever experienced, before or since. I was barely functioning and had no will to walk this earth anymore. It was as if all the years' of abuse and trauma had finally managed to break me and I couldn't fight back anymore.

Then one fateful day, just as I thought I could not find any more strength to go on, I found myself sitting in a swing that hung from a tree in the front yard of the house I was sharing with two other friends and colleagues. I was holding a razor blade, weeping, feeling totally broken and tattered. I was staring at my wrists as the tears rolled down my face and onto the ground, trying to imagine what it would feel like to die.

While I finally cried, releasing what felt like the very last tear that I have been given for this lifetime, something strange happened. A great calm came over me, like I had been covered with a cloak of love and understanding. I took a few deep breaths and felt extremely exhausted. Then I heard a voice in my head.

It was a comforting and understanding voice that felt almost like my future-self talking to me and it said,

"Dearest Jo, if you want your life to be different and if you want change, then you are the only person who can make that happen. No one else can do it for you".

So, I asked myself a question,

"What is the biggest, boldest, scariest thing I can think of doing with my life?" I have been at the bottom, feeling like I didn't want to live anymore, now I would live a life worth living and do it in the biggest way I possibly could, no matter how scared I felt. I loved adventure and travel and wanted to do something extraordinary.

And in that moment, I made both a decision and a promise to myself.

I would be the first woman in history to travel around the African continent solo and I promised myself that I would never again even consider giving up on myself! (I would break that promise later on). And just like that, I made up my mind that I would stop everything I was doing and focus all my energy on my goal to travel around the African continent alone. An epic adventure that would push me to my limits physically, mentally and emotionally.

The next morning, I went to work and resigned from the last office job I ever held. Upon handing in my resignation to the person to whom I reported, he just looked up at me and said, "You're an asshole". Those were the last words I heard as I walked out of the office.

Then the planning began.

I was left with no employment - by choice - and a very big, audacious dream. My idea was to start small and prove myself capable of being able to travel long distances on my own so that potential sponsors might feel more willing to invest in me. The plan was to start off with cycling from Johannesburg to Cape Town on my own. I managed to make the journey, on my own, in 15 days. This was in 2008.

Time to step it up. In the form of a cycle around South Africa. Yes. With some help from friends and friendly volunteers, all my accommodation was sponsored by lodging establishments en route. The event also starting getting a bit more coverage in the media by way of newspaper articles and radio interviews. The journey lasted exactly 100 days over a distance of 5951 kilometers. That was in 2010. (I know... I should have gone around the block a couple of times to make it 6000, but I didn't and it's something I have to live with for the rest of my life). But, it was 5951 kilometers closer to my goal.

I felt that I was ready to finally tackle the African continent and decided to focus all my attention on getting the funding and sponsorships I needed to make this happen. Between 2010 and 2011, my time was spent working as a waitress at a local restaurant in town, writing proposals and having meetings with potential sponsors. The money wasn't forthcoming and the money I made in tips at the restaurant barely kept me going.

I tried to arrange a number of fundraisers with help from some of my friends. These all helped but never really brought in anything substantial enough to get me going. At one point, I was so broke that I would eat mieliepap (A south African porridge) every day, hustle pool tables to try and make some money (I was pretty good at the game of pool at the time) and steal toilet paper out of the toilets at the bars where I played pool. Not something I am proud of, but I needed to survive.

I never gave up and finally a couple of sponsors started to get on board. A company based in Australia called 'Apres Velo' (meaning 'after cycling' in French) wanted to sponsor my clothing. A stranger, named Guy Pearce, who I had never met before, sent me an email one day, after hearing an interview I did on the radio and he said that he would like to sponsor me R10 000 - approximately US$1250 at the time. He explained that he did not want anything in return and wanted purely to see me succeed. I was at a loss for words.

The restaurant where I was working at the time, Picobella, in Melville, Johannesburg, got on board with sponsoring the panniers for my bicycle and a friend of mine, Hanret Snyman, bought my tent! Things were moving, I could start to get excited, all the hours spent fundraising were starting to pay off. I had all the essentials needed for this venture, bar the money. I couldn't help but feel that if I waited until I had everything needed for this journey, I would be waiting for a very long time. I didn't even have enough money to see me through two months on the road, let alone around the entire African continent. I knew that, somehow, if I stayed the course, everything would work out.

It was after I had conducted one of numerous radio interviews, on my plans to cycle around the African continent that another very useful sponsorship came in the form of some tactical training. I received a call from an unknown number, the man on the other side explained that he had heard my interview over the radio, that he felt very concerned about my safety and that his company would like to offer me some training in self-defence. To this day, I don't know how they came by my number, but for the next two months I underwent tactical training provided by two ex-Special Forces Officers in Pretoria. It was the most gruelling - and only - combat training I had ever undergone, but I loved every second of it as I knew that someday, it could potentially save my life.

Training consisted of hand-to-hand combat, handling numerous types of weapons, hostage situation training and I was even physically kidnapped one evening as the final task in my training. I will forever be grateful for what I learned from those men during that time.

In April 2011, I flew to Cape Town - also known as the Mother City - from Johannesburg, to finally set off on accomplishing my dream of becoming the first woman to travel around the African continent, solo. I would set off from Camps Bay and some friends gathered on the day to see me off. It was early morning as we gathered at the Vida Cafe facing the promenade. There were loads of cyclists out for their morning run, joggers and people out to have an early morning coffee, along with reading the newspaper. For them, it was a normal day. For me and my team, a tangible excitement hung in the air.

When the time finally came for me to push off and start my mammoth journey - or maybe just another step in my mammoth journey - some friends made it extra special by sending me off playing on their Djembe African drums. The drums attracted some attention and all of a sudden, I felt very self- conscious. It dawned on me that a lot of people would be keeping an eye on me from then on. As I made my way past the famous Victoria and Alfred Waterfront and headed toward the N7 highway that would carry me all the way to Namibia, I started settling in and retreated to a place in which I would become familiar and comfortable in the months to come, while in my own mind, it was "okay, so this is it, I'm finally on my way. Am I supposed to feel nervous? Because I don't feel very nervous. I don't feel very well either. In fact, it might be my imagination but it feels like I'm coming down with something? Maybe it's just nerves".

It wasn't nerves. I suspect that after all the preparation and build up to this momentous day in my life, my body had let go of all the stress and worry it had coped with for so long and was going into shut down mode. The timing was impeccable! This was just the first day and I could barely reach my first destination, Malmesbury, a mere 80 kilometers from Camps Bay! By the time I did, I checked into a guesthouse, along with my friend, Hanret, and her Mom, who had driven the first day with me for moral support, and collapsed on the bed. Was this some kind of sign?

I had come down with a bad bout of flu and would be unable to continue the next day. I felt miserable and so emotional, but not deterred in any way. From then on, it wouldn't matter what the Universe threw at me, I would bat it as best I could. I took this small glitch to be a sign that said,

"This is going to be anything but easy, so you had better be very sure that this is what you want to do".

I had made a promise to myself and as sure as day and night succeed each other, there was no way in hell that I would even consider giving up! I might not have been blessed with the most robust immune system, but I have been blessed with enough stubbornness to last ten lifetimes!

And so, after a day's rest, I set out again, heading towards Piketberg, 67 kilometers away from Malmesbury. My health wasn't anywhere near where it should have been to be cycling long distances with a loaded bike as well, but I also felt that I needed to get a move on. As long as I kept moving forward, I'd get a little closer to achieving my goal. My focus was now solely on making it to Namibia, previously part of and now a neighboring country to South Africa. . I'd never been to Namibia before and felt very excited about crossing the border to new frontiers.

The gear that I was carrying on my bicycle weighed in at about close to 50 kilograms! This included everything I needed to carry with me to be self-sufficient. Clothes, water, food, camping equipment, spares, tools, toiletries, maps and my journals. My equipment consisted of:

Camping:

1 x 2 man, 4 season tent
1 x -5 grade sleeping bag
1 x ground sheet
1 x set of cooking pots and utensils
4 x 1,5 liter water bottles
1 x headlamp
1 x MSR Expedition camping stove
1 x Thermarest air mattress;

Clothing:
5 x change of clothing for on and off the bike
1 x warm jacket
1 x compact rain jacket
1 x pair cleated mountain biking shoes
1 x camelback hydration pack
1 x cycling helmet
4 x gloves
Underwear and socks;

Toiletries:
Basic toiletries
Mosquito repellant
Comprehensive first aid kit - sponsored by ER24
Malaria testing kit.

I spent two nights in a town called Springbok, a town situated 120 kilometers before the Vioolsdrif border crossing to Namibia. The Masonic Hotel very kindly sponsored my stay and I used this time to inspect my bicycle to make sure that everything was in good running order, doing some laundry and catching up on writing in my journal. I learned that it takes great discipline to keep up a journal while travelling. It's something that requires real commitment. The rest was just what I needed to finally shake off the flu and regain some much-needed energy for the road ahead.

CHAPTER 2

The day finally arrived where I would be crossing my first official border! I felt so excited that the 100 and something kilometers to the border felt like nothing. I was just enjoying the sights and imagining what it would look like on the other side of the border. You know how you try to imagine what the landscape might look like on the other side of a border? That's exactly what I was doing. I was imagining myself traveling through a portal to another dimension.

Having my passport stamped out of South Africa and into Namibia took all of 10 minutes. No fuss, no hassles, easy peasy. As I pushed my bicycle across the border with anticipation as to what I might see, it soon became very clear that it looks pretty much exactly the same on both sides of the border. Even though this was a slight let down, I still found myself in high spirits as I had just successfully crossed my first official border on my journey. This was good progress!

Because I had very little in the way of finances, my plan was to camp as much as possible from there. I knew I'd have to come up with a plan to secure more money soon as I hardly had enough to see myself through Namibia. I had already decided that I would try to get in touch with the same man (we'll call him Mr. Grey) who helped a fellow South African adventurer, when he cycled around the African continent, hoping he might be able to do the same for me. I was desperate for any help and would try (almost) anything to get some funding to enable me to continue my journey. All I knew was the man's name and that he worked for Namibian Breweries. My plan was to visit Namibian Breweries' head office once I arrived in Windhoek, the capital of Namibia, and ask to speak to this man. What could possibly go wrong, we ask?

I had been cycling from Springbok and so, by the time I crossed the border, I had already done more than a 100 kilometers for the day. I needed to pace myself and not overdo it and, with this in mind, I decided to carry on until just before dark and then find a suitable spot along the road where I could set up camp. This would be my first time camping, on my own, in a foreign country - out in the middle of nowhere! Yikes!

Of course, I could pretend that I was brave and all that good stuff, spending a night next to the road in a place I didn't know, all on my own, that it didn't bother me at all, but I'd be lying. In reality, I felt pretty nervous. I did feel excited and adventurous as well, but more nervous than anything. What if I was attacked in the middle of the night? Or what if someone stole my bicycle while I was asleep. To counter my latter worrisome thought, I decided to tie one end of a piece of string around my ankle and the other end to my bicycle, hoping that this would alert me in the event of some 'up-to-no-good-middle-of-the-night-vagrant' tried to steal my beloved

Luna. Yes, they could just cut the string, I am aware of that - but can we just move along here because the string made me feel more at ease, okay?

I was, however, very excited to try out all my new outdoor equipment. It would be my first night in my new sleeping bag. My first time lighting up my very cool MSR Expedition Stove that can burn using just about any flammable liquid! What I didn't realize before was that when you get this lightweight, compact, sophisticated camping stove going - it sounds like a jet engine! This did not bode well for my efforts of blending in with my surrounding and engaging incognito mode! There wasn't much I could do about it so I figured I'd just to have to be quick in preparing dinner for myself, which consisted of canned corned beef mixed with a can of mixed vegetables. Yum! Not.

After dinner, I settled into my sleeping bag and crawled halfway into a drain pipe running underneath the road, feet first, hoping that this would help conceal me in some way. It was cold and I struggled to fall asleep. You know how when you go to bed after you've watched a horror film and you start hearing all kinds of things? This is exactly how it was for me. I lay there with my sleeping bag zipped up to my chin, listening to the sounds of the night and allowing my imagination to play with me. Are those footsteps? Surely not. I held my breath to try and be as quiet as I possibly could. Then, I hear it again. Something is definitely approaching or nearby. What do I do? My pulse is thumping in my head.

It's dark and I can only make out silhouettes against the night sky. I heard something overhead and there's something scurrying about close to my head. There really is. My heart was pounding in my throat and adrenalin rushing through my veins. Then it swooped down and nearly brushed against my face as it caught a moth and flew off. It's a bat! For goodness' sake, woman! Get a hold of yourself! I calmed myself down to a mild panic and forced myself to just breathe and listen and recognise the sounds for what they were. I heard bats overhead flying past, using their sonic chirping as radars to catch their dinner. A cricket was jumping around near my head and there's an owl hooting somewhere not far off as well. On this night, I invented it. "Gutter Camping!" The real deal.

I finally managed to convince myself that nobody was going to come to kill me in the middle of the night and that there was a very good chance that nobody actually cared that I was there. I was really cold and got out of my sleeping bag to put on more clothes, then crawled back in. I finally started to get tired and lay on my back, staring at the stars, thinking about the journey already behind me and the one still stretched out ahead of me. I wonder what Angola will be like?

I woke up with sunrise the next morning, absolutely frozen! It's still too early for the sun's rays to offer any warmth. I got up anyway and started up the jet engine to make myself some coffee and oats porridge. Oats porridge is great as a slow energy releasing food. I've never really minded oats, but this particular batch could have done with some butter, the kind of thing one too easily takes for granted in life. Nevertheless, I have my porridge and a cup of coffee, watching as the world around me awoke and a vehicle or two passed me by, people hooting and waving. People sure are friendly in Namibia. Next stop - Grünau!

For some reason, I had it in my head that Namibia would be a pretty flat country with little in the way of climbing on my heavily laden bicycle. Wrong answer! What I forgot to take into consideration is that Cape Town is pretty much at sea level and Windhoek, the capital city of Namibia, is 1700 meters above sea level. So I'd be climbing all the way to the capital city. The worst of which would be getting to Grünau! I thought maybe I was just imagining this never ending hill I seemed to be on while heading to Grünau, until I heard big freight trucks gearing down and struggling as well! The trucks were going so slow that I could just about grab onto one of them and coast up the hill, but resisted the temptation on account of fear of slipping and landing under one of said trucks' many wheels. So with that, we all struggled our way up the hill, my lungs making a similar sound to that of the trucks' engines!

When you're going at snail's pace for kilometers on end, on your own, day in and day out, you have a lot of time to think. It's amazing how many thoughts can go through one's mind in a day. Everything from your past, to your present and on to your future. Wondering what the road ahead might hold, pondering what you want to achieve beyond the current goal, whether love will find you again someday, whether you'll get blown to smithereens by a landmine in Angola. But, when the going gets tough, all your focus and energy goes from universal to pin-point focus on the task at hand. I learned what worked for me during these times was to keep my head down, count every pedal stroke and focus on my breathing. In those moments, the only thing that mattered was self-motivation.

I made it to Grünau in good time and with a few hours to spare before the sun would set. I decided to camp at the Grünau Shell Service Station Chalets. Booking a chalet was way above what my budget would allow, but I was happy to have a sheltered camping stand and not a drain pipe under the road. No brainer really.

I pitched my tent for the first time on this trip, not realizing that there would be an unexpected surprise to celebrate the occasion. I had put up my tent and was busy preparing my dinner when one of the ladies working at the service station came over with a white take-away cup in hand. She handed it to me with a note and a smile, then turned around and left. The note read: "Welcome to Namibia! Raymond." Raymond Spall was referred to me by a mutual friend who believed that Raymond might be of some help during my time in Namibia as he worked in the Tourism industry. I had been keeping him up to date of my progress via SMS messages, which is how he knew I was camping out in Grünau. He had obviously phoned the cafe situated inside the service station and told them to bring me a cup of hot chocolate. It's amazing how such a small gesture can mean so much. It made me smile and great, big tears of appreciation welled up in my eyes as I thought to myself: "Everything is going to be just fine!"

I started getting used to 'life on the road' and became really good at scouting out suitable camping spots, setting up camp in world record times and preparing my dinner equally fast, on account of not wanting to have the jet engine sound its alarm for too long. I also started 'becoming one' with my surroundings. It's also incredible how our senses are heightened when we are 'out in the wild'. In the mornings, as I set off after I had had breakfast and packed up camp, I could smell what was going on inside the vehicles that passed me on the road. I could smell when the occupant of the vehicle was drinking coffee or smoking, I could smell perfume as vehicles passed me by. It's amazing how heightened my senses became!

People are also extremely friendly on the roads in Namibia with almost every vehicle that passed me hooting and waving with smiles beaming from within the cars and trucks. It made me feel at home. Namibia is a country of vast, open spaces. It is the 34th largest country in the world with a population of only 2 million people. You can go for days without seeing a single soul, if you're on some of the roads less travelled.

Which is why I decided to stick to the main road... just in case.

Raymond kept track of my progress throughout Namibia and offered me a place to stay with him and his housemate when I arrived in Windhoek. I had mentioned to him that one of my priorities, while in Windhoek, was to get in touch with "Mr. Grey" of Namibian Breweries. When I told Raymond his real name, he said, "well, you won't believe it but I actually know him. I'll set up a meeting, no problem. He actually works for First National Bank now and not Namibian Breweries anymore". I could hardly believe it! Of all the people in the world, the Universe connects me with the one guy who happens to be friends with the one person with whom I desperately want to talk, in Windhoek!

When I finally arrived in Windhoek, after about two weeks of cycling since I crossed the border, Raymond met up with me on the outskirts of town in his green Jeep and showed me the way to his house. It was great being able to take care of some laundry and gave my bicycle a good wash and a service while getting to sleep in an actual bed! I also didn't have to start up the jet engine to prepare breakfast or dinner, which really pleased me. It's an amazing piece of equipment, I just don't really get why it needs to be so loud? Or maybe I was just doing it wrong?

I had three points of order while in Windhoek.

1. Set up a meeting with the Marketing Manager at First National Bank,

2. Apply for a visa for Angola,

3. Stock up on supplies.

Raymond helped to set up the meeting while I headed straight for the Angolan Consulate the next day. Sadly though, what I thought would be an easy, in and out Visa application process, was anything but easy. Upon submitting my application, I was informed that I had to apply for said Visa in my own country of residence and could not do so from Namibia. Regardless of how much I pleaded, I was met with refusals to make application for an Angolan visa, from Namibia. This posed a major problem as it meant that I would have to fly back to Johannesburg to apply for the visa, with money that I simply did not have! Now, it was of even more importance to convince Mr FNB Marketing Manager to help me.

The meeting was set to take place over breakfast the following day. Raymond would accompany me to the restaurant, where it was agreed we would meet, as I had no idea how to get there. When we arrived, it became obvious that I wasn't just meeting with Mr. Grey, but his whole team too! I was going to have to convince not only one person, but half a dozen people, that I was worthy of their help. I felt very uncomfortable and unsure of myself. I kept thinking to myself, "Why would these people actually buy into the idea of giving me money to live my dream?"

Nevertheless, I was set on giving it my best shot and told my whole story to the group. Mr. Grey listened intently and, when I had finished, simply said: "Our policy states that we do not hand out sponsorships to individuals or non-Namibians". My heart sank and I could see my dream unravelling before me when, suddenly, he added,

"But... I do admire your courage and, because you have such a remarkable story, we will give you R10 000 in return for talks given by you to schools on your route throughout northern Namibia". Eureka!

I could hardly believe my ears! They were agreeing to help me, even though they had just told me that their company policy stated that they would not give sponsorships to individuals or non-Namibians and I just happened to be both! I could just about jump over the moon. It wasn't a million bucks, but it gave me enough breathing space to be able to focus on the next leg of the journey. With this money I could fly back home, apply for my Angolan visa and then return to Windhoek within a week or two to continue my journey north! Things were looking up!

I booked my flight to Johannesburg and spent two weeks back in South Africa to obtain the visa for Angola. I figured, while I was at it, I may as well apply for more visas for the countries on my planned route going forward. After securing visas for all countries up to Cameroon, I figured that it would give me enough leeway to negotiate acquiring the other visas on route. When planning such an extensive trip, crossing multiple borders, visas pretty much become the biggest nightmare. I returned to Windhoek with my passport boasting new tourist visas for Angola, the Democratic Republic of Congo, the Republic of Congo and Cameroon. South African passport holders do not require a Visa for Gabon for a stay of up to 30 days. This meant one less Visa needed, which was a huge bonus! Outstanding!

With my newly replenished bank account, thanks to First National Bank Namibia, I could direct all my focus on reaching the next border which would be the border between Namibia and Angola. Before I left Windhoek, Raymond introduced me to a man who seemed to know Angola better than any non-Angolan resident should. He explained that he used to work for a company that operated throughout the country, lifting active landmines that still remained after the civil war that lasted from 1975 until 2002. He was a tall man with a deep voice, a long grey beard and ruffled grey hair. An 'out-of-Africa Santa', if you will.

He welcomed me with a cup of tea and listened intently, while puffing on a pipe, as I told him my plans to cycle around the African continent. After I had finished he put down his pipe and looked at me with soul-piercing eyes, searching for the real reason behind this journey. He told me that he thought I was a little off my rocker and that I would need all the help I could get if I was to survive 'out there on my own'. He took out an old, well-used paper map of Angola and that bore the mark of numerous scribbles made over years of use. Together, we pored over the map as he showed me the best and safest roads (to his knowledge) to take me north. Furthermore, he gave me the names and phone numbers of friends of his living in Lubango with whom I could stay, and the name of the Proprietor of a guesthouse situated right before the Angolan border.

"Ask for Dona Maria... and tell her Hendrik sent you. She will give you a room for the night. This used to be a well-known stop over for diamond smugglers from the north, so just be careful and don't go out on your own at night". Move over, Blood Diamond.

With all this new information, my freshly stocked panniers and visa-filled passport, I set off from Windhoek - due north. From there, I would travel through Okahandja, Otjiwarongo, Otavi (which I would later learn has the best spring water in Namibia, according to two Namibians, whose path I would cross in Angola, another story for later), Tsumeb, Ethosha National Park, Ondangwa and finally Oshikango, before crossing the border into Angola. In each major town where I stayed on route, where a First National Bank branch existed, I would be welcomed and taken in by the bank's staff, while the local media would do an interview with me for their local newspaper and a presentation arranged at the local primary and or high school that same evening.

It's a very rewarding thing, sharing your dreams with youth and seeing their eyes light up with wonder and amazement. You can just about see their imaginations conjuring up their own epic adventures in their fertile, young minds. Each presentation would end with all the pupils falling in line to give me hugs and ask for photographs and my autograph. Somehow, I would become their hero and they would probably be telling their parents, that night at home, about the girl from South Africa who is cycling around the whole of Africa on her own! It gave me great joy to know that my own journey might have sparked a daring dream or two in some of those kids' souls.

Just beyond Oshivelo, next to the Etosha National Park, lies a control post that divides northern Namibia from the south. More than half the Namibian population lives in this area in the north that covers just 6% of Namibian territory, named 'Ovamboland' by English-speaking visitors, relating to the Ovambo people living in this region. This area in the north is far more rural than southern Namibia. On either side of the main road that stretches all the way north to the Angolan border, you are surrounded by wide, open plains, dotted by small groups of huts with smoke coming from an internal fireplace and chickens and the odd goat roaming outside. Every so often, there are little cafes on the side of the road, or a little bar or 'cuca shop' (shebeen or small rural shop selling mainly beer and maybe some cold drinks and snacks).

I grew a little anxious as I was moving further away from home and further away from my comfort zone and everything that is known and secure. I had no idea what to expect as I travelled further north but decided to take one day at a time. There isn't much in the way of hotels or guesthouses to check into as you travel through the north of Namibia, not until you reach the more populous towns right up before the Angolan border. I spent one night in the Etosha National Park at Mokuti Lodge, where a ranger working at the lodge, and yet another of Raymond's friends, organized a night's stay for me at no charge. The Etosha National Park is amazingly beautiful and I would recommend for anyone planning to visit Namibia, to put this national treasure on their list!

The rest of the way north, I continued camping wild in the veld (flat open country with few trees). My tent's flysheet just happened to be orange, not the best colour to use when one wants to go unseen, so I would wait until it got dark to pitch my tent, before I'd put the flysheet up. My jet engine expedition stove became a real thorn in my side as I went to a lot of effort not to attract attention and it was the one thing that would always potentially give me away. I'd light it up and cook whatever food I was having for dinner, as fast as I possibly could. Then I'd crawl into my sleeping bag, with my headlight strapped to my head, to update my journal and end the day's routine with tying one end of a string to my bicycle and the other end to my ankle, in the hope that it would serve as an 'early warning system' in the event that anyone tried to make off with my most valuable possession. I would then place my CRKT tactical pocket knife under my pillow, my headlight next to me and then zip myself into my sleeping bag for the night. This became my daily routine. Heaven only knows what I actually would have done if that string around my ankle had been pulled taut one night...

I spent two night camping wild, on the side of the road, before reaching the town of Ondangwa, which is a larger town with more infrastructure and the second last town I would stay in before reaching the border with Angola. I spent the night at the Ondangwa Rest Camp. Their slogan is, "a place where you can overnight in peace", and this is exactly what drew me to this establishment. I felt the need for a place where I could lay my head down and not have to worry about anyone tugging on that piece of string around my ankle in the middle of the night. I also made use of this opportunity to wash some of my clothes, while having a proper shower and even treated myself to a steak and an ice cold Windhoek Lager at the camp's restaurant. They do serve a pretty good steak!

My final stop would be Oshikango, the border town between The Republic of Namibia and Angola. This is where Hendrik, in Windhoek, told me to search for a place called "Piscas" and ask for 'Dona Maria' who would supposedly give me a place to stay for the night if I told her that Hendrik had sent me. Entering the outskirts of Oshikango gave me my first taste of what a true African border post is like. You reach an invisible line, a point of no return, and once you cross that line, the town will quite literally swallow you up and all of a sudden you are surrounded by a cacophony of sounds and smells and bustling activity. It's a sensory overload and if you don't keep your wits about you, you'll end up leaving with less than what you arrived with.

I stopped on the side of the road to take a look at my map and to just take a breather and gather up my courage, which seemed to have fallen to the floor at that point. I felt completely overwhelmed and out of my depth. It's funny how the right people always seem to show up in these scenarios. This would happen to me on a regular basis, going forward, and even now, I am always in awe of just how amazing the Universe is and how everything is intertwined.

As I stood there on the side of the road slowly gathering my courage up from the floor, a young boy, also on a bicycle, approached me. This teenager had spotted someone who was in obvious need of some help and, with a beaming smile, came over to offer it. He asked me where I was heading and I gave him the name of the place where I intended to stay for the night, to which he simply replied, "follow me, I'll take you there", and zoomed off on his bicycle ahead of me. I quibbled with myself for a split second as to whether I could trust this young boy but also instantly knew that my gut was telling me to follow him. Which is exactly what I did.

He led me through the chaos that is the trade market of this border town. Stalls packed to the rafters, with all sorts, lined the streets, all the way up to just before the border. Thousands of people go about their business, buying goods to be taken to Angola or back home to Namibia. The streets are packed with people and cars and trucks and goods and taxis and dogs and chickens. You name it! At this point I felt extremely grateful to have this young boy guiding me to where I needed to be. When we reached Piscas, he turned to me and said,

"Okay, now you're safe. Good luck", and off he went. How bizarre... and yet absolutely befitting of the whole scenario.

I walked up to the entrance of Piscas which is covered by a carport. On the wall the words: "Piscas Rest & Hotel" are painted in black letters. I felt very nervous because I realized everyone around me was speaking Portuguese and my Portuguese was limited to, "Bom dia" and "Obrigada". These are useful words to know, but how would I explain who I was or why I was there if Dona Maria didn't speak English? I parked my bicycle against the wall outside and carefully stepped inside the building. The room was dimly lit and it took a moment for my eyes to adjust. There were only a few people sitting inside, drinking beer and smoking cigarettes. I realized that I'd stepped into a bar. I made my way up to the barman and just uttered two words, "Dona Maria", to which the barman disappeared through a door leading to the back of the building.

Moments later, a woman appeared who I presumed to be Dona Maria. It was only at this moment, while pondering my total lack of Portuguese vocabulary that I realized that 'Dona' probably stood for something and was, in fact, probably not a double-barrelled name. Turns out 'Dona' means 'proprietress or dame' in Portuguese. Live and learn.

Turns out, Dona Maria could speak some English, huge relief. I explained to her who I was and where I was heading. I told her all about my plans to cycle around the African continent and that I had met Hendrik in Windhoek and he said that she would be able to give me a place to stay for the night. She seemed a bit puzzled, but listened to my whole story. When I had finished she asked,

"Did Hendrik say he would pay for you to stay here tonight?"

He hadn't... and I told her that he didn't mention anything about paying for me to stay there. She asked me to have a seat and wait so she could try and get in touch with Hendrik. I went outside, so I could keep an eye on my bicycle and all my gear while awaiting news. While inside the establishment, I felt okay, but as soon as I stepped outside, that nervous feeling from earlier would fill the pit of my stomach again. I stood with my back against the wall, under the carport, watching the throngs of people passing back and forth in the street in front of Piscas. Two security guards sat outside, speaking Portuguese to one another while shooting glances over to me every now and then. Feeling extremely uncomfortable, I just wanted to get this border crossing over and done with!

A few minutes later, Dona Maria appeared and told me to come back inside and to bring my bicycle with me. She told me that she could not get hold of Hendrik but would give me a room for the night anyway. This was very kind of her. She showed me through the door in the back and, to my surprise, it led out onto a gorgeous courtyard with a rich and well-kept garden. There was even a swimming pool, with the rooms situated right at the back. Joy. I felt a huge sense of relief as she showed me to a single room as, for a moment, I had thought she might turn me away. I thanked her for her generosity and then settled into my room.

I wanted to get some supplies before crossing over into Angola the next day. I had no idea what the infrastructure would be like on the other side of the border in Santa Clara and whether I'd be able to buy the things I would need for the road ahead. So, thinking it best to stock up with as much as I possibly could, before crossing the border, I went shopping. Right across the road from Piscas, there is a little shopping center with a supermarket, an ATM and a couple of fast food stores.

As I walked out of the front entrance of Piscas, two Namibian Border Police Officers approached me. They wanted to know where I was going and expressed their concerns of my walking around on my own.

"It's not safe here, especially for someone like you on your own. We will escort you to where you need to go and make sure you get back here safely".

With their words still lingering in the air, I looked around me and all of a sudden, it was like I was only seeing people giving me sly stares from everywhere. It felt like I had a great big target painted on my forehead. The officers were very friendly and helpful though. They escorted me to the shopping center and back, never leaving my side. They asked what time I was planning to cross the border the next morning and offered to escort me to the border as well. I wanted to get it over and done with as soon as possible, so I told them that I planned on crossing the border as soon as it opened.

"We will be waiting for you here at 08h00". With that, I turned in for the night, filled with both feelings of anxiety and excitement of what lay in store for me on the road ahead.

CHAPTER 3

The day finally arrived that I would cross the border into Angola! This was a big deal to me because Namibia felt more like a province of South Africa than a completely foreign country. People still speak a language I can understand in Namibia. The culture is still familiar and the infrastructure similar to that in South Africa. So, I never really felt that far removed from home, while in Namibia. I was now about to enter a country that would be foreign to me in every possible way. The food, the culture, the people, the language. This was the true 'unknown' to me and I felt both exhilarated and numb with fear.

Wait! First things first - getting myself stamped out of Namibia. One would expect this to be a fairly straightforward procedure, and I'm sure under normal circumstances, it's exactly that. After I had my passport stamped, I was subjected to having myself and my belongings checked by Customs staff, when a female Customs officer approached me and demanded that I unpack my panniers. Although slightly annoyed by her attitude, I thought it best to just smile and do as I was told. I unpacked all my pannier bags for her to see as well as my camping equipment. Then she asked,

"Do you have papers for this motorcycle?"

For a moment, I wasn't sure I had heard correctly, so I asked her to repeat the question. Sure enough, there it went again,

"Do you have papers for your motorcycle?"

I really was not sure whether she was joking or not, so plainly stated that it was a bicycle and not a motorcycle. She took a few steps backwards, inspecting my Luna for a moment. I could see the realization set in as a look of embarrassment came over her. She told me to carry on, turned on her heel and walked away briskly. I thought it very amusing and this encounter actually helped settle my nerves a bit.

Next up - getting my passport stamped to enter Angola. I could not foresee any hiccups as I now had a valid visa in hand so there was no reason to deny me entry into the country. Thankfully the customs Officers at the Santa Clara Border Control could not see any reason not to grant me entry either and I found my passport stamped into Angola in no time. The Angolan side of the border is just as chaotic as the Namibian side, with throngs of people, cars and trucks filled with goods being transported back and forth across the border on nearly non-existent roads, all while the eyes of every passerby are fixed on Yours Truly! If ever you feel yourself suffering from a lack of attention, go and cross the border at Oshikango between Namibia and Angola. Instant cure!

From the border, I would make my way to a town called Ondjiva, just 50 kilometers away. The very helpful carrier of information about all that is Angola, Hendrik, also gave me a contact name and phone number for acquaintances of his who happen to live on a little piece of land just before Ondjiva. A husband and wife, Martie and Hendrick Lottering, who were forced from their farm in Zimbabwe and who were now trying to make ends meet in Angola, was just one. I phoned the number given to me and Martie answered. I explained to her who I was and that I was heading to Ondjiva, as we spoke. She sounded very excited and said that I would be most welcome to stay with them for the night. She explained to me how to get to their house and said to wait for them if I arrived before they got back home from work.

The road from the border is shocking, with countless potholes. I think it classifies more as a load of potholes with some road in between. Being on a bicycle made it a bit easier for me to negotiate my way around the potholes, though it made the going a bit slower and more intense as I had to dodge the odd car, which, in turn, would be dodging a pothole. About halfway to Ondjiva, I had to stop as nature was calling. Normally, this would not be an issue at all. I don't mind having to 'go' in the bush. I actually prefer it to a dirty toilet. No, it wasn't the state of the natural lavatory that was bothering me. What was bothering me is that I was then in Angola and even someone who knows absolutely nothing about Angola will know two things about

Angola, at the very least. Those being: Civil war and Landmines! I'll admit that I was a bit nervous about veering off the beaten track, so to speak. So, when the need arose, I left Luna on the side of the road and very carefully moved just a short distance from the road, carefully planning my steps. Not like it would help, but it somehow did. It was while in the middle of going about my business, when a group of ladies appeared from nowhere in the bushes ahead and walked past me towards the road, giggling, that I realized I probably didn't have to worry about landmines in this area. Good to know!

The ex-Zimbabwean couple stayed in a little one-bedroom house about 10 kilometers before Ondjiva. It was easy to find as Martie had told me to look out for the biggest Baobab tree in the area and their house would be the one right next to the tree. Sure enough, it would be impossible to miss the magnificent, giant tree in front of their house. As I suspected, they weren't home yet when I arrived so I parked Luna against the tree and found myself a cosy seat next to her where I could just relax a bit and take in my surroundings.

When Martie and Hendrick finally arrived home, they welcomed me like I was an old friend. They invited me into their home and Martie got straight into making me a cup of tea and then on to preparing dinner. It was my first night in this foreign country and there I was being provided with some comfort and familiarity to ease me into the swing of things. I felt right at home and enjoyed chatting to the Lotterings, telling them a few tales from my time spent on the road so far until late at night. Before turning in, Martie informed me that Hendrik would be accompanying me into town the next morning and that she would meet me at her office, which just happened to be situated right on the main road that I had to ride out on, heading north. Knowing that I'd have a bit of company the next day, before leaving town, made me feel happy and grateful.

The road leading up to Ondjiva from the border is mostly a gravel road, being worked on by the Chinese. From Ondjiva to Xangongo, some 100 kilometers away, the Chinese had finished working on the road and it's all beautiful, newly tarred road. Then, as Hendrik informed me, from Xangongo to Cahama, I'd be facing another 100 kilometers of very bad road that used to be tarred but was now more of a gauntlet of potholes and sand traps. I figured it would take me a day to get to Xangongo and then another two to make it to Cahama, so I stocked myself with enough food and water to last me for another three days, before hoping to replenish my supplies in Cahama.

The next morning I rode in to Ondjiva with Hendrick leading me to Martie's office. She helped me, over the next hour or so, to get all the supplies I needed. Once fully stocked again, it was time to say goodbye and get going towards Xangongo. The fabulous new tar road proved to be a royal treat from the moment I rolled Luna's wheels onto it. Now I could maintain a steady pace and it looked like I'd make it to Xangongo with loads of time to spare. I also wasn't the only cyclist on the road anymore as I started noticing more and more locals on bicycles, transporting goods between villages. Said goods ranged from stacks of wood, to chickens hanging upside down from the handlebars and goats draped around the cyclist's waist. Suddenly my load didn't seem so odd after all.

There's very little in the way of traffic on the road between Ondjiva and Xangongo. I found myself enjoying the solitude and steady pace that I was able to maintain on this road. I would stop for a break every hour or every 20 kilometers, whichever came first. I was in no rush and took my time to just take in all the new sights and sounds. Beautiful, lush, green bushveld lined both sides of the road. I also encountered the first of many abandoned military tanks on the side of this road. These rusted monuments serve as a permanent reminder of the brutality that was the Angolan Civil War. I found them rather eerie and fascinating at the same time.

I made it to Xangongo with loads of time to spare before sunset. Although I had initially planned to find a suitable place to camp on the side of the road, fate had other ideas. I didn't know where the town would be exactly, seeing as I didn't have a GPS, so my idea was to keep on going through town, once I'd reached it, and then find a quiet place somewhere on the side of the road a few kilometers out of town where I could set up camp. Just before I got to the little town, a man approached me, asking me where I was going, in Portuguese,

"Vai pra onde?"

I knew the word 'where' by now, so could pretty much decipher what he was asking. I pointed ahead and said,

"Cahama".

He obviously knew that it was too late in the day for me to reach Cahama before nightfall and so he indicated that I should follow him.

A lot of people were now gathering around, curious about who the strange girl is and what she's doing in Xangongo on her own on a very heavily loaded bicycle. Or, I imagine, that's what they were wondering. I wasn't sure whether I should follow this man or not and had to rely on my instincts again. My instincts seemed to tell me to go with it and so I did, up a hill to what seemed to be a compound for local workers, overlooking the Kunene River. We reached the top of the hill just in time to witness a spectacular sunset over the river. The compound had a number of shipping containers in it that had been converted into living quarters. The man showed me to one of these containers and inside stood a single bed with an adjoining bathroom with a toilet and a shower in it. He was offering me a place to sleep for the night! He said something in Portuguese, pointing at the bed, then gave me a key and left. I found myself at a loss for words! I didn't ask for anything and yet this stranger recognized that I might need a safe place to spend the night and provided it without expecting anything in return. Angola is a far friendlier country than I would ever have expected! Oh, the prejudices that we allow to build up in our own minds!

The next morning as I started getting ready to hit the road again, a couple of the workers staying in the compound approached me, gesticulating that they would like to have a photo taken with me. Of course, I gladly agreed and, after some posing and photo taking, I thanked the guys for allowing me to stay over for the night and started making my way to the road back down the hill again. Next up - Cahama!

I had been told that the road from Xangongo to Cahama is in need of some maintenance, but I wasn't quite prepared for what I was about to witness. The best description for it would be a road that stretches for almost one hundred kilometers and rather resembles countless potholes connected by a bit of tar in between, here and there. Some of the holes were so deep that I could probably stand in in them up to my knees. On the bicycle, it's not as bad as in a car or in a truck, as I could obviously weave between the potholes, but it sure made for slow progress.

A detour had been laid out parallel to the existing road by Chinese construction workers as they were making preparations to build a new road. The only problem with the detour was that it was a thick sand track, more than anything else. Which is better than the potholed, riddled road for four-wheel drive vehicles, but have you ever tried to peddle a heavily loaded bicycle in thick sand? My 20/25 km/h average speed came down to a painstaking 5 - 10 km/h. I would swap between weaving through the potholes on the existing road, until I got tired of it and then veer off to the detour just for a little something different, until the sand got so deep that I couldn't maintain enough momentum to keep the bike upright and then I'd get back onto the road of a million potholes.

I had three modes at this stage. Snake mode on the road of a million potholes. Snake mode on the road of the lesser known, southern Sahara. Or walk mode. I had to engage walk mode quite often when the sand got so deep that I could stand still on the bike with its wheels planted in sand up to the axles. It was while taking a break, under the much needed shade of some threes on the side of the road, that I noticed a big Coca-Cola truck approaching on the sandy track. It could obviously not even consider risking it on the road of a million potholes, as its precious cargo would just be obliterated.

The truck came to a standstill next to me, with the driver hanging halfway out the window, asking me where I'm heading. I point up the road and utter one word, "Cahama". I find I am absolutely exhausted. The going has been tough and the heat has not helped at all. I've been rummaging through my food and water supplies to keep my energy levels up and, at this rate, I would run out of supplies just before reaching Cahama.

The truck driver must have taken pity on me, sitting in the sand, on the side of the road, this foreign girl on her own. So, next thing, he climbed out of the truck and onto the back, slipping in under the truck's side sails. When he appeared again from under the sail he was carrying four bottles of Coca-Cola. One for himself, one for his co-driver... and two bottles for me! What's even more is that he said something to his co-driver, as he was climbing down to give me my two bottles of Coca-Cola and, next thing, the co-driver jumped out the truck and handed me a blue, plastic bag. It is only when I felt the cold that I realized what it was. He'd just given me a bag of ice to go with my two bottles of Coca-Cola! Gobsmacked! And all they asked for, in return, is a photo, which I take on my camera and they don't even get to keep!

It felt like someone had just handed me the elixir of life, sent straight from heaven! I didn't open a bottle immediately, but rather savoured it for a bit later down the road. It would be my prize for a little more effort put into conquering the sand! That and the fact that the contents of the bottles were lukewarm, so I put them in the bag of ice and into one of my panniers so it could cool down for a bit later. I only covered about 40 kilometers that day and finally veered off into the bush to find a suitable camping spot about an hour before sunset. I was spent and had very little energy left. All I wanted was to have a bush shower, which consisted of wiping myself down with anti-mosquito wet wipes, cook my dinner on my jet engine camping stove, set up my orange tent and then fall asleep staring at the stars!

Before doing any of that though, I settled on a spot in a little clearing about 30 meters away from the road and sat down to enjoy one of the bottles of Coca-Cola. It was pure heaven and I sipped and savoured every single drop as if it might be my last! Never had a soft drink tasted so good! I wasn't quite prepared for what was about to transpire next!

There was I, sitting somewhere in the middle of the Angolan bushveld, sipping my Coke and minding my own business when, the next thing, a herd of cattle came barging through my camp site-to-be. They just stomped past me like I wasn't even there! And following them were three herdsmen, who obviously also weren't expecting me to be sitting there. I suddenly felt a bit awkward, betting that these blokes had never seen anything like this before. I greeted them with a friendly smile, though my greeting only got blank stares, in return. Next I had to endure the longest, most awkward five minutes (which felt more like 30) of my life as they just kept standing there and staring at me, not saying a single word! I tried asking them how they were, in both English and Portuguese, but no luck. I tried asking their names and still no luck. In the end, we all just kind of stood around engaged in a pretty intense staring competition. Thankfully, they eventually got bored of the game and moved on without any warning. For a moment there, I felt worried that we might be locked into an infinite staring competition. They would've won! These guys are absolute pros!

That was one of my favourite evenings on the entire trip. After I had eaten my supper and finished writing in my journal, I lay down on my sleeping bag in my tent. I didn't put the fly sheet over the tent as it was way too hot for it and I enjoyed the slight breeze gently blowing over me. As I lay there, staring up at the millions of stars twinkling overhead, a feeling of utter contentment came over me. For the first time in a very long time, I felt at ease with just... being. To top it all off, I had obviously set up camp near a village as, the next thing I knew, drums started playing not far away from me. This made me smile and I feel immensely grateful that I got to fall asleep looking at the stars overhead, listening to drumming nearby with a full belly and the knowledge that I was on the greatest adventure of my life!

The next morning, I was up before the cows and back on the road for another day of alternating between riding on the road of a million potholes and the Southern Sahara detour. I wasn't in a rush and took my time to save my energy. Although I wasn't pushing it, I was still making my way through my supplies at an alarming rate. I figured I'd probably run out of food and water before the next morning. Still, I wasn't feeling panicked as I would be close to Cahama by the time I'd run out of supplies and I could just stock up in town again. I hoped.

I spent another night camping in the bushveld and the next morning I was up early as I had indeed, run out of pretty much all my supplies, bar, maybe a liter of water. As fate would have it, I'd get to stock up even before reaching Cahama that day.

I had just packed up camp and got on the road heading to Cahama when I spotted two large freight trucks up ahead, about five kilometers from where I had spent the night. As I approached the trucks, a sense of excitement filled me when I spotted the Namibian registration plates on the back of the trucks. They were parked on the side of the Southern Sahara detour road, one behind the other. As I approached the truck parked at the back, I could hear voices further up ahead. I then noticed two men standing between the two trucks, sipping, what I assumed to be, was coffee out of their mugs and busily cooking themselves some breakfast. I stopped next to the two men and greeted them in my native language, Afrikaans. I just knew they had to speak Afrikaans, and sure enough, they did!

Both of them had a puzzled look on their faces and immediately asked where I was from. They were surprised to learn that I was from South Africa and said that they would have expected me to be from Europe, because a South African girl can surely not be as naïve as to think she can travel through Africa on her own. They meant no offense and I could tell that they were just really surprised to see me, a girl on her own, here in the middle of the Angolan bushveld. I didn't blame them.

We got chatting and I told them where I was from and everything about my plan to cycle around the African continent. They thought me mad. Courageous, but mad nonetheless. I stood around chatting to them for a while and then asked if I could maybe fill up my water bottles from their water tanks. I knew they'd be carrying drinking water with them, these truckers are usually stocked to the rafters while on a run up in Africa. Without hesitation, they both jumped up with a

"Yes of course".

They took my water bottles from me to fill them up with fresh, cold water. While one of the drivers was filling up my water bottles, the other climbed up into his truck, rummaging around for something. As I was handed back my now filled-up water bottles, I was also informed that the water I was about to taste, came from a fresh water spring in Otavi and that it is the best drinking water in the world! It was pretty good tasting water, I have to admit.

When the other driver emerged from the front of his truck, he walked over towards me, carrying a whole bunch of supplies in his arms.

"Here you go, girlie, we can't have you starving up here in the middle of nowhere".

He handed me a kilogram of 'boerewors' (a traditional type of sausage, originating in South Africa), two cans of mixed vegetables, a couple of packets of crisps, three chocolates, a bag of biltong (another South African speciality, similar to beef jerky) and a few cans of Coca-Cola! Wow! I felt like I had just won the lottery! More than that, I was about to learn that this guy knew just about every trucker south of the equator and he put out word to all truckers making runs into Angola, asking them to be on the lookout for a girl on a bicycle heading up to Luanda and, if they came across me, to give me something to drink and eat!

I was left speechless, yet again. I thanked these two good Samaritans and bade them farewell as I wanted to try and make it to Lubango within the next three days. Lubango lies about 190 kilometers north-west of Cahama. I figured I'd be able to make it within three days and, thanks to our friend, Hendrik, back in Windhoek, he had given me one last contact with whom I could get in touch, friends of his from Namibia, who happened to live and work in Lubango. I figured I would phone them when I was a day away from the city to ask if they could possibly help me with a place to sleep for a night or two.

The road leading up to Lubango from Cahama is surrounded by beautiful scenery with lush, green bushveld on either side of the road. Though the scenery is something to behold, the elevation is an entirely different story. If you want to practice hill climbs on a bicycle, this is the place to do it! It soon became clear to me that it would take me at least three days to make it to Lubango. From Cahama to Lubango, it is about a 1000 meter climb in elevation over a 200 kilometer stretch. Not too bad, but it'll give you a workout.

I did get in touch with Hendrik's friends in Lubango and they were friendly enough to let me stay with them for two days so I could have a rest and take care of a few things like doing my laundry, giving the bike a service, having a proper bath and stocking up on supplies, etc. Even more than that, they took me on a sightseeing tour of the famous 'Tundavala', the Christ statue (Cristo Rei) and the engineering marvel that is Leba Pass. Tundavala is a viewpoint situated some 18 kilometers from the city. The difference in altitude from the rim of the viewpoint to the escarpment below is about 1000 meters, which makes for a pretty breathtaking view of tens of kilometers. The Cristo Rei, or Christ the King statue, is a Catholic monument and shrine that overlooks the city of Lubango and was inspired by the Christ the Redeemer statue in Rio de Janeiro in Brazil. It is one of only four in the world.

The Serra de Leba Pass is situated some 30 kilometers outside of Lubango and is famous for its altitude and its beauty. It is one of the famous hairpin roads in the world and one just needs to do a Google search to find countless stunning photos of this spectacular mountain pass. This beautiful mountain road spirals down from 1 845 meters above sea level to almost sea level in just 10 kilometers, literally traversing 3 or 4 climate zones during any ascension or descent climb of the Pass. Legend has it that the Pass is named after the woman who designed and built the road, who died after she viewed it on the very day the project was finished.

I kept updating my blog as I went along and when I wasn't able to update it myself, my friend Hanret, back in South Africa, updated it for me. I would type up an update on my phone and then send it to her via text message along with a couple of photos. While in Lubango, I received a personal message on Facebook from Pedro Bandeira, of Hoteis Angola. He had read about my journey on the Bradt Angola site (which I didn't even know had published a post about my trip) and had also read on my blog site that I was seeking sponsors in each country that I planned to travel through. He said that his company wanted to sponsor the Angolan leg of my trip, that the company was situated in Lobito and wanted to meet up with me if I hadn't passed Lobito yet. I immediately replied, saying that I was a few days from reaching Lobito and would love to meet up once I arrived in the city.

This really lifted my spirits as it would mean a healthy $1000 deposit into my account, which would certainly go a long way on my trip!

It is nearly 400 kilometers from Lubango to Lobito and I figured it would probably take me about 5 or 6 days to reach the coastal city. Armed with the knowledge that I could count on some much needed funding coming my way, I felt far more at ease. My route would take me from Lubango to Cacula, through Quilengues and Chongoroi, before reaching Benguela, the capital city of the province bearing the same name. The road from Lubango, all the way to pretty much Quilengues, resembled something similar to that of the road of a million potholes between Xangongo and Cahama. Progress was slow, but steady, and after five days of cycling, I finally reached Benguela!

Within those five days I, met a group of South Africans traveling between Lubango and Lobito for work. They specialized in installing air conditioners for big firms and shopping centers. They passed me on the first day after I had left Lubango and stopped to ask the usual questions. They handed me a hamburger and a can of Coca-Cola and said they'd be seeing me again within the next day or two as they were traveling back and forth between Lubango and Lobito for work. Another chance encounter took place about halfway between Lubango and Lobito, as I had just started a climb up a particularly long hill. Suddenly, I heard a truck hitting its brakes on approach from behind me. A monster of a freight truck came to a stop about 50 meters in front of me on the opposite side of the road. The driver jumped out of the truck and started jogging across the road, heading straight for me. When he reached me he asked,

"Are you Jo, the girl cycling around Africa?"

I thought it pretty obvious but answered with a short yes and smile nonetheless.

"We've been asked to stop and give you something to eat and drink if we saw you on the road."

He handed me a bag of biltong and two cans of Coca-Cola and then turned right around and headed back to his truck. All I could do is shout thank you after him. Someone out there was certainly looking out for me. I figured my poor Guardian Angels had their work cut out for them, this felt like a very personal 'looking after', if you know what I mean. It made me smile and feel all warm inside. Again, I experienced that feeling of gratitude and utter contentment and that everything is going to be just fine.

I kept updating Pedro on my progress and by the time I reached Benguela, he was there waiting for me and would lead me to Lobito, driving in his car in front of me. He led me straight to the Restinga Promenade and to a well-known restaurant called 'Zulu'. The name suggested to me that this establishment had probably been started by a South African and indeed, when I asked, Pedro confirmed that it had indeed been opened by a South African expat, originally. We spent the afternoon having a wonderful lunch, looking out over the Atlantic Ocean. I told Pedro all about my plans to cycle around Africa and he confirmed their plans to sponsor the Angolan leg of my journey and they also wanted to arrange some radio interviews while I was in town. I had no problem with this as I figured it would help spread the word and drum up some publicity and support further down the road.

While in Lobito, I stayed with the new South African friends who I had met on the way from Lubango. Pedro would pick me up in the mornings and I'd spend the day with him and his wife Lu. They'd take me out for breakfast and show me around town. I really fell in love with Lobito while I was there, there is something about this town and to this day, it remains my favourite city in Angola. Pedro organized a day with the press and this was spent posing for photographs and numerous questions for a number of radio and newspaper interviews. In return for the sponsorship Hoteis Angola gave me, I would put their company logo and link to their website on my blog site and conduct said interviews. In the meantime, a friend of Pedro's in Luanda, and fellow entrepreneur in the tourism industry, Candido, got in touch after he heard about my quest over the radio. Candido offered to arrange for more publicity, in the way of interviews, when I reached Luanda and offered me a place to stay at his girlfriend's house.

Things were steadily falling into place and I felt very positive about the journey that lay ahead. After a few wonderful days spent in Lobito, it was time for me to get going again. According to my calculations, it would take me about a week to get to Luanda, which is just over 500 kilometers from Lobito. I remembered Hendrik telling me about the road leading out of Lobito, towards Luanda. I remembered him saying what a steep hill climb it is and that once I got to the top, I should be very careful as the road gets pretty narrow from there on, all the way to Luanda. He wasn't kidding about the steep climb! With my newly stocked food and water supplies, my bike was so heavy that I had to push Luna almost all the way up the 10% grade incline!

Once at the top and once out of the city, the road quietens down, though I was facing a new challenge. This road had no shoulder, which meant countless close encounters with cars and trucks passing me. I was forced to cycle on the gravel stretch on the side of the road most of the time, which wasn't too much of a problem expect when that part of the road was taken over by the trees and shrubs growing close to the edge of the road. In those few days, I became an absolute pro at judging how fast a truck was approaching from behind and could calculate with pinpoint accuracy just how much time I had to stay on the road before I'd have to swerve off to the right to avoid being hit. It was a tense couple of days of cycling, insane traffic and more hill climbing!

Candido kept in touch with me via text messages, keeping tabs on my progress. He had arranged to meet up with me when I got closer to Luanda so they could guide me through the city and to where I would be staying while in Luanda. He arranged for me to stay at Kwanza Lodge, a lodge owned by yet another South African, situated just 70 kilometers south of Luanda. This is where Candido would meet me and they would accompany me on the road to the capital. The lodge is a really magical place, the kind of place you go to, to break away from everyday life. Situated right at the mouth of the Kwanza River with air conditioned cabins, a restaurant and bar, it is simply fantastic. Great food, fantastic view, what more could one ask for?

After my night's stay at Kwanza Lodge, I was really looking forward to meeting Candido and his long-time girlfriend, Linda. What I wasn't expecting is that they'd be arriving with a whole welcoming committee in tow. I was up early and having coffee on the deck of the restaurant when a Nissan Patrol, sporting an Angolan flag and a South African flag hanging off the back of the vehicle, entered the Lodge. I had to assume that this was Candido and Linda. With them, they had two more vehicles filled with journalists and cameramen. My morning was about to start off with a number of interviews before we'd even hit the road! Said journalists would also follow us all the way to the capital where they would then conduct a final interview before handing it over to their respective editors for print.

Candido and Linda are two fantastic human beings. They welcomed me with open arms and as part of their family from the get-go. The fact that Candido had a South African flag hanging off the back of his Patrol told me that he was the kind of person that makes friends wherever he goes. He has an amazing energy about him and also runs a tourism company called Trevogel. It's dubbed a 'rural tourism and adventure' company. I would soon come to learn that Candido knows just about every person living in Angola, which would come in handy for me a bit later on. But first...

I spent a few days in Luanda being ushered to and fro by Candido for numerous interviews on radio, for newspapers and even as a guest on the famous Hora Quente talk-show on Angolan television. I was like his new prized toy that he had to show off. Not that I minded too much. I figured the publicity would help me more than do me any harm, so I went with it.

Luanda is a very busy city filled with over 6.5 million people. If you can negotiate the traffic in Luanda, you can negotiate traffic anywhere else in the world. I've heard of traffic nightmares like India and Vietnam, but I couldn't imagine it was possible that any other country in the world could suffer worse traffic conditions than Luanda. It was easy enough for me to negotiate traffic on my bicycle, but when entering the city I had to wait for Candido and would sometimes ride alongside, holding on to the car, we were moving that slow. Hooting and shouting, thousands of people crossing the streets, the odd ministerial procession chasing cars off the road with blaring sirens, then the return of hooting and shouting as they went past. Absolute madness. I was trying to imagine if cities like Lagos and Cairo could be any worse. I've read about the traffic being just as bad in these capital cities. It would remain to be seen.

After a couple of wonderful days spent with Candido and Linda, exploring all that is Luanda and attending countless interviews, the time had finally arrived for me to start thinking about moving on. My visa would be expiring soon and I had to get to the Democratic Republic of Congo. It was decided that Candido and Linda would accompany me out of Luanda and guide me to yet another friend's lodge in Barra do Dande. Here, they would spend the night with me at the lodge before we'd all bid one another farewell the next morning. They would return to Luanda and I would carry on towards N'zeto.

Leaving Luanda proved to be far easier than entering it. With the newly built 'Ring Road', one need not enter the capital city when traveling north or south. You could simply travel on this bypass road, which made for far less of a headache. When we did hit traffic, I would travel ahead until Candido would pass me in his Patrol. He would then travel ahead and stop every 10 kilometers or so to wait for me to catch up. They took me to see a military memorial that portrayed South African soldiers in the Angolan Civil War in Panguila, on route to Barra do Dande. I have to admit, it gave me a strange feeling when asked to pose in front of these memorials for photographs.

We would stay at the Pasargada Resort in Barra do Dande. On arrival, I was welcomed by the owner of the resort, Arlette Jardim, and her staff, who all wanted to shake my hand and have photographs taken with me. In the entrance, photographs of me were on display with a write up about my trip. As we entered the resort, I could see a long table, set for a feast. Fresh fish was being grilled and local delicacies being carried to the table. I do enjoy Portuguese food, so tasty and rich in flavour. I felt a bit like an imposter. It felt like I was being welcomed like a hero, when in reality, I hadn't achieved that much yet. Well, I had achieved a lot but I was still a long way from achieving what I set out to do. Either way, I felt incredibly spoilt and thanked my hosts for their amazing generosity. After a feast of a lunch, we all went on a cruise of Rio Dande and Candido took me to meet the local Tribal Chief of the area, who happened to be an elderly woman. He asked her to bestow her blessing on me for protection on the road ahead, I thought it very special. When we returned to the lodge and turned in for the night, I lay in bed thinking about the road ahead and what it would have in store for me. Tomorrow, I'd be on my own again. This made me feel happy as I needed to recharge on my own after all the interviews and social gatherings in Lobito and Luanda.

The next morning, I would be escorted by the local Chief of Police for a few kilometers out of town, as a sign of goodwill and for protection, I thought it was a nice gesture. I bade farewell to Candido and Linda. It felt like I was saying goodbye to friends I had known for years. These two incredible people had taken care of me, a stranger, in more ways than one, without ever expecting anything in return. I would forever be in their debt and the best way I could think of honouring them was to continue with my journey.

The road north deteriorates pretty rapidly once you leave Barra do Dande. A rocky, poorly maintained gravel road with, yes, you guessed it, a million potholes! What's worse is that as the day went on, I started feeling like I was coming down with a cold. I started feeling worse with each passing kilometer. Another sign that didn't bode well was that I started seeing more and more 'beware of landmines' signs on the side of the road the further north I travelled, which felt a bit disconcerting.

It also became obvious that all the interviews I had conducted had indeed created more awareness of my trip, more and more people stopped, when they passed me on the road, to talk to me or to take pictures with me. All very friendly people.

Despite not feeling well, I was making good progress. I spent my first night back on the road on my own, sleeping under a very big Baobab tree. I always chose my camping spots based on the tree to which I felt drawn. That night was spent tossing and turning, fighting off mosquitos and a growing fever. I would spend another night on the side of the road before reaching N'zeto. Initially, I thought I'd try and find a place where I could spend the night in town, but as I cycled through the town on the main street, I got this feeling that I should keep going and rather camp wild some kilometers outside of town to the north, which is exactly what I did.

I spent another feverish night in my tent. This time, I had my flysheet up as it was raining softly throughout the night. It made me feel more at ease as someone had once told me: "criminals don't like getting wet". Though nothing could've prepared me for what lay in store the next morning!

Camping in Namibia   *Near Keetmanshoop*

Speaking at a school   Nearing Ondangwa

Cycling in Angola   *Cycling in Angola*

CHAPTER 4

When I awoke the next morning I felt like death warmed up. I was convinced that I had contracted malaria. I had a pounding headache and a fever and all the muscles in my body felt like they were seizing up. I decided I would get out my first aid kit and test myself for malaria. I could test myself and I could treat myself with Coartem. It was still very early and I lay in my tent listening to the rain, still softly falling outside, as I tested myself. It takes a few minutes to get a result, so I started getting dressed. I felt stuck between a rock and a hard place. I felt that I couldn't remain in my tent on the side of the road and at the same time, didn't feel like it would be a good idea to be cycling in the rain.

How my day would turn out would soon be revealed. The malaria test showed negative and I figured I just had a bad bout of flu. I packed up camp and decided that I would take it easy out on the road, making whatever progress I could for the day. I had to push on as the expiry date on my visa for Angola was drawing closer.

The rain had stopped and I had just got on the road, when a black Ford pickup truck pulled over and stopped a few meters ahead of me. People stopping on the side of the road and wanting to chat to me had become somewhat of a normality, after all the publicity

I received in Luanda, so I thought little of it. Four men got out of the vehicle and approached me. I got this uneasy feeling in the pit of my stomach and when they revealed that they were carrying machetes and knives, I knew why. Adrenalin shot through my veins within a split second and a dozen thoughts flashed in my brain, considering every possible outcome. I remained calm and waited for them to make the first move.

The leader of the pack spoke to me in French. I couldn't understand all of it, but the gist of it was that they wanted me to hand over all my belongings. They were very obviously under the influence of alcohol. I was seriously outnumbered and although I did carry a knife, I knew it would be suicide to try and fight. Scenarios practiced during my self-defence training came flashing back and I knew the best possible solution for me would be to make a run for it. I slowly prepared to hand over my bicycle to these guys and planned to grab one of the front panniers off the bicycle, which contained my journals, and make a run for it into the bushveld. I counted to three in my head and then turned around and ran away as fast as my legs would carry me.

It was only when I reached thicker cover that I dared to look back to see if any of them were in pursuit. They weren't. None of them had even bothered to run after me. I immediately got the feeling that this was more of a practical joke to them than anything else. Of course, I didn't think it was very funny at all.

On the upside, I still had my Camelbak, within which was my cellphone, passport and bank cards. I had also managed to get away with the pannier bag with all my journals in it. All was not lost!

As I watched the spineless "C-words" disappear over the horizon with pretty much all my possessions in the world, I took a minute to try and process what had just happened. It's amazing how many thoughts actually go through one's mind in just a few seconds. Standing there behind some bushes, I thought to myself, well, I guess I could still become the first woman to walk around Africa! Ha! I quickly crunched some numbers in my head and figured out that, at a pace of about 5 kilometers an hour, on average, for 8 hours a day, including rest days and possible delays in requiring visas, it would take me roughly 4 years to complete the journey. And that is when I had the thought that,

"There has got to be an easier way".

I'm not sure how my brain even came to the next thought but, boom!

"I want to start over on a motorcycle".

This thought was a bit curious for a number of reasons. Most of all, for the reason that I had never been on a motorcycle in my life before, except that one time when I was allowed to go on the back of my uncle's motorcycle, when I was a little girl. I'd never ridden a motorcycle before and didn't even know how to change gears!

It's hard to explain, but somehow, I just knew that this was what I was supposed to do. It was like everything had led to this fateful point and now I finally knew what it was that I was supposed to do. I wasn't supposed to travel around the African continent on a bicycle! I was supposed to travel around the African continent on a motorcycle! Hooray! Now I just needed to find the money to buy a bike and learn to ride it and Bob's your uncle!

After considering all these thoughts for a few minutes, I figured it would be wise to notify someone of what had just happened. As I said earlier, I thankfully still had my Camelbak with me which had my mobile phone in it, so I took it out and sent text messages to my friend Hanret in South Africa, to Pedro in Lobito and Candido in Luanda, explaining to them what had just happened.

Next, I had to start making my way back to the nearest town, which happened to be N'zeto, about 8 kilometers away. And so, with my hydration pack on my back and pannier bag in hand, I started walking towards N'zeto. My phone rang and it was Hanret. She offered her condolences and support in whichever way she could give it. She has also experienced some horrific attacks on her person and told me that I needed to get rid of some of the adrenaline running through my body and that the best way to do this would be to stomp like a wild animal and scream at the top of my lungs. I'm not a screamer and don't easily show my emotions unless I feel comfortable doing so, but I figured I didn't have anything to lose , so I gave it a try. I jumped up and down on the side of the road and screamed until I didn't have any air left in my lungs. And then I burst out laughing at myself as I could only imagine what I must have looked like!

Both Pedro and Candido called me and expressed how sorry they were for what had happened. Then, another call, unidentified Angolan number. I answered. On the other end, a man's voice greeted me in Portuguese. He then switched to broken English and introduced himself as Pedro Sebastião, Governor of the Zaïre province of Angola and former General in the Angolan Army. He told me that he had just been informed of what had happened to me and asked that I remained where I was as he had instructed the local Chief of Police from N'zeto to fetch me. He informed me that he was on his way from his home in M'Banza Congo and would meet me in N'zeto. That was it.

Sure enough, about half an hour later, a police vehicle arrived to pick me up and took me back to N'zeto. There were three police officers in the car and, at first the driver took off in a northerly direction, away from town. I realized that he probably intended to go after the perpetrators, but I explained to him, in my best English with a Portuguese accent, that they'd be long gone by now. He seemed to understand and turned around, heading back to N'zeto.

Once back in town, I was taken to the Police Station. It seemed like everyone had heard the news as, seemingly, every Police Officer in the near vicinity was standing outside the Station, wanting to get a look at the girl on the bicycle who had been robbed. I was led to a small room inside the Police Station. The Chief of Police offered me a seat and asked if I'd like something to drink. He sent for a translator and started writing on a notepad. When the translator arrived, the Chief asked him questions, to be translated to me in English, and the answers relayed back to him.

"What did the vehicle look like?"

"How many people were there?"

"What did they look like?"

"What were they wearing?"

"Did you manage to catch the vehicle's license plate?"

Yeah right.

With the adrenalin wearing off, I could feel the flu settling back into my bones again. For a moment there, I had completely forgotten about the flu. I realised that I was suffering from on almighty headache and felt terribly exhausted, all of a sudden. When the Chief seemed content with my answers, he spoke to the translator, who, in turn, told me that I would be taken to a hotel in town and was to remain in the hotel until the Governor arrived. He had left M'Banza Congo in his airplane and should arrive within the next two hours or so. With that, I was taken to the hotel and shown to a room. Two guards were to remain outside my door at all times. It felt a bit like I'd been enrolled into a witness protection program.

I stood outside on the balcony for a minute, just taking it all in, I guess, when two men on the opposite side of the street called out to me,

"Hey, aren't you that girl who's cycling around Africa on her bicycle?"

"Not anymore", I answered back. I told them that,

"I've just been robbed of my bicycle and gear".

"What scum!" they exclaimed and then told me that they're from South Africa and doing some contract work in Angola and that they were on their way to Luanda. They wished me good luck and then they were on their way.

I welcomed the silence as I lay down on the bed and almost immediately fall asleep. I only woke up when one of the guards knocked on the door to tell me that the Governor had arrived.

Outside, a whole procession of police vehicles and officers are lined up to meet the Governor on arrival. It's pretty obvious that he's a very important man in these parts and suddenly, I felt nervous again. I was shown to a table in the hotel's restaurant and watched as the officers stood in line outside, saluting as the Governor arrived. For a moment, I felt like perhaps I should get up and salute as well, but remained seated.

Governor Pedro Sebastião is a tall man with a strong frame and well-kept moustache. His presence demanded respect and I could sense, from the get go, that he is not a man to be messed with. He walked up to me and shook my hand and the first thing he said is,

"I am sorry".

He apologized for the behaviour of his people and expressed that this is not the way of the Angolan people. He told me that something like this had never happened before and assured me that he will do everything within his power to return me to safety. He then informed me that two helicopters had been dispatched from the Angolan capital to search for the perpetrators and requested that I accompanied and stayed with him at his home in M'Banza Congo, until the end of the weekend. If by then the search turns up empty handed, I could choose to where I would like to be transported and he would make sure an airplane is made ready for me. He then ordered a burger and a Coke for each of us and started interrogating me.

I felt like I should click my heels or that I needed to be pinched or something. My head was spinning, this was all too much for me. Inside, I am laughing deliriously but I do not dare show it on the outside because I somehow didn't think that the Governor would get my twisted sense of humour. Or maybe I'm just in denial. Either way, the flu is really starting to act up on me.

I wasn't feeling very hungry and after the Governor had finished questioning me, he told me that I would be returning with him in his private airplane to his residence in M'Banza Congo, where I was to remain for the next two days. I told him that I wasn't feeling very well and that I thought I might have the flu. As we got into the plane, he got out his radio and spoke into it in Portuguese. For the next two hours, I silently stared out of my window, trying not to vomit from the pain as the change in air pressure made my ear drums hurt something terrible! When we touched down in M'Banza Congo, three vehicles waited for us on the runway. One for the Governor, one for his bodyguards and one for the doctor he called for over the radio. The Governor opened the door of one of the cars for me and apologized as he suddenly realized that there were two semi-automatic rifles lying on the floor of the car on the passenger's side. I simply replied saying that I'd handled such weapons before and that they didn't bother me, and then got in the car. He looked at me for a few seconds with a slight smile and then closed the door to get in on the driver's side. He obviously preferred driving himself. Without knowing anything about him, this man had my trust and respect.

Not surprisingly, he lived in a mansion of a house and the only paved road in the town happened to run from the front of his mansion to the airport. He showed me to a room up the stairs on the first floor, where the doctor then took a look at me. I told the doctor that I had tested myself for malaria, it was negative and he also suspected that it was the flu. He gave me some medication and told me to get some sleep. When he left, I followed doctor's orders and lay down on the bed to take a short nap. I woke up the next morning as the sun was rising and birds were chirping outside my window.

I felt embarrassed for not having had the decency to at least thank the Governor and say good night. I had a quick shower and headed down the stairs, to find the Governor sitting with a newspaper at his breakfast table. I offered my apologies for having disappeared during the night and explained that the medication the doctor gave me must have knocked me out. He doesn't make a big deal of it and asked me to sit down and have some breakfast. The next two days were spent waiting for news from the search parties which were out looking for the criminals who stole my Luna. The Governor asked me to come up with a figure of how much it would cost to replace all that which had been taken from me.

I had no idea what to tell him and messaged Hanret later on, when I was back in my room, asking her what she thinks I should say. She advised me to grab the opportunity with both hands as the Angolan government has lots of money and advised that I should say it would cost $20 000 to replace what had been stolen.

"I can't say that!" I tell her, to which she simply replied, "of course you can".

Sunday morning arrived and still the search party turned up no leads to the perpetrators. The Governor sat me down and asked me for a figure. I felt panicked and could hardly look him in the eye.

"Say $20 000. Just say it!" I said to myself, in my head.

My heart was racing and my mouth was dry. I counted to three, took a deep breath, looked him in the eyes and said,

"$20 000".

He didn't even blink, merely called his Assistant over and whispered something in her ear and then she disappeared through the front door. In my mind, I was seeing images of my being thrown in jail, never to be heard from again. The Governor's facial expression wasn't giving away anything and I felt panicked. Only minutes later, his Assistant returned with a white envelope and a piece of paper.

The Governor read over the piece of paper, signed it and then handed it to me, asking me to please sign it as well.

"In order for you to be able to take this money out of the country, you will need to declare it. This document is to state that it is a gift from me so you will not have any trouble from Angolan Customs".

He handed the envelope over to me and I nearly fell off my chair when I looked inside. $20 000 in crisp $100 bills. I was speechless! I could hardly believe my own audacity and that I'd actually just been handed $20 000! I couldn't say thank you enough! What's even more is that an airplane was ready and waiting for me on the runway to take me to Lobito. I had mentioned to him the previous day that, should my belongings not be found, I'd like to return to Lobito. I felt like I had a bit of a support structure there with Pedro and Lu and my South African friends and I could use a day or two to just take it all in and decide on a course of action.

With that, the Governor escorted me to the runway and bade me farewell. He asked that I notify him when I returned and I, again, thanked him profusely for his amazing generosity. I felt like I'd never be able to thank him enough in my lifetime. Although he is a very stoic military man, he hugged me before I got in the plane wished me the best of luck. As I boarded, I realized that I wouldn't be the only passenger. A man and woman sat buckled up in their seats. The man introduced himself as Alfonso, Personal Aid to the Minister of Tourism for Angola. He informed me that he would be escorting me to Lobito, where the Minister would be waiting to meet with me at the Hotel Terminus, a four star hotel situated on the beachfront. This time I did laugh out loud.

I spent the next few hours sleeping on the plane as we headed for Lobito. In some way, I sort of expected to wake up and find that I was back in my tent on the side of the road and that this had all been just one crazy dream!

I woke up as we touched down in Lobito, to discover that this crazy dream happened to be my reality. Pedro met us at the airport and also accompanied us to the hotel where I'd be meeting with the Minister of Tourism. The short ride from the airport gave us some time to catch up on all that had transpired over the last few days. Pedro was extremely supportive and understanding. On arrival at the hotel, the Minister had not yet arrived and I was shown to a room where I would be staying for the next day or two. Later on that evening, the Minister arrived and we all had dinner together, including Pedro and his wife. The Minister also expressed his disappointment in the events that had transpired and offered his apologies. He asked me if I had decided what I wanted to do and I told him that I wanted to return back to South Africa to start over again. I had already spoken to my South African friends in Lobito and could hitch a ride with one of them back to Windhoek and catch a flight back to Johannesburg from there. Riding back to Windhoek would also give me a bit more time to come to terms to all that had happened and start formulating a plan of action for when I returned home.

The next two days were spent on the road, heading back to Windhoek, in a 4x4. A distance that took me weeks to cover on my bicycle, only took two days in a vehicle. As we drove to Windhoek, I could pinpoint every single spot where I had set up camp. It made me feel pretty nostalgic, although I didn't say much. I didn't feel like talking much. I had the $20 000 in my Camelbak which lay on the back seat of the 4x4. I got to feel what it's like to be a smuggler as we crossed the border back into Namibia. I didn't feel the need to declare the money, unless asked, as I felt it might cause unnecessary drama that I'd have to deal with. I had had enough drama over the last couple of days. No one ever asked or searched the vehicle. I think I have potential as a cross-border smuggler.

When we arrived in Windhoek, I went straight to the airport to catch my flight back home to Johannesburg. Do not pass Go, do not collect $200. Go straight home. Flying had become my least favourite mode of transport, at this point, as I was still suffering from the flu and being up thousands of feet in the air really hurt my ears! I now get why babies are forever crying on airplanes.

Back home in South Africa, I took a few days out to just relax, to process the past week's events and to come up with some kind of plan in my head. I knew I wanted to start over again on a motorcycle, although I didn't know the first thing about riding or overland travel on a motorcycle. I spent days scouring the internet, searching for online motorcycling and adventure travel forums. I read every article I could find on adventure motorcycle traveling and learned about dual-purpose motorcycles.

After extensive research, the list of potential motorcycles finally came down to three possibilities: I would choose between a Honda Africa Twin, a Kawasaki KLR or a BMW F650GS Dakar. My personal preference leaned towards the BMW, although I ultimately went for the cheaper option and bought a brand new Kawasaki KLR 650. It had to be delivered as I could not yet ride it home. Amazing that one can buy a motorcycle on a learner's license in South Africa!

Since he had been riding motorcycles since his teens, I asked my younger brother if he could teach me to ride a motorcycle. My brother can be pretty sweet, I'll give him that, but he has no patience whatsoever! He explained to me, in theory, how the gearing on a motorcycle works and how to pull away. A few rimes, he stood by and watched me struggle to try and pull away on a little Yamaha 250 and then gave up. I kept trying until I finally got it. At first, I would practice pulling off, stopping, and then pulling off again. Then I started riding in circles. It's just like riding a bicycle, except it is less taxing physically and you can go much faster!

I was so scared of riding the Kawasaki for the first time. It's a tall bike for a short girl like me. I'm of average height at 5'5", but what helps is that I have fairly long legs, which helps a lot in being able to ride just about any bike, no matter the height. That being said, when you are a novice it makes for being very nervous. I knew that to get over my fear, I needed to get on the bike and ride somewhere. Anywhere! Easy peasy. So, for my maiden ride, Hanret took pictures as I was about to pull out of the garage. I swung my leg over the bike and nearly dropped it on the opposite side, but just managed to keep it up. With Hanret's help. Then, with my heart pounding in my throat, I pulled off out of the garage and headed down the road. After my heartbeat returned to a more reasonable rate, I was able to start getting used to the bike. Riding was easy, stopping and pulling off were the tricky parts!

I spent the next few weeks getting used to the bike and doing tons of research on what I'd need for the road ahead. I researched spares and tools and watched how-to videos on YouTube on how to change a tyre and clean an air filter on a motorcycle. I started the application process for visas all over again, this time, I'd apply for all my visas up until Cameroon. I learned about a Carnet de Passage, which is basically the motorcycle's passport that needs to be carried when crossing borders and allows the temporary 'import' of a motorised vehicle into a foreign country and the removal of it within a certain time. Exactly in the way that a visa works for a human. It's a pretty expensive document though. Depending on where one means to travel, one can expect to have to pay up to 300% of the value of your vehicle as a deposit on a Carnet de Passage. The good news, though, is that one gets this back after one's return to country of residence.

I knew from the outset that I didn't have enough money to make it all the way around the African continent, factoring in all the visas required. Even with the Governor's amazingly generous sponsorship, I'd only maybe be able to make it half way, if I worked really sparingly. Then, something happened that I could never have foreseen!

One morning, while sitting in front of my laptop and reading yet another ride report on overland motorcycle travel for research, I received a message on my personal Facebook profile from Bornito de Sousa, Minister of Local Government of Angola. He introduced himself in his message and expressed his wish to apologize for what had happened to me in Angola. Further to his message, he conveyed that if there was anything that the Angolan government could do to help me, I should let him know.

I read the message over and over again and could hardly believe my eyes. I doubt very much that, had these events transpired in any other country in the world, I would ever have received this type of reaction. The kindness and support from the Angolan people, in general, just blew me away! I also took this as a sign to grab the opportunity with both hands and wrote back to the Minister, explaining my predicament of lack of funding to complete the journey. I told him that my decision to start over again on a motorcycle now meant that I needed way more funding than what I would've needed on the bicycle. He replied with an understanding tone and asked me to send him a proposal with a figure of what I would need for the entire project. My heart jumped back up into my throat again! Another Eureka moment!

Over the next 48 hours, I slept very little and stayed up trying to figure out exactly how much I would need for the entire project. Including fuel, spares, tools, new camping equipment, riding gear, visas, food the Carnet de Passage, the works. I put together a proposal with my intended route and names of the countries I intended traveling through. I tried to explain as best I could why I wanted to do this and at the very end, I included a financial breakdown with a final amount of $60 000 for the entire trip around Africa, all inclusive. After I compiled an email to the Minister and uploaded the proposal, it took me forever to hit the send button. What if he said no? What if he thought me a total crook? I felt like I was taking a fat chance! But I had to try. I took a deep breath, counted to three and hit send. I just needed to wait for an answer.

I hate how time slows down when you are forced to wait for something. A minute feels like an hour and an hour feels like a day! The next two days felt like the longest wait of my life. I just about wore out the Refresh button on my laptop's keyboard, hopeful that the next time I hit it, a reply from the Minister might appear.

Finally, he did reply. It took me longer to open the email than to send it! I felt afraid of what I might find in the email. I'd eventually have to check though and when I finally scraped together the courage to read his reply, I nearly fell off my chair!

He said yes!

He said yes!!

The Angolan Government would sponsor my dream to set the record as the first woman in history to circumnavigate the entire African continent on a motorcycle!

Simply unbelievable! How lucky can one girl get? The best thing that ever happened to me, in my life, was being attacked in the middle of nowhere in Northern Angola. Literally.

CHAPTER 5

Isn't it amazing how all of life's woes seem to fall to the wayside when one has a lot of money? Well, I guess maybe that only happens when you're not used to having a lot of money? After receiving that email from the Minister, I felt as light as a feather all of a sudden. Like everything was absolutely awesome and nothing could bring me down. All because I had a bit of money.

The euphoria was unfortunately short lived as my brand new Kawasaki let me down shortly after its first service. It had only 3500 kilometers on the clock when the engine seized one day as I was on my way to meet a fellow adventure rider to pick his brain on his experiences traveling alone through Africa on his motorcycle. A big fight with the manufacturer ensued and in the end, I had lost all confidence in the bike. I decided to go for the BMW F650GS Dakar instead. Best decision ever!

The next few weeks were spent preparing for the relaunch! I was introduced to someone who helped me get the bike 'overland ready'. Kurt Beine taught me how to change a tyre on my motorcycle, how to fix a puncture and how to do a basic service myself, as well as what tools I'd need. He even gave me an impromptu, basic, off-road riding lesson in an open field near his house. I was very grateful for the help and felt more confident knowing that I'd be able to maintain the bike myself. I've always been the kind of girl who likes to be able to do things herself and I'm pretty good at figuring things out. This is how I knew that I'd be fine. No matter the problem, I'd always be able to find a solution.

I booked for and officially passed my motorcycle driver's license two weeks before setting off on my journey around Africa again. Yes, that's right - I only got my motorcycle driver's license two weeks before re-embarking on the greatest adventure of my lifetime. People always seem amazed when I tell this story, but it didn't faze me at all, at the time. In my mind, I was as ready as I'd ever be.

I made my way back down to the Western Cape Province, making a two-day trip of the 1300 kilometer journey from Johannesburg. I would stay over with new adventure motorcycling friends I had met on the *Wild Dog* online forum. A group of adventure riders had very kindly organized a send-off for me, followed by a group ride to the southernmost tip of the African continent the next day, where I'd officially start my journey again. I was filled with both excitement and a bit of impatience as I just wanted to get going again. I knew what lay ahead and, in my mind, I wanted to get to past the point where my previous trip came to a halt. Mentally, it felt like I was stuck at that point and I wanted to get over it so I could get on with the rest of the journey. At the time, in my ignorance, I might not have realized that it was all part of the bigger journey that I was on.

The morning of the 11th of April, 2012 arrived and a dozen riders from all over arrived to accompany me to Cape L'Agulhas, about 200 kilometers away. The weather was miserable. Cold, wet and windy. It didn't bother me though. I was filled with adrenaline and anticipation. At this stage, I still had very little experience of riding on a motorcycle and keeping the bike going in a straight line, while also fighting strong crosswinds, which proved to be pretty challenging. At one point, we stopped for a break and one of my riding companions, Rudolf, came to me and told me not to ride too close to the edge of the road. Being a local, he was obviously used to this kind of weather and he advised me to try and stick closer to the middle of the road to avoid being pushed off the side of the road by the strong crosswinds. Something that had apparently happened to a friend of his before.

Making it to the Southernmost Tip of Africa was a joyous and exciting occasion. The miserable weather didn't dampen our spirits and the group huddled together at the Cape L'Agulhas landmark for a swig of locally made champagne, to celebrate the start of my journey around Africa. Again. We stopped off for breakfast in Napier, after which a few members of the group would accompany me as far as the Cederburg Oasis, where we would spend the night. That made for about 550 kilometers of riding on the first day. I felt absolutely exhausted, both from the ride, fighting against the elements and also mentally and emotionally tired after the build-up and anticipation of getting going again. But more than this, I felt very happy and content to be back on the road again.

Day one had come and gone and, over the next two weeks, I would make my way back, north to where I had previously (been forced to) leave off. I had decided to not follow the same route as before as I could go faster now and explore a few areas that would have taken too long before, on the bicycle. I crossed the border back into Namibia again, three days after leaving Cape L'Agulhas and, instead of heading straight up the B1 towards Windhoek, I wanted to visit the renowned Fish River Canyon, this time round. The Fish River Canyon is the largest canyon in the southern hemisphere and the second largest canyon in the world after Arizona's Grand Canyon. The canyon is about 160 kilometers long, up to 27 kilometers wide and 550 meters deep in some places. It really is something worth putting on one's bucket list and I can understand why it is the second most visited attraction in the country of Namibia, with its stark beauty and amazing views over the breath-taking ravine.

Although I had covered a bit of dirt/gravel riding on route to the Cederberg Oasis, on the first day, the road leading off the B1, towards the Canyon, offered the first substantial stretch of off-road riding that I'd have to tackle, on my own, on this journey. With adrenaline pumping through my veins, I took a deep breath and decided that I'd take it easy and try my best to not write off either myself or my motorcycle, this early into the journey. Anyone who has ever travelled in Namibia will know that their gravel roads are well known for being very well maintained. They are more like 'gravel highways' really. These well-maintained gravel highways can be a bit deceiving sometimes, as patches of loose sand can jump out of nowhere, just as you're daydreaming about adventures that still lay ahead, and give you a bit of a wake-up call. I hit a patch of loose sand at about 100 kilometers/hour and had a bit more of an adrenaline spike than I would have liked. I nearly had a heart attack as the sand patch caused the bike to go into a nasty tank slap. With eyes as big as saucers and my heart thudding in my chest, I remembered tips I'd been given by numerous riders to not let of the gas, but to rather open up to get the bike to pull straight. The bike and I swerved all over the place and when I finally managed to gain some control, I had to stop for a few minutes, just to get my heartbeat to come down to something close to normal again. It gave me a big fright, but it also taught me to never get too comfortable, to always be on the lookout and to always expect the unexpected.

I did drop the bike a bit later on that day, just before I reached the Canyon. Coming around a corner, I hit another patch of thick sand and struggled to keep control. The bike started veering off towards the side of the road and I just could not get it to head in the direction I wanted it to. I just did not have enough experience, at the time, and decided to rather put it down than risk a bad fall. I put the bike down at low speed, right in the sand. No damage to either myself or the bike and, seeing as nobody was around to bear witness, even my ego remained intact. My next challenge would prove to be far more difficult than I originally expected. Picking up the bike became an impossible task in the thick sand. I spent so much energy trying to get the bike up, and because it was so overloaded with all my gear, I couldn't even get it to budge. Lucky for me, a family of German tourists came to my rescue when they saw me standing on the road with my bike on its side, and very kindly helped me pick up the bike.

I spent that night camping at the Ais-Ais resort, situated close to the Canyon and treated myself to a well-deserved steak and a beer after my very eventful day on the road. DAX the bike, obviously drew a lot of attention as not a single person in the campsite walked past without stopping and asking some questions, as curiosity got the better of them. I didn't mind though, as I enjoyed the conversation and sharing my goals with everyone who stopped by. I also had the good fortune to meet two ladies traveling across Africa in their Land Rover Defender. Jen and Bel, together with their Border Colley, named 'Peggy', documented their journey on their blog site named 'Djin and Tonic'. Meeting other women traveling on their own through Africa gave me a sense of relief, as if to say 'it is possible after all'.

From Ais-Ais, I would make my way back to the main road leading up north through Namibia, the B1, towards Windhoek, the capital of the once-German colony. I enjoyed the long, empty stretches between Keetmanshoop, Mariental and Windhoek. With little in the way of traffic for miles and miles, it felt like I had the road to myself at times. I spent a lot of time in my own head, admiring the scenery and thinking about the journey that lay behind me and the journey that still lay ahead. I felt anxious about entering Angola again and even more anxious about what countries like the Congo and Nigeria would hold for me. I forced myself to put away my anxiety and focus on getting through one day at a time and to enjoy it as much as I could.

I knew I could find a nice camping spot at the River Chalets, just outside of town. As I rolled in through the entrance, I noticed two 4x4 vehicles, equipped with every travel accessory you could possibly need, parked at a chalet near the entrance. Both cars bore South African number plates. As I slowly rode past them, one of the men stopped me and struck up a conversation, wanting to know the usual. He offered me a room in one of their chalets, as they had a spare room that they wouldn't be using. It saved me having to pitch my tent and would assure me of some company and probably food, so I thanked them for their generosity and took the spare room. As they were on a fishing trip, heading to Henties Bay, a well-known little fishing town situated on the coast just north of Swakopmund, they spent the evening regaling me with their angling tales. They suggested that if I passed by Henties Bay, I could stay with them, and so I agreed to meet up with them again a few days later.

I headed up to Windhoek and met up with Ray again, before heading west to Swakopmund to say hello to my brother and his girlfriend. They were living in Swakopmund, as my brother was working as a contractor at the Walvis Bay Harbor. The town is a well-known tourist destination on the desert coastline with shops, hotels, restaurants and a pier. What I love most about the town is its predominantly German colonial architecture, which gives it a feel of a town with a rich history. The town was founded in 1892 as the main harbour to German South West Africa. A small percentage of its population is still German-speaking today. I spent a few days with them, catching up, before heading north to meet up with the guys in Henties Bay on their fishing trip, before carrying on north, on my own again, towards the Angolan border.

Following the same route I had previously ridden on my bicycle, my route would lead me back to Swakopmond, back through the desert towards Omaruru and on to a greener bushveld milieu, as I headed to meet up with the B1 at Otjiwarongo. I welcomed the greener, lusher environment in the north, after having made it through the more arid, desert-like environment of the south and the West Coast. I decided to make the run from Henties Bay to Ondangwa in one day, a total of 875 kilometers.

I was eager to get back to Angola and pick up where I had left off. I had stayed at the Ondangwa Rest Camp previously, so that was exactly where I was heading. This time I wouldn't have to guess or wonder what it would be like, as I already knew.

It was a long, tiring day and I knew that getting into camp before dark would be cutting it fine, so I didn't take a lot of time when stopping for a toilet break or to fill up and stretch my legs. Just on the other side of Oshivelo, about 150 kilometers from Ondangwa, I was pulled over by a Traffic Officer, for speeding. The Officer had me get off my bike and said that I would have to pay a fine. Though reluctant, I had no problem with paying a fine as I was, indeed, over the speed limit. The Officer was adamant that he would have to take me all the way back to the Police office in Tsumeb to pay the fine. I just looked at him with bewilderment as I knew there was no way on earth I would make it to the camp before dark, if I had to go back to Tsumeb first. The sun was already starting to set and so I tried to persuade the Officer to let me go. I played the, "do you really want me to ride in the dark as a woman alone" card, and it worked! I told him that if something happened to me, it would be on his conscience. A bit manipulative, I know... but desperate times call for desperate measures! So he let me go, without a fine. I thanked him and shook his hand before jumping back on my bike to continue towards the Ondangwa Camp, with plenty of time to spare before sunset!

I arrived at the camp and went about setting up my tent, when I heard two motorcycles approaching. I turned around to see two bikes pass the campsite. With a weathered look, their pannier boxes covered in stickers of different African countries' flags, tents strapped onto the back seats along with roll bags, the bikes had "overlanders" written all over them. I got so excited that before I could help myself I was waving at them, with maybe just a tiny bit too much enthusiasm. Imagine Forrest Gump waving at Lieutenant Dan from his shrimp boat, when he saw him sitting in his wheelchair on the pier. That's a bit what I looked like.

It didn't appear that they had seen me, as they turned around and left. Or maybe they did see me and turned around and left! Either way, I felt disappointed as I really looked forward to picking the brains of some fellow overland travellers. Luckily my disappointment didn't last as they returned before long. They checked into the camp and rode around to where I had set up my tent. They introduced themselves, Chris from Switzerland and Andrei from Romania. They had made their way down the west coast of Africa and were on their way to Cape Town. This really excited me as it meant I could pick their brains for some information on the road that lay ahead.

After they had set up camp, the three of us went on a walkabout, exploring the town a little bit, something I wouldn't have done had I been on my own. When we returned to camp, we bought a few cold beers and sat down at a table with our individual notebooks and maps of Africa. The guys were incredibly helpful and went through the map with me from where we were, all the way to Morocco, giving me valuable information on what to expect and look out for and with whom to get in touch. It is here that I learnt that there's a whole network of motorcycle clubs leading all the way up North! In return, I gave them what little information I could on the route options and information heading down to Cape Town.

It is also here that I learned the invaluable lesson that once you ride a motorcycle, you automatically become part of the biggest family on this planet! There is this unwritten code amongst bikers that bikers always look after their own. This made me feel a little more at ease, knowing that there were people with whom I could get in touch for support along the way. It meant that I would never 'really' be on my own. It took the edge off my anxiety of what may lie ahead.

The next day, I bade Chris and Andrei farewell and headed north towards the Angolan border. I expected my crossing back into Angola to be quick and easy, considering that I now had personal ties to the Angolan government after all. Things would not go exactly as I had planned. Upon my arrival at the border, I found that the infrastructure I had previously seen had been bulldozed and new buildings with fresh paint stood in their place. I had to figure out where to go all over again, which wasn't too difficult, at least. The other positive was that the newly erected fence, guarded entrance and exit gates meant that border crossings could proceed in peace and away from the chaos that is the town of Oshikango on the Namibian side of the border and Santa Clara on the Angolan side of the border.

Passport stamping out of Namibia is easy enough, but stamping into Angola is a whole other story. I was shown to a new white building where I needed to show my passport with the required Visa for Angola in it, which I had, of course. What I wasn't expecting was for the Customs Officer to have a problem with the type of visa I had acquired. I had an 'ordinary' Visa in my passport and not a 'tourist' Visa. This was the same type of Visa with which I entered previously and that is why I applied for the same Visa again. When it became obvious that the Officer wasn't going to budge, I explained to him that I had been instructed by the Minister of Local Government in Luanda to meet with an appointed fixer at the border who would lead me to Ondjiva. I gave the Officer the Minister's number and asked him to phone him to determine that I was, indeed, telling the truth.

The Officer disappeared into his office to phone the Minister as I requested he do. He emerged a few minutes later, handed me my passport back with an entry stamp and said that I was free to go. I asked if he knew who was supposed to meet me, but he had no idea. I waited around for a while and eventually decided to head to Ondjiva on my own. It's not like I didn't know the way.

A few things had changed since I had last ridden the road from the Santa Clara border to Ondjiva. The same hustle and bustle still existed just beyond the border. I stopped to buy a local sim card and some airtime, and something cold to drink. Once my phone was sorted with a new working sim card, I carried on toward Martie and Hendrik's home, where I had stayed previously, while making my way north on my bicycle. A whole new road appeared on this stretch of the journey, since I had last been here. This meant that I made it to Martie and Hendrik's in no time. I didn't even need a GPS. I could identify their house underneath the big baobab tree anywhere.

These people are such gracious hosts and, once again, Martie went out of her way to make me feel welcome. She had prepared a wonderful home cooked meal and dessert for the occasion. We sat around their small dining room table and I brought them up to speed with all that had happened in the time I'd been away. We were just tucking into the lovely dessert that Martie had made, when the unthinkable happened.

My spidery senses were triggered and all of a sudden it was as if everything was happening in slow motion. Martie was still speaking to me as I watched Hendrik get up from the table across from me. He was heading for the front door, his eyes filled with an expression of fear. I was standing on the other side of the table, behind the couch when Martie let out a loud scream. Before I knew it, a hand holding a crowbar come through the door. Hendrik tried to push the door back so he could close it, but then another hand appeared through the gap, holding a pistol. Four men in total pushed their way through the door and into the house. One holding the crowbar, one with the pistol in hand, one with a can of mace spray and the last one was empty handed and played the role of lookout.

My mind was racing and went over dozens of different scenarios in a matter of seconds. The little training I had received previously kicked in and I summed up the situation for myself: we're outnumbered 3 to 4 with two females on our side and two elderly people. There was no way we could fight back and win, so giving over control was the only logical plan of action.

The man with the gun was obviously the main aggressor and instructed us to sit down in the chairs while the man with the crowbar started going through the kitchen drawers. He found some packaging tape and started taping us to the chairs. I was first and considering the amount of tape he used, he must have considered me a possible threat. He taped my legs to the chair and my hands behind my back, taped around my body and the chair and finally he taped my mouth shut. They turned on the television and turned the volume way up. This made me uncomfortable as it meant that they didn't want anyone to hear what was going on in the house. Plus, seeing that we were far away from any other houses or building, I could only think that they didn't want anyone to hear anything as loud as a gunshot!

After they tied us up, the guy with the crowbar and mace started going through the house and grabbing anything of value. The man with the gun grabbed my mobile phone off the table, where it was charging, and stuffed it in his trouser pocket, while the lookout was outside, trying to get into Hendrik's truck. As all of this was going on, the main aggressor kept shouting the word 'money' in English, Portuguese and... Afrikaans. This is when I realize that these guys were not Angolans. I also then noticed the KFC beanie that the guy with the gun was wearing. I felt even more violated, knowing that we were being attacked in Angola... by non-Angolans. Go figure. I don't know quite why this was such an issue for me when criminals do that all the time.

My motorcycle jacket, with US$1000 in cash, the keys to my motorcycle, my passport and credit card, was lying at the front door. I simply refused to give them a single cent. KFC beanie guy pointed the gun at my head and kept shouting,

"We know who you are!"

This made me feel awful! Did I lead these horrible people to Martie and Hendrik's home? Even so, I remained resolute and refused to give in, I would not give them anything. Even if it cost me my life. (I know it may sound silly, but you just don't know how you will react until you're actually faced with such a situation).

My mobile phone started ringing in KFC beanie dude's trouser pocket. It kept ringing and ringing and I knew it was probably the local chief of police trying to check in with me. You see, I sent him the details to my whereabouts the minute I arrived at Martie and Hendrik's home, so they would know where to find me. And now, they were trying to get hold of me and my phone just kept ringing in this idiot's pocket.

The situation started escalating as we weren't giving them what they wanted. They had already taken a video camera, all our mobile phones and some jewellery from Martie's bedroom. Hendrik offered up the cash in his wallet that was in his truck, parked outside. But these bozos didn't have enough know-how to open the truck. I mean, seriously? What a joke.

And then it became anything but a joke. Mr KFC beanie had had enough and wanted to make his feelings clear. It is then that he pulled a magazine out of his trouser pocket and loaded the gun. It was never even loaded! But it was now. He stepped in front of me and put the gun right against my head. You know they say your whole life flashes past when you're about to die? That didn't really happen for me. I distinctly remember, and will never forget, what I felt in that moment.

One the one hand I felt like, "well, if this is my time, then this is my time", but on the other hand, I closed my eyes and shouted "HELP" with all that I could muster. Bound and taped, it couldn't be out loud, but, with all my heart and soul, I guess.

The next minute, the lookout came storming in and said something incomprehensible. He seemed panicked and the others dropped what they were doing and ran out the door. None of us knew what had just happened. We stared at one another, still tied to the chairs and our mouths still taped shut. The tape around Hendrik's mouth was pulled off so that he could explain to them how to get into his truck. Yeah right, not happening, dude.

Hendrik broke free from his bounds and cautiously moved to the front door. I had no idea what to expect but, the next minute, the door is flung open again and a big burly man in a police uniform was standing in the doorway. We all let out a sigh of relief, it was the Chief of Police! He had come and searched for me because I wasn't answering my phone! The look on his face was one of bewilderment and a touch of, "You have got to be kidding me right now! Not again!"

He made a call and within minutes, the place was swarming with police vehicles and included the local Governor who had come to see what was going on as well. Now released from our bonds, the Chief of Police embraced me in a big bear hug and kept repeating,

"I'm so sorry, I'm so terribly sorry".

I couldn't help but burst out laughing. I guess different people have different reactions to near-death experiences. I had so much adrenaline pumping through my veins that I couldn't stand still and couldn't help but giggle like a little girl the whole time. I stood outside on the veranda smoking one cigarette after another

(I have quit smoking since then), watching the Police Officers scouring the area for the perpetrators, feeling like I'd had ten cups of very strong coffee. Never in a thousand years could I have guessed that on my first night back in Angola, something like this would happen.

As for how people react differently to stressful situations, Hendrik came and stood by me outside, watching the spectacle of flashlights and dozens of policemen still scouring the area. In unnecessary detail, he told me a harrowing story about when he was in the army, back in the day, and he and two fellow soldiers had killed a man in cold blood, behind enemy lines, in Mozambique. I know it was probably his way of dealing with the whole situation, as well, but I felt a bit like I was stuck in a bad dream. A dark-humoured nightmare that something from a movie. I also found out later that Martie was keeping the monthly wages for the company she works for at home. So, it wasn't my fault after all, but an inside job instead. Why the guy with the gun said he knew me, nobody knows.

The police didn't find the perpetrators, but they did find a lead that they said they were going to follow to see if it delivered anything. In the meantime, we were instructed to stay in the house and two guards were placed at the front and back doors to keep watch throughout the night. Not surprisingly, I struggled to fall asleep that night.

The next morning, the Chief of Police escort me into town and Martie joined us to help with translating where necessary. To my surprise, our first stop was for an interview with the local news station. Nothing was said about the previous night's events. To be honest, as the people had been so good to me, I didn't want any more bad press leaking about traveling in Angola. To prove my point, our next stop was at a phone shop to buy me a new phone, compliments of the Chief of Police.

Before I was allowed to carry on, I was informed that I would be given an armed escort for the rest of my journey through Angola. I didn't even protest as I could completely understand their fears. None of us wanted yet another incident, I seemed to be to criminals in Angola as a moth to a flame. As I bade all my new friends' farewell and started making my way out of town, I stopped off at a fuel station to fill up for the road ahead. My newly appointed armed escort surrounded me and ushered everyone away from the bowsers so I could fill up first. I felt so awkward but just went along with it but when I went inside the little store to buy a cold drink and got to the counter to pay for it, the man behind the counter looked at the heavily armed men outside, then looked at me and asked,

"Hey lady, did you do something wrong"?

With all that drama behind me, I was back on the road again. It felt great to be moving again, though I remembered that a particularly bad stretch of road still lay ahead between Xangongo and Cahama. The same piece of road that took me three days by bicycle. Work was still being carried out on the road so we had to take the alternative route, which was basically a thick sandy route, winding its way through the bushes and thorn trees. I was still a beginner rider at that stage and really struggled in the thick sand. My escort rode ahead of me and I struggled along at snail's pace, until we reached some hard pack again, where I could go a bit faster. We passed countless freight trucks stuck in the sand and the heat made the slow progress almost unbearable. No Coca-Cola truck this time to offer us some refreshment.

Whenever we reached a major town, we'd head straight for the Police office where I would be signed over to become the responsibility of the next Chief of Police and so on and so on. I felt like a DHL package being transported to borders beyond. One thing was sure, I was as safe as houses. Nobody dared to come within a 50 meter radius of me. With my escort leading the charge, we made our way to Lubango, where I was graciously hosted by a friend of the Governor of the Cunene Province. Previously, on my bicycle, I had headed up to Benguela from Lubango. This time, I wanted to take a different route and ride down the famed Serra de Leba pass and stay overnight in the coastal town of Namibe.

Namibe is a desert coastal town that was founded by the Portuguese in the 19th century. Its arid environment and vegetation is due to its proximity to the Namib Desert. My good friend, Candido, from Luanda, had given me the name and number of a good friend of his in Namibe who, he said, would happily host me during my stay in the town. My police escort handed me over to the powers that be in Namibe and then made their way back to Lubango.

I spent the afternoon enjoying some time to myself without any police escorts to lead me anywhere or government officials to meet. I walked through the city and down to the beach. It must've been a beautiful town in its day. Right in the centre of town, I walked into, what must have been, a beautiful park in its day. Remnants of old Portuguese style monuments remain, paying tribute to important figures of yesteryear. The beach is lined with artsy benches, on which to sit, with their arched canopies in an array of vibrant colors and where artists sometimes exhibit and sell their work. A mix of old and new, rich and poor. A beautiful town of contrasts, wedged between the desert and the ocean.

That evening, I was to meet with the Governor of the Namibe province at the city hall in order that he could welcome me to his provincial area, followed by an interview with the local press, the next morning, before I could be on my way, heading up further north towards Benguela Province. The first 20 kilometers would be on an apparently brand new tarmac road, until I would hit gravel again for most of the way to Benguela. As has become the custom, an armed police escort would lead the way and accompany me all the way.

The first 20 kilometers on the beautiful new road flew by, so fast, that I almost regretted not going slower and savoring it a bit longer before getting onto the gravel road again. I was still getting used to riding off-road with a fully loaded bike. And when I say fully loaded, I mean that when it came to packing for the trip, I threw in everything including the kitchen sink! My poor motorcycle was more like a mule than anything else. Rookie mistake!

The fully loaded bike made it hard to handle in some sandier and technically tricky areas. My DAX was packed to the rafters and I sometimes struggled to keep the bike upright, when I was forced to stop on a camber, to wait for big, burly construction vehicles to pass me. They were obviously still busy working on the road, tarring the rest of the road from Namibe. In some places, big, loose rocks would hinder my momentum and I'd put the bike down. It would be in these instances that I'd be grateful to have an escort as the guys would get out of the car, help me pick the bike back up and then we'd slowly carry on again. This went on for most of the way until the gravel road became more hard-packed, which made for easier going and I could go a bit faster.

The cool ocean wind, coming over the dunes on my left, provided some much needed relief from my hot, sweaty stickiness brought on by wrestling the bike back up from its horizontal position, every now and again, on the dirt road. The scenery is quite spectacular with sheer drop-offs to the left and down to the beach below and arid desert-like scenery to the right. It's a different kind of beauty. We made fairly good progress, though by my calculations, at our pace, we'd only reach Benguela in the dark. What didn't help is an hour-long wait in Dombe Grande, when we had to wait for the Chief of Police to arrive so my escort could hand me over to the next escort that would be with me until Lobito, where I would once again stay at the Hotel Terminus.

It's only 90 kilometers from Dombe Grande to Lobito. My surroundings had gone from arid desert to more greenery, the road lined with thorn trees and Baobabs. The gravel road was in fairly good condition. While waiting in Dombe Grande, I was given a plastic chair to sit on in the main road, right across from the Police Station. Actually, it was the only road in town. From what I could gather, the town was made up of a Police

Station, a few houses and a small shop. And the red soil gravel road that ran through it.

When the Chief of Police finally arrived, I was signed over and we could get going again. The only problem was that it was starting to get dark and the police car, that was now my escort, didn't have working headlights. So, instead of the vehicle driving in front of me, I now rode in front of them, to show them the way. This meant that the pace came right back down again. We finally arrived in Lobito at midnight, in pouring rain. It didn't really matter though. I was safe and making good progress. I just kept focusing on reaching my next destination, the Republic of Congo. I wanted to, at least, make it further than my last attempt.

While in Lobito, I met up with the Minister of Tourism and with Pedro Bandeira again. The Hotel Terminus graciously hosted me once again for the two nights that I spent in my favorite town in Angola. Pedro and his wife Lu took me out for dinner to the Zulu restaurant again. I have such fond memories of this restaurant situated right on the beach, where they serve the most delicious Portuguese influenced food and seafood! Fresh fish, langoustines, shrimp, crab, mussels and more. Delicious!

The next day I would meet up with a local motorcycling club called, 'Moto Clube 9'". They were a very friendly group of guys who immediately went about helping me, by way of having my bike checked and given a wash. It was decided that they would accompany me to Barra do Cuanza the next day. There, we would meet up with the motorcycle club 'Amigos da Picada' from Luanda and they'd ride with me the rest of the way into the capital. We tried getting out of having to have a police escort with us, but they wouldn't budge. Orders are orders and the local Chief of Police had orders to send an armed escort with me to Luanda, where the next group of police officers would take over. The biking guys really didn't like the idea of having an armed escort holding us up, but we really had very little or no say in the matter.

Early the next morning, I stood outside waiting for the guys next to my clean, fully loaded bike. Pedro had come to bid me farewell again. He is such a good person. Both he and his wife are really wonderful, giving and caring people. When the guys arrived, it was time for us to get going and so a few last photographs were taken and then we were off, with our escort leading the way with blaring sirens. The 'President' of the motorcycle club had a chat with the police officers in Portuguese before we left. I don't know what he had said to them, but we went much faster than I had been traveling with my previous escorts. The boys obviously didn't want to be held up and somehow convinced the policemen to quicken the pace.

Again, it felt strange to be riding on roads that I had previously cycled. The massive uphill leading out of Lobito toward Luanda was a monster, with no end, when I was on the bicycle. Now, on the motorcycle, it almost didn't feature as something worth remembering. I was overcome with nostalgia pretty much all the way to the meeting point. I tried to imagine what the welcome would be like, but never in my wildest dreams could I have expected what was about to happen next.

Before you arrive in Barra do Cuanza, you cross a long bridge over the Cuanza River, which brings you to a check point. After the checkpoint, you enter Barra do Cuanza. As I passed the checkpoint, I saw this long line of motorcycles with riders in yellow t-shirts waving at me. As I approached, they started cheering loudly and as I stopped I was sprayed with champagne from all sides. It felt like I had just won the Grand Prix! I was taken by surprise, I had no idea that all of this had been organized in my honor. Once I wiped the champagne out of my eyes, I spotted my good friend Candido Carneiro, standing ready with his camera and a massive smile on his face. He had organized the welcoming party for me with the Motorcycle Club, along with a radio interview, on arrival. I couldn't believe that they had all gone to so much trouble. I felt very special and humbled by the experience.

The boys from Lobito bade me farewell and turned around for their ride back home. The Amigos da Picada Motorcycle group would see me in to Luanda along with Candido and our ever present police escort. I had quite the convoy heading into Luanda. We had two policeman on motorcycles in front, then a police car behind them, Candido in his 4x4 with Angolan and South African flags hanging off the back of the car, the Amigos da Picada Group Leader behind the car, then me and the rest of the group behind me. We caused quite the uproar coming into Luanda.

If you've never experienced the traffic in Luanda, let's just say it is right up there with some of the world's listed cities with the worst traffic! I don't know if our entering the town made it any easier or worse, but I'm guessing it would've made it worse for the locals. Police vehicles led in front, with sirens blaring, the bikes pushing cars off the road to make way for me and my convoy. You'd expect something like this for a presidential procession in most African countries. A cacophony of sirens, hooting and shouting, as we slowly edged our way through the jam-packed traffic. I wasn't anything official, apart from a package to be delivered to the next neighboring country as soon as possible! I felt both very important and horribly guilty, at the same time, for wrecking people's daily commute home. I could see the look in some of the drivers' eyes like they were thinking,

"Who in the hell is this person and what is all the fuss about?"

Once back in the city, I had a full program, it seemed. When we made it into the capital, we headed to Miami Beach Bar where a mountain of food and drinks was waiting for our group. I was required to pose for a gazillion photographs, with as many people, while a television crew followed me around. After some food and drinks, Candido, the TV crew and I headed to Candido's house for more photographs by his pool. And then... peace, at last. Well, for a little while at least.

The rest of my program while in Luanda included a meet and greet with most of the Angolan government ministers and officials, a number of radio interviews and a personal meeting with Minister Bornito de Sousa, who was responsible for my getting a sponsorship from the Angolan government. The meeting was set up at my request, mainly to thank the Minister for all his help and for the Angolan government's incredible generosity. The Minister and his wife were very gracious in receiving us and we spent a wonderful evening talking about our countries, about my journey and just getting to know one another.

I spent two days with Candido and then moved to stay with one of the senior members of the Amigos da Picada Motorcycle Club, George Almeida. George and his family welcomed me into their home as a friend. I enjoyed George's company as he talked more about politics and Angola's history. I enjoyed learning more about this beautiful country and its people, through which I just couldn't seem to travel without having to have protection. Even so, I really do love Angola. It is any adventure traveller's dream. A great portion of the country remains raw in its beauty and unspoiled by tourists, which makes it all the more exciting in which to travel.

I really enjoyed my stay in Luanda, for a second time, but it was now time to start moving on. Although pretty much in the opposite direction from where I was supposed to be heading, the guys from the motorcycle club suggested that I join them on a social ride to Huambo, before I started making my way back up north. Huambo is almost 600 kilometers from Luanda, almost in line with Lobito, on the map. The boys were going on a trip from Luanda to Huambo, then Lobito and back up to Luanda. I figured it was a good opportunity to get to see even more of the country and agreed to join them. I had enough time on my visa and I'd be safe with the club guys. Even so, we had to ask Minister de Sousa for permission for me to tag along and although he'd allow us to travel without my ever present police escort, we would have to check in with local police in both Huambo and Benguela. So, in a group of about 20 motorcycle riders, we left at 05h00 the next morning for our little excursion to visit the town of Huambo.

Huambo, formerly known as Nova Lisboa or New Lisbon, is located about 220 kilometers from Benguela and 600 kilometers from Luanda. It is the second largest city in the country, after the capital, Luanda. The road from Luanda to Huambo is in fairly good condition, tar/black top all the way. The route between the two cities is dotted with smaller towns or settlements. What

I really loved about the ride down to Huambo was the scenery. Untouched, thick green bushveld as far as the eye can see. Exploring nature in all its glory is probably one of the top reasons why people embark on adventures, I think, apart from personal growth and experiencing local cultures, food, traditions etc. I never really saw any wild animals as I'm guessing most of them have either been eaten or eradicated by the former civil war, which is a tragedy.

Once in Huambo, Lilio accompanied me to the police station to check in and report that I was, indeed, still in one piece. We met up with the riders from the motorcycle club who had ridden in from Lobito and the whole group went out for dinner and clubbing that evening. These guys sure know how to party and I had a lot of fun! The next morning, we all saddled up and headed to Lobito for one more night's stay before returning to Luanda, where three guys from the Amigos da Picada Club had decided that they would like to ride with me all the way to Soyo. I didn't complain as this was the stretch during which my journey came to an end the last time round, and even with the police escort, I felt like I could do with all the protection I could get.

Once back in Luanda, I phoned the man who had come to my rescue previously, the Governor of the Zaire Province, and let him in know my plans for riding north to Soyo. He sounded very surprised and happy to hear from me and we arranged to meet up when we reached

N'zeto. I'm guessing that he probably thought that he'd never see me again. It always feels good to be able to surprise people and I was looking forward to being able to thank the Governor for all that he had done, once again.

The aftereffects of the Angolan Civil War, that lasted until 2002, can be seen everywhere you travel in Angola, even to this day. War memorials that have been erected in towns and cities, demolished or blown-up buildings and abandoned tanks are still evident, all over the country. Warning signs, to stay on the road and avoid landmines, are prevalent. Yet, the people are some of the friendliest I've ever met. I think that when you've experienced so much pain and grief, all you want is peace and joy in your life.

I had three guys accompanying me north to Soyo. We would meet with Governor Pedro Sebastiao in N'zeto before carrying on to Soyo, about 480 kilometers from Luanda and 200 kilometers from N'zeto. The road north of Luanda to Ambriz would be tar and thereafter, it remained the same as before, a gravel road until just before N'zeto. I was still going much slower than the other guys on the gravel, but had the police escort with me at all times. At one point, we had to stop as one of the guys' bikes sprung a radiator leak. They fixed it in no time with some Pratley's Steel Putty and then we were on our way again. I loved this part of the country, it felt more isolated, with very little between towns, except for an open gravel road lined with gigantic baobab trees. I slept under one of those trees when I was still on my bicycle and the fact that I would soon be standing at the same place, where my journey came to a halt before, felt both daunting and strangely nostalgic at the same time.

As we approached the town, we were met by another police vehicle that led us to the equivalent of the Town Hall. On the steps outside the building, stood a group of about two dozen children, aged 10 and up, all dressed in red t-shirts and singing songs to welcome us (me back) to their town. In front of the children, stood Governador Pedro Sebastiao, dressed in a suit, as usual. As I got off my bike, he came down to meet me and my traveling companions and then led us inside the building. We all gathered in a boardroom, accompanied by some members of the press and other officials from the area. The Governor handed me a bunch of flowers and an envelope with my name on it, while the press took photos, video and short statements.

After all the official business had been taken care of, we told the Governor that we needed to fill up our bikes with fuel. He told us to leave it to him and instructed his assistant to fetch fuel for the bikes. In the meantime, we were led to a nearby restaurant, where a spread had been prepared for our party. Delectable fresh seafood, plantain, beans, Portuguese rolls and whatever we wanted to drink. We were so spoilt and completely lost track of time as we sat talking around the table. By the time we had finished, we realized that there was no way that we would reach Soyo before nightfall and so we decided that we would carry on for as far as we could and then camp on the beach for the night before carrying on to Soyo the next morning.

We carried on for about another 100 kilometers, before we stopped off at Manga Grande, which is where we would stay for the night. We pulled off and followed a short footpath toward the beach. Manoeuvring my heavily loaded bike through the thick sand towards the beach, proved to be quite a challenge. Everyone got stuck and, as it was getting dark, we decided to help push the bikes through, one by one. Finally on the beach, we pitched our tents and the guys arranged with the locals for some buckets of water (to wash with) and some food (a pot of spaghetti) for dinner. The guys all washed themselves on the beach while I found some cover, behind bushes, where I washed myself with the cold water in the bucket. We then sat on our sleeping bags, eating spaghetti, under the stars and drinking Amarula liqueur that one of the guys had brought with him, with the sound of waves breaking onto the beach behind us. One of the simplest days on my trip and one of my favourites. While lying in my tent, listening to the waves, I suddenly remembered the envelope that the Governor had given me. I put my headlamp on and pulled it out of my jacket's inner pocket. As I opened it, I could see that there was money inside. US$2000 in cash! Like he hadn't done enough already! This man's generosity truly knew no bounds. I put that money aside as my fuel fund for the trip.

At dawn the next morning, we got up and packed up camp before pushing the bikes back to the main road through the thick sand again. Once back on the road, we stopped at a roadside food stall for some breakfast which consisted of more fresh grilled fish, plantain, beans and bread. We took our time as we only had about 80 kilometers to go to Soyo. In the meantime, I received a call from Governor Sebastiao to inform me that he had arranged for us to stay in a hotel in Soyo and that he would be meeting us there later in the afternoon. He had flown from his home in M'banza Congo to meet us in N'zeto, flew back home and then he'd be flying to Soyo to meet us again.

Soyo, formerly known as Santo Antonio do Zaire, is situated at the mouth of the Congo River, the border between Angola and the Democratic Republic of the Congo, or DRC, and is the single largest, oil-producing area in the country. My initial plan was to travel through Zaire, cross the border at Matadi and then ride north to cross into the Republic of Congo at Mfouati. Recent reports of heavy rains and impassable roads made me change my mind and I elected to catch a ferry from Soyo to Cabinda, which is an exclave and province of Angola, with a population of less than a million people. I had received a number of messages and letters from readers who had been following my journey, expressing their concern for my safety in Cabinda. I figured, whether I travelled through the DRC or Cabinda, both would be fairly equally risky and my instinct was telling me to head through Cabinda. If there is one thing I've learned from traveling alone, it is to always, always, always trust your instincts.

Entering Soyo we were directed to a nearby, fairly snazzy hotel, where the Governor had arranged for us to stay for the night. He hadn't arrived yet and so we used the time to meet up with another friend and member of the Amigos da Picada Club, living in Soyo, Tó Basilio. A big, burly bear with a heart of gold, Tó received us with open arms, offering us food and drink while catching up on our little adventure from Luanda and my ride, which had now officially reached its furthest point! I felt elated having made it further than before. I think it also helped overcome a bit of a mental block I had been struggling with and had me excited about what was still to come.

We spent the evening dining with the Governor over a, once again, fantastic spread of amazing fresh Angolan/ Portuguese fusion food, when he informed me that he had arranged me a place on the first ferry leaving for Cabinda the next morning. This both excited and terrified me as it felt like I would be leaving a safety net, to which I had become accustomed, in Angola. When the Governor informed me that his Personal Assistant would be traveling with me on the ferry and that the Governor in Cabinda had been informed about me, I felt a whole lot better. It's amazing just how quickly one becomes accustomed to a comfort zone.

So, the next morning arrived and it was time for me to say farewell to all my friends, including the Governor. He accompanied me to the port, where a group of men helped load my motorcycle onto the boat. It took quite some manhandling as the boat was filled with people and their goods, also traveling to Cabinda. Once on board the ferry, I climbed to the roof of the boat and waved farewell to the Governor for, hopefully, the last time. I'm sure he didn't want to see me back again, except for social visits, of course.

We weighed anchor and slowly started heading out of port and on to Cabinda. It's a two hour boat ride to Cabinda and I spent the whole two hours staring out over the open sea and imagining what the road ahead might hold for me. Every now and again, I could spot the offshore oil drilling platforms out at sea. Angola is ranked among the 15 biggest oil producing countries in the world. It is no surprise then, that the daughter of the Angolan President is the youngest and only female billionaire in Africa. Angola suffers the same problem as so many African countries, where a handful of people share most of the country's wealth, while the majority of the country's population live in poverty.

As we arrived on the shore to Cabinda, I was informed that all the passengers on board needed to get into a smaller boat, with their belongings, and would then be transported to the shore. This meant that my motorcycle had to be manhandled from the boat we were on into a smaller boat by four men who stood at the ready. This made me very nervous as one misstep would mean that DAX could be dropped into the ocean. I stood watching with bated breath as my bike dangled over the side of the boat, while two men stood ready, below, in the smaller boat. It seemed like this might not have been the first time that they had transported unwieldy goods from one boat to another and, in no time, DAX was safely in the boat below and I could breathe a sigh of relief.

Once on the shore, Governor Sebastiao's Personal Assistant went about finding the local police who had come to meet us. She stood talking to them for a few minutes and then came over to where I was fitting all my luggage, back onto the bike, to tell me that she would be heading back to Soyo and would leave me in the capable hands of the local authorities, who had been instructed to look after me. I thanked her for making the journey with me, bade her farewell and followed the police car into the town. They led me to the Hotel Por Do Sol where I would be spending two nights, before heading to the Congolese border. At the hotel, I met up with a friend of a friend from Angola, Julio, who treated me to lunch. After lunch, I took a nap in my room and only woke up at 18h00 that evening, when the phone in my room rang and the Receptionist informed me that there were people waiting for me in the foyer.

Downstairs, the Vice Governor, the Head of Sport and other members from the Sports Ministry along with a translator, awaited me. They had come to officially welcome me and to inform me that I was now in the care of the Ministry of Cabinda. I thanked them for their hospitality and we planned the next day's events. I was informed that I was scheduled to take a ride around town with a group of local riders, accompanied by a local television crew. I asked to be taken to a supermarket as well as I had some shopping to do and needed to do some basic maintenance on my motorcycle, such as cleaning, lubricating the chain and cleaning the air filter.

The next morning, the boys arrived in droves, on all sorts of two wheeled machines, as well as quads or ATV's, to show me around, with the television crew in tow. We took a ride around town, with a police escort leading the way, as usual. The guys liked showing off and would pop wheelies around me to show off their skills. After the ride, they joined me outside the hotel for a drink, before heading off to get back to their normal lives again. I never felt threatened at all, not even for a second. But then I was very shielded and protected, thanks to my previous run-ins with the wrong sort.

The next morning, I would head to the Congolese border, again, with the police escorting me out of town, with sirens. I could see the vegetation starting to change as we were heading further north and the tarmac road was in good condition. It started to feel more jungle-like, as one would expect when approaching the Congo. The trees were less familiar in this region and the undergrowth started becoming denser. Once through the border to the Congo, Julio would escort me to Pointe Noire, where I would meet up with Patrick Lobo, a man who had contacted me via Facebook, offering me a place to stay, while Julio would return to Cabinda.

My police escort continued with me all the way to the border, through Customs on the Cabinda side of the border and then bade me farewell, once I stamped into the Congo. I imagined in my head that they were probably thinking,

"So long suckers, now she's your problem".

Starting over - Agulhas

Starting over

Namibia

Djin & Tonic

Tropic of Capricorn

Camping in Ondangwa

Angola, Martie on the right

Angola – My police escort

Angola - Namibe

Angola - Namibe

Angola - Interview

Angola – Lucira

Lobito – With Pedro Bandeira

Angola – gathering mementos

Angola – with the two motorcycling clubs

Angola – Heading north with friends

Angola – Welcomed by Governor Pedro Sebastião

Angola – Heading to the north to Soyo

Angola – Camping on the beach

Angola – stuck in the sand

Angola – typical road side food stall

Angola – Loading the bike in Soyo on the ferry

Cabinda – Transferring the bike mid sea

Cabinda – with my welcoming committee

Cabinda – road to the Congolese border

Congo – with Nando, Stephanie and Ilona

Congo – Pointe Noire with Lobo family

Congo – En route to Gabon via Dolisie

Congo – dusty face

Congo – Bob falls stuck

CHAPTER 6

Stamping out of Cabinda and into the Republic of Congo proved to be fairly painless, as local onlookers stared at my heavily-loaded steed with a dumbfounded expression on their faces, pointing and talking in French. Finally, I'd be able to put my very limited French to work all the way up into Northern Africa, where, there are 21 French-speaking countries in Africa, one of the widest spoken languages on the continent after Arabic, Hausa and Berber.

Once stamped through, I met up with Julio again, who could basically walk through and together, we covered the 40 kilometers to Pointe Noire. The road leading up to Pointe Noire is another tarmac road in good condition. We stopped at a little bistro for brunch and I phoned Patrick, to let him know that I had arrived in town and the address of where we were. When he arrived, the funniest thing occurred. It just so happened that Patrick and Julio actually knew one another and neither of them knew that I'd be meeting up with both of them! I guess it somehow proves the 'six degrees of separation' theory, it is a small world.

Julio handed me over into the care of Patrick and Patrick, in turn, introduced me to his brother, Fernando, and his family, with whom I would be staying while in Pointe Noire. Originally, my idea was to spend only a few days in the Congo, while applying for a Visa for Nigeria, but my immune system had other plans. I fell ill with what felt like another bad dose of the flu and was woman down for almost a week. After a few days, my host family started to get really worried about me and took me to the hospital to have blood tests, fearing that I might have malaria. The communication between the doctor, Stephanie (Fernando's wife), who had taken me to the doctor and myself, wasn't exactly clear, but from what I understood, I was suffering from some sort of internal infection. The doctor prescribed antibiotics and a few more days' bed rest. I used the time to send my passport to Brazzaville to apply for a Visa into Nigeria. A message came back though, requesting that I apply for it in person. As I wasn't really planning on traveling to Brazaville and still had other opportunities to apply for a visa ahead, I decided to give it another go in Libreville, Gabon.

I spent about two weeks with my Congolese family: Fernando, Stephanie and their two daughters, Ilona and Jessica. These people took me in and treated me like family. I lived with them, ate with them, went out with them and they always went out of their way to make me feel welcome. Stephanie looked after me when I was sick, took me to the hospital and for follow up visits. Fernando and Patrick sat with me at night going over maps and giving me pointers and advice on the road ahead to Gabon. They helped me send my passport to Libreville and get it back again. They did so much for me, even though they, initially, didn't know me from Adam. Their empathy and generosity truly humbled me.

As I got better, it became time to start planning my leave of Pointe Noire and move on to Gabon. However, two days before I planned on hitting the road again, I received a message from my biker friends in Luanda, informing me that there was another traveller on his way up north on a motorcycle. Bob - not his real name - was also heading up the West Coast of Africa, towards Morocco, and then on to Europe, to end his journey in his home town of Prague, in the Czech Republic. I asked my friends whether it would be okay if Bob also stayed with us for one night, before we'd both be heading towards Gabon.

I still felt nervous about heading up further into Central, then Western and finally, Northern Africa, on my own. I had no idea what still lay ahead and, with this in mind, I decided that it might not be the worst idea to have a travel companion for a while, especially a man who could perhaps help and protect me, if necessary. I was about to learn that I am well capable of holding my own.

I got in touch with Bob and arranged to meet him at a beach bar not far from the Lobo's home, when he arrived in the Congo. I was still not feeling 100% but well enough to be able to get back on the road again. Besides, my Congolese visa had already expired and been renewed once. I didn't want to chance having it expire again and then face the possibility of not being able to have it renewed again. Bob arrived on his yellow and black BMW F800GS and we got chatting. I told him that I had arranged with Fernando (or Nando for short) and Stephanie for him to spend the night at their home. The first warning light went off when he didn't seem grateful whatsoever and couldn't, evidently, bring himself to say thank you. First impressions were that this guy seemed pretty self-involved, but then who am I to talk, I'm writing a whole book on my own journey?

I decided not to make too much of it and we agreed to travel together up until Ghana or so and see how it goes. Nando and Patrick gave me the names and numbers of friends who we could look up, and stay with, in Gabon in Ndende, Lamberene and Libreville. We agreed to leave at 06h00 the next morning and would try and make it to Ndende, across the border in Gabon, that same day. It is 435 kilometers from Pointe-Noire in the Congo to Ndende in Gabon. We would follow the road from Pointe-Noir to Dolisie, on the N1, and then take the National Highway, the N3, all the way up to the Gabonese border.

At 05h00 the next morning, we were up, to load the bikes and get ready for the road ahead. I was really looking forward to getting back on the road again after my long break. At the same time, I felt sad leaving my Congolese family behind. We had grown very close in a short period of time and when it came to saying goodbye, there were even some tears shed. As Freddy Mercury would say: 'the show must go on'. A last check to make sure everything was securely fastened to the bike and then it was time to go. I waved goodbye to Nando, Stephanie and the girls as we rolled out of their garage and on to the open road. Off to Gabon we go.

Bob and I never really discussed who should ride in front, or at what pace we would be riding. He seemed happy to take the lead, with which I had no problem. Off we went, making our way out of Pointe Noire and onto the main road toward Dolisie, which was easy going as it was so early and there was no traffic on the roads. The road between these two towns is a new tarmac road built by our friends, the Chinese. I wasn't expecting the road to be in such a pristine condition and really loved every mile we rode, with jungle-like vegetation lining both sides of the road. Fog resting in the air lent an eerie feeling to the day, while I was thoroughly enjoying the curvy corners with no other traffic in sight. We stopped about halfway to Dolisie for a short break and stretch of legs.

Arriving at Dolisie, it seemed like a truck stop and main layover between Pointe-Noire, Brazzaville and the border with Gabon. We didn't go into the town but rather stopped at the crossing for some fresh fruit and a bottle of Coca-Cola each. I tried to find out from some of the local stall owners what the condition of the road ahead would be like. Everyone seemed unanimous in their conviction that the N3 is a National Highway and that many trucks travel this road between the Congo and Gabon. So, I saw no reason why we shouldn't be able to make it past the Gabon border to Ndende, well before nightfall.

After a snack of bananas, washed down by some Coca-Cola, we were off again, heading north toward the border. The first couple of kilometers looked like a promising, good, tar road... until the Chinese seemed to have run out of tar. In no time, we were on a narrow, dirt road, lined with hundreds of little roadside villages with children and animals running across the road. They had obviously had a bit of rain, as I had to dodge the odd water puddle. Bob disappeared up ahead and I decided to proceed at my own pace. I didn't want to risk causing damage to either me or the bike and I, at least, wanted to take in the scenery a bit as well.

It soon became evident that Bob was fairly talented at riding gravel roads in good condition, but lacked the same skill when one adds water to the mix. Mud didn't seem to be his forte, I learned, as I was approaching one of the many roadside villages and a group of people flagged me down, just before the village. Bob had fallen off his bike and the villagers were helping him up. Once back on the bike, he raced ahead again. I thanked the villagers for their help and then carried on at my own pace, going about 50 kilometers per hour on average, dodging potholes all over the show.

The road is so narrow that when a truck, carrying cargo, approached from the front, I'd have to almost stop on the side of the road for it to not run me over. I'd then be surrounded by a cloud of dust that would bring visibility down to zero. Once the truck had passed and I could see again, I'd carry on, trying my best not to run over any animals, when passing through little villages. At one stage, I was just exiting one of said villages when a chicken came from nowhere and did a kamikaze dive right in line with my bike's front wheel. There was nothing I could do. I knew that trying to avoid it could send me flying and possibly, breaking bones and damaging the bike. So, I did the only thing available to do... I closed my eyes and kept course, shouting, 'désoleeeeeé' (sorry, in French), as I exited the village. I felt horrible, but I also knew that stopping would bring a whole host of problems with it, as I would be made to pay for the chicken, which, although I didn't have a problem with, being on my own, meant I would be really vulnerable and largely outnumbered by a number of angry villagers. So, to the villagers, I offer my apologies for running over one of your chickens.

CHAPTER 7

It took much longer than anticipated to cover the distance from Dolisie to the border and, according to the information that I had, the border would close at 17h00. Thereafter, we would not be able to cross and would possibly have to camp at the border, which wasn't really a train smash, but also not ideal. I hardly ever saw Bob during the day except for when I'd catch up with him after he had stopped to take a break in one of the little roadside villages. I only caught up with him maybe twice and, for the rest of the time, I was on my own mission, which actually suited me.

Our last (planned) stop before the border remains memorable to me, to this day, as I saw Bob's bike parked on the side of the road and a bunch of children standing around it. As I approached to park next to his bike, the kids ran away, obviously a bit afraid of these machines. I'm sure that they don't see people passing on big capacity motorcycles too often. By the time I got there, Bob seemed to have already made friends with the locals. We hung around for a while, mainly exchanging smiles with the locals and, as we were about to leave, the women of the village started surrounding me, gesturing that they wanted money. They would point at their breasts and then to mine and then cup their hands, suggesting that I should give them money because I am a woman like them. I felt outnumbered and would love to help empower women, but I'm not convinced that by just giving someone money, you are really empowering them. So I apologized to them and graciously refused their request.

It was around 15h00, by the time we left that village and we looked good for time as the border was only another 50 kilometers away. Of course, it would not be that straightforward. Literally 10 kilometers from the border, I came across Bob, bogged down in a mud puddle. It's not that there wasn't a way around the mud so much, but he seemed, always, to choose the wrong lines through the mud, through the deepest parts. It's called target fixation. Basically, it means that you become so focused on an object or obstacle that you inadvertently end up colliding with said object or obstacle. Which is what happened to poor, old Bob and as a result, he got himself as stuck as a ring on a fat finger.

I parked my bike on the side of the road to help poor Bob. My choice of terrain for parking wasn't the best as I heard my bike topple over behind me while heading towards Bob and his bike. I turned around to pick it back up again, when Bob suddenly shouted at me,

"Leave your bike and come help me".

Strike one. I ignored him and went to pick up my bike, then I returned to try and help him get his bike out of the mud. As I got closer, I sank knee-deep into the mud and had a hard time getting my foot out it. This is when I realized that we were going to have our task cut out for us, trying to get his bike unstuck with just the two of us.

Nevertheless, we tried our best. I tried pushing him, while he sat on the bike, trying to ride it out. No joy. I tried pulling him, no joy. I went in search of some pieces of wood to wedge under the tires for some traction. This helped a bit but still not enough to get the bike out. Eventually, covered in mud and exhausted after having wrestled the bike for more than half an hour, our salvation arrived in the form of two locals who came walking towards us from the border's direction. As they arrived at the mud hole, I used my very limited French to ask them for some help. Without hesitation, they jumped in and helped us get Bob's bike unstuck. It took us another ten minutes of struggling, but we finally got it out. This was the good news. The bad news was that we only had about twenty minutes left before the border would close! So, with that, Bob rode away and left me to deal with the locals, who were now asking for remuneration for their efforts. Strike two, Bob!

I gave the guys some Francs and then got on my bike to join Bob at the border. Arriving at the border, I could see Bob's bike parked on the side of the road, but no Bob. Upon closer investigation, I found him sitting at, what could only be described as, this tiny border village's bar, having a beer. Not only was he sitting at the bar having a beer, instead of having his paperwork stamped, so we could get through the border, but he didn't even bother getting me a beer as well! Strike three.

Starting to really get annoyed, I walked up to Bob and asked for his passport and Carnet de Passage, so I could get our paperwork stamped. I knew if I didn't do it, we'd be spending the night sleeping at the border. Once stamped, I went to get myself a beer too and told Bob we'd have to get going right after finishing our beers.

While finishing the beers, the Head of Customs arrived for a similar refreshment. We started talking and he asked where we were from and where we were going. He explained that the border had already closed and that we would not be able to cross over into Gabon. I pulled out my best smile and asked, as nicely as I could, whether he might consider allowing us to cross the border if I bought him a beer. He seemed to like this prospect and agreed to let us cross if we left immediately... which is exactly what we did.

Back on the bikes, we got to a boomed gate, which is the Congolese border. The Officers let us through and we proceeded to the Gabonese border with haste. I noticed something fall off Bob's bike in front of me and stopped to pick it up. It turned out to be his sleeping bag that had fallen off. When we arrived to the border with Gabon, Bob noticed that he has also lost his tent. As I handed him his sleeping bag, he shouted at me, asking why I hadn't picked up his tent as well. I told him that I hadn't seen it and only saw the sleeping bag fall off. I told him to give me his passport and Carnet de Passage again so I could have us stamped through, while he went back to search for his tent. It was getting dark by now and I was starting to feel a little concerned about us reaching the town of Ndende in the dark, not having a clue about what the road ahead looked like.

There was a little hut on the side of the road which, I assumed, to be the Customs Office. Inside, there were three men sitting and having some beers as well. I handed over our passports and the Customs Official told me that we could not cross the border as it was already closed. I tried to explain, in my Frenglish, that we had been given permission to cross, but the Officer would have none of it. When Bob arrived back with his tent strapped on the back of his bike, I told him to wait at the border so I could go back and ask the Head of Customs to give us written consent to cross the border. Another beer and fifteen minutes later, I was back with written consent in hand and we were free to cross into Gabon. By that time, it was pitch black dark and, without the bikes' lights, I could not see my hand in front of my face.

Bob took the lead, but stopped every 10 minutes – literally - saying that he was too exhausted to go on, that he had very little fuel left and that we were not going to make it. I kept trying to motivate him to continue on to Ndende, where we could get fuel and I could phone the number Nando and Patrick had given me for a place to stay. It became really tiresome to get Bob to keep moving as he had little emotional breakdowns every couple of kilometers. He fell into another mud puddle again, about 5 kilometers from where we crossed the border. By that stage, I was also getting really tired, both of digging Bob out of mud holes and draining my energy with his negativity, so I had had enough, at that point and was close to having a sense of humor failure.

I stopped to take out the towing rope from my tools and fastened it to Bob's bike and to mine so I could pull him out of the mud. I should have thought of doing it when Bob fell in the mud before the border, because pulling him out with my bike was so much easier.

We finally rolled into Ndende and headed straight for the first fuel station we could find on our GPS'. By that time, it was already well past 20h00 and everything seemed to be closed. The fuel station had no fuel, a bummer, but something we could worry about the next morning. I phoned the number I was given but it seemed to be out of service. A young boy walked by and admired our motorcycles. He walked up to us and asked where we were from in broken English. Fantastic, someone who could speak English! I asked him if he knew the person we were looking for and showed him the piece of paper. He said he did and that he would show me where he lived. I told Bob to stay put as he didn't seem fit enough to go searching for anything anymore, while I walked with the boy to find 'Pinheiro', which was the only information I had to offer.

In the dark, we walked in search of Pinheiro's house, while this young boy asked me about where we were from and where we were going. The usual questions. I would guess that he was maybe 16 years old and a well-mannered young man. When we finally arrived at the house of Pinheiro, the boy knocked on the door. A voice from inside shouted,

"Who is there?" in French, to which the boy answered that he was with a lady named Jo and that I had been given his name by Nando and Patrick in the Congo. The man opened the door and I tried to explain that we were two weary riders looking for a place to stay for the night. The man very generously agreed that we could stay in his living room and, with that, the boy and I went back to find Bob.

I thanked the boy for all his help and then led Bob to Pinheiro's house where he had put a mattress out for us, on the floor in the living room and showed us to his bathroom with a hot shower! Score!

Pinheiro didn't hang around and left us to do our own thing. Without asking and in typical fashion, Bob went for a shower first. I used the time to let people back home know that I was safe and used my satellite phone to make a quick call to South Africa. Since it was costing me so much, I felt that I ought to use the satellite phone every now and then. Or, rather, it cost the Angolan Government so much money! After finishing the call, I went back inside the house to find Bob fast asleep on the mattress. The immediate problem was that there was only one mattress and there was just no way in hell that I was going to share it with... Bob! I had a shower and then got into my sleeping bag on the floor next to the mattress. I begrudged Bob for being a dick, but I also felt grateful that he had shown me that I was perfectly well off on my own and could handle myself just fine. Thanks to Bob, I felt a little less concerned about travelling through Western Africa on my own!

We were up, the next morning, at 06h00. Pinheiro had graciously prepared breakfast for us which consisted of fresh baguettes, cheese, cold meats and yoghurt. I was truly thankful for the food as I hadn't really eaten much since the day before. After breakfast, we thanked him for his incredible generosity and set off to find some fuel. We rode to the Total petrol station in town but they, unfortunately, had no fuel. I asked if any of the neighboring towns might have fuel and it was explained to me that the bridge over which the fuel trucks have to cross to deliver fuel to the town, had washed away, hence the shortage of fuel. This posed a bit of a problem. The only thing I could think of is to head back to Pinheiro's and ask him if he might have some fuel for us.

Not only did he have some fuel for us, but he filled both our bikes from fuel canisters he had filled up to see him through the fuel shortage and refused to take payment for it. The selflessness of some people will never cease to amaze me!

You have to check in at the local Police Station to have your passport stamped before you can make your way through Gabon, something that no travel guide will tell you. Without this stamp, you are not able to exit Gabon as you don't get your passport stamped at the border.

With our stamps in our passports and our bellies and bikes filled up, we were finally ready to hit the road again. From Ndende up to Mouila, on the N1, there is a good dirt road on which you could easily average 80 kilometers/hour or so. Bob shot ahead and I figured I'd meet up with him intermittently when he stopped for a break. When I reached Mouila, I opted to not go into town, as Pinheiro had explained to us that there would be a Petro Gabon station just outside of Mouila, en route to Lamberene. I stopped at the fuel station but, you guessed it, no fuel! I wasn't too concerned as I still had enough fuel to make it to Lamberene, a bigger town where I was sure we'd be able to find a place for fuel.

From here-on out there's a beautiful tarmac road that goes all the way to Libreville! Just before Mouila, there is a big roundabout. If you head straight, you'll be going into town, but if you go left you head towards Lamberene. I turned left and carried on until I reached a police check point on the side of the road. The police officers approached me and as always seemed quite surprised once I'd taken off my helmet to reveal that I was a women. The only officer asked me where I was from and when I answered South Africa, he let out a big 'Wow' and welcomed me to Gabon. That was it for the questioning as they wished me well on my journey ahead. I still hadn't seen Bob anywhere and asked them whether another motorcyclist had come the same way. They confirmed that they did let another biker through and so I figured I'd meet up with him in Lamberene.

I adored the jungle-like surroundings of Gabon, I felt like a real adventurer, riding through that country, like a real-life female Indiana Jones or Lara Croft even. I admired the scenery and took my time, taking it all in. I stopped for a break just before Lamberene and stood staring at the beauty that surrounded me. The dense vegetation, the sounds of birds, frogs, crickets and monkeys surrounding me. I had never seen such tall trees in my life, some trees tower as high as 60 meters! About 85 percent of the country is covered by tropical forest that holds more than 6000 species of plants, 300 species of trees and 190 species of mammals including gorillas, forest elephants, chimpanzees, hippopotamus, a huge variety of monkeys, leopard and lots of dogs. I haven't been chased by as many dogs as I was in Gabon. The country has some of the most amazing 'twisties' I've ever ridden on, the only problem was that there would be a dog around every bend wanting to catch you.

Just before reaching Lamberene, I stopped at a petrol station for fuel. At least this time I was able to fill up and, a moment later, Bob pulled up beside me. I felt confused as I thought he was ahead of me. He told me that he had gone into Mouila to find fuel but was unsuccessful. At least now, we were able to fill up and I made sure my fuel cells, in which I could carry an extra 10 liters, were also filled up.

I had already decided that I would want to continue, on my own, when we reached Libreville. While at the filling station, Bob informed me that he had seen a hotel on the side of the road just before Lamberene and had decided to call it a day and book himself into the hotel. We would now go our separate ways and I would carry on to Libreville while Bob would head straight for Cameroon. This suited me perfectly. Needless to say our farewell was short and sweet and I carried on towards Libreville while Bob stayed behind.

The road between Lamberene and Libreville is one of the best roads for riders who love twisties! There probably isn't a straight stretch of road for over 200 kilometers. Small villages dot the sides of the road, but they're not at road level as you would expect. No, these villages are mainly a level below the road and disappear into the jungle and its dense undergrowth. Cars cannot get down to the villages, so they park up on the road and people then walk down to the villages. At road level, local women sell mainly fresh fruit. People walk to and fro between villages on the road and every village has at least one dog and that dog will chase you, guaranteed. In Lamberene, there are two crossings over a fairly big river, the Ogooue River. I got a little lost in town but thanks to my trusty GPS, I was able to find my way back again.

I knew it would be a push to make it to Libreville before dark but, what I was really looking forward to, was crossing the Equator for the first time! I was so excited and remained very aware for the sign on the side of the road. I was getting closer and closer to Libreville and the sign was nowhere to be found. Eventually I gave up. I was so tired that I just wanted to make it into town, find a cheap hotel for the night and go to bed early for a good night's sleep. It was getting late in the day and I started feeling nervous about the prospect of arriving in the capital at night. I had no idea what to expect and had no idea where I would stay. I had the contact details of friends of Patrick's, but felt it would be better to phone them the next day instead of just dropping in on them. Besides, I could also do with a night by myself.

I opted to stop for a break at the edge of the city to give myself a pep talk as I was really getting more nervous, with every passing kilometre, about not having an idea where to go. I should've phoned the contacts Patrick had given me but then I also felt like they may not understand what was going on, with my limited French and I felt shy all of a sudden.

I was standing on the side of the road, waving at cars and trucks that were honking at me as they passed, when a big cargo truck pulled off onto the side of the road right next to me. A man got out of the truck, laid down a towel on the ground and proceeded to start praying. I felt very awkward and didn't know what to do, so I just stood quietly, waiting for him to finish his prayers. When he had done, he got up off the ground and turned to me to introduce himself. He spoke perfect English and asked me the usual 20 questions. I explained my dilemma to him and he offered to help me out. He instructed me to follow him into town. He would go and park his truck at his factory and then get his car to show me to a hotel. I know that under normal circumstances, this might seem a bit dodgy, following a stranger at night into a town you don't know at all. I consulted with my instincts for a second and I felt like it would be okay for me to trust Duklua, his name. And so I followed Duklua into chaotic traffic streaming into the city at a snail's pace with lots of hooting and shouting going on, I just made sure to keep behind the truck.

It took us a good part of an hour to make it through the traffic and to Duklua's factory, where he swapped his truck for a car. I then followed him to a hotel where he negotiated a good rate for me (CFA 30 000, which is about USD60), a safe place to park my bike and helpers to carry my bags to my room. After I had settled into my room, Duklua just disappeared. I figured maybe he had to get home, but 15 minutes later, there was a knock on my door and there stood Duklua with a bag. He had bought me some food and something to drink.

My voice was a bit hoarse, as I had a sore throat, so he also bought me some lozenges. I was totally gobsmacked. I mean, I didn't ask him to do any of that, but he just wanted to help, because that was his nature. I didn't know how to thank him and he didn't want thanks. These are the types of encounters and experiences that I will cherish for the rest of my life. I ended the day, looking out over the city of Libreville, from my room on the 5th floor, feeling like I had accomplished something for making it this far and grateful for people with big hearts.

The next morning, Duklua came to check in on me to make sure I was safe. I asked if he could help me by phoning the number that Patrick had given me and explaining to the person in French, who I was and what I was doing. He did so, without hesitation and, 30 minutes later, we were on our way to meet Nando and Kathy.

Fernando (or Nando) and his wife, Kathy, are two open-hearted, fun-loving and vibrant human beings in their fifties. Nando is originally from Portugal and Kathy from France. From the moment I met them, I felt welcome in their home and as if they really wanted me to stay with them. I fell in love with them instantly and would be staying with them for at least a week while I sorted out my visa for Nigeria. Later on in the afternoon, a friend of theirs, from France, Vanessa Vincent, arrived and the four of us spent the afternoon playing pool and generally chilling out. Kathy and Vanessa helped me learn more French and Nando spoke Portuguese to me while I helped them with their English. The four of us were as thick as thieves in no time! That evening, they took me out for pizza and beer at Gigalou restaurant and we chatted away until the wee hours of the morning.

The next day, we spent most of the day relaxing in their pool, to escape the heat and humidity. Another friend of theirs', Bruno, joined us in the afternoon and he could speak perfect English, so he helped translate when I didn't understand Kathy or Nando and vice versa. I spent the afternoon giving my bike some needed TLC, give her a wash, cleaned the air filter, tensioned and lubed the chain, etc. Later on, Bruno took me sightseeing around town and past the Presidential Palace. He told me that it was forbidden to take photos of the building, to which I responded by taking some photos, of course. He told me that if I landed up in jail, he wouldn't help me!

Bruno took me out for dinner and told me that he was a member of the French Foreign Legion and about how he had been kidnapped, while on a mission in Liberia, and help captive for months. The French Government had to send in Special Forces to break him out of captivity. This was all very sexy and adventurous! He told me that he worried about my safety, going through Nigeria and northern Africa, and told me horror stories about what has been known to happen to people who are captured and held hostage in these areas. It didn't deter me, of course and so, to make himself feel a bit better, he gave me the biggest knife I've ever seen in my life, a Special Forces combat knife, which was as long as from my finger tips to my elbow. He asked that I carry it with me at all times and told me,

"I haven't killed anyone with this one".

Vanessa helped enormously by going with me to the Nigerian Embassy, where I could apply for a Visa. I was expecting long queues and lots of red tape but, instead, was very pleasantly surprised when there was no queue, I was helped by friendly staff and spent only ten minutes filling in some paperwork. It cost me USD60 and I could collect my Visa the next day. If I had applied for my visa in South Africa, it would have cost me USD300 and a week to get a Visa. Go figure.

Vanessa and I grew really close as friends and we would hang out together for most of my time spent in Libreville. We'd meet up with friends of hers at a café for lunch, then we'd go to listen to her and her brother, Alexander's band, called the Sand Quarry Band, practicing at night at Alex's house. After band practice, we'd all meet up with a group of their friends at the 'Guengette', a French word for a local get-together spot, like a restaurant. There, I met more people, Muriel Gilardetti, Marie, Jack and Christophe. A local motorcycling club joined us and gave me two t-shirts and stickers to add to my collection of souvenirs. It was decided that the group of motorcyclists would ride with me out of town the next Sunday, along with Nando,

Kathy, Vanessa and Bruno, who would follow us in a car. We'd all have lunch outside of town and from thereon, I'd be on my own again.

I left Libreville on the morning of Sunday, 3rd of June, 2012. Kathy had prepared breakfast with croissants, coffee and juice, while Nando and Bruno went over the map with me. They had phoned ahead to friends of theirs in Oyem, a town situated about 105 kilometers from the border with Cameroon. I would stay with them, for the night, before crossing over into Cameroon the next day. Bruno asked me if I had my knife and I showed him that I indeed did have it on me, tucked into my riding boots. It felt like I was being deployed on some undercover mission, although I didn't feel all that nervous. I had come to learn that everyone is suspicious of their neighbors. In Angola, the people warned me about the Congolese. In the Congo, the people warned me about the Gabonese. Now, the people in Gabon were heeding me against the Cameroonians.

It was mid-morning when we left Libreville. The gang rode with me until outside of the city, where we stopped for a coffee and to say farewell. I would certainly miss my friends in Gabon as they had taken me in as one of their own, just like in the Congo! I loved these people and would cherish them always.

I would have to backtrack the way I had entered Libreville, as this was the only road in and out of the city. The 20 kilometers getting out of the city is badly potholed, with a bit of road in between. I made better progress riding on the side of the road, which also helped dodge the gazillion trucks with their cargoes, crawling in and out of town. This time, I actually found the sign on the Equator and figured out that I had missed it previously because there were roadworks on that particular stretch of road and the trucks had obviously blocked the sign! I was so happy to have found it and would cross it a third time, for good measure, as the road out of Libreville heads back in Lamberene's direction, before turning north to the border via the N2. I was so happy to see the sign! It was like a confirmation of accomplishment. It's a sign of progress and, in my case specifically, an opportunity to prove naysayers wrong.

You see, there's this cycling club back in Port Elizabeth, South Africa, that took online bets that I wouldn't make it to the Equator. When I got to the sign, saying that I had officially crossed the Equator, it helped solidify my conviction that I would be able to make it around the African continent. Even though this was a journey I was undertaking on my own, I was never really alone.

Before I had left, Kathy had packed me some croissants and cheese for lunch, which I had on the side of the road as I sat staring into the jungle, imagining what wonders lay beyond. There were very little, in the way of police control points, on the road and, by the time I made it to Oyem, it was around 19h00. After I had unpacked and had a shower, my hosts, Henry and Yvette Weber, also from France, who were managing a large brewery situated in town, took me on a tour of the brewery. I got to see the process of making beer from scratch to the end result. Men, in white coats, stood in a closed-off laboratory, testing the end result in little test tubes. I was given a few samples to try, the beer tasted very fresh and almost like it needed a bit of maturing. That night, I enjoyed a wonderful meal with my hosts, drinking beer from the brewery next door, of course.

The next morning, I headed north towards the border with Cameroon. Just outside of Oyem, there is a Police Patrol Point, where I was stopped by the Officer on duty and who took down all my details in a ledger. From there, I would stay on the N2 all the way to Bitam, which is situated about 30 kilometers from the Cameroonian border. What I didn't know at the time was, as Customs was not situated on the border, I was required to stop at the Police Station in Bitam, in order that my passport could be stamped, as with entering in the south at Ndende. I should have figured it would be the same for exiting, but didn't.

At the border, I made my way to the 'Duane' Office to have my Carnet de Passage stamped, which was quick and easy. Then, as I tried to get my passport stamped too, I was advised that I needed to have had it done in Bitam! This meant I'd have to go back to Bitam, get my passport stamped at the Police Station, then return to the border. Bummer.

On my return, I exited Gabon and entered Cameroon. At the Customs Office, the Officers on duty invited me to have a seat inside, while they flipped through the pages of my passport and chatted to me. They were very friendly and all of them asked me for my number before I left. I didn't like giving my number out to strangers and would either make up a fake number (which didn't always work as they would try to phone it in front of me) or I would explain that I was planning on getting a local sim card and then my number would change. They seemed to accept this information and let me be. It didn't seem like there was much going on at the Duane office. I knocked on the door as I entered, just to find the Officer inside lying on his folded arms, asleep at his desk. He wiped his eyes and lazily stamped my Carnet and then I was free to enter Cameroon officially.

I had now officially entered the fifth country on my journey and felt a mixture of excitement and nervousness about making my way through Western Africa. I contacted an acquaintance I knew in Cameroon and the idea was that we would meet up in Yaounde. Back when I was peddling through Africa, Divine Ntiokam and I had 'met', via email, while both supporting the same charitable organization. We had not yet met in person before, but I could tell, from our email communication, that he is a stand-up guy. He sounded very happy and excited when I phoned him to tell him I had entered Cameroon. I would soon find out whether my instincts were wrong.

As I crossed the border, I could, almost immediately, notice some differences between Gabon and Cameroon. It's amazing how a place can differ completely by just crossing an imaginary line! For one, the building style was different in Cameroon, compared to Gabon. In Gabon, you were likely to come across wooden houses lining the roads in the villages while, in Cameroon, you have more brick-face houses. In Gabon, the villages seem to be built right into the jungle on the sides of the road and in Cameroon, the dense jungle seemed to start thinning out. In Cameroon, every second person who passed me, no matter whether on a bike or in a car, would flash their lights at me to signal me that my lights were on. This turned out to also be the main reason why I was pulled over at every single military and Police Control Point – and there are a lot of them! Turns out, that in Cameroon, it is illegal to ride/drive with lights on. This posed a problem, I couldn't turn my lights off and had to explain at every control post that the lights 'c'est automatique!' (Technically, by pulling out the switch, I could have switched the light off, but I didn't feel like doing this as I had fitted aftermarket lights and there was a whole lot of duct tape holding the unit in place, which I was loathe to undo. So, I opted to rather explain my way out of it each time).

Although I had aimed on spending my first night in Cameroon in Yaounde, it soon became clear that I wouldn't make it to the capital before dark. Time spent at the border, and being stopped at the numerous control points en route, caused far too many delays. I phoned Divine to inform him that I wasn't going to make it to the city and it just so happened that he had to travel that evening anyway. He had to travel north to a town called Bamenda for a convention, but, before he left, he phoned a friend of his in Mbalmayo, who has a guesthouse that I could stay in. He sent me the name of the guesthouse and said that the owner would be expecting me.

The main roads in Cameroon are all tar roads, well maintained and in good condition. The roads leading off the main roads and into the villages, for example, is another story. When I arrived in Mbalmayo, I kept a lookout for a sign for the guesthouse and finally found a sign saying the guesthouse is located 500m from the main road. I followed the little jungle track off the main road in the direction I thought I should be going. I asked for directions a few times and people kept pointing down the road. At one point, after putting the bike down too many times, I ran out of energy to pick it up by myself. Two young men, walking past, helped me pick up the bike and the three of us then pushed the bike to the guesthouse, which was, literally, 50 meters from where they had helped me pick up the bike.

The guesthouse was just a little house, with a few available rooms. The owner and her staff, (or maybe some neighbours), were kind enough to help me carry my bags inside. I washed myself in a bucket of cold water and enjoyed a plate of fish, tomatoes and rice that the owner had made. I hadn't eaten all day and definitely welcomed the food! That night, I woke up in the early morning hours, as a thunderstorm broke loose outside. It wasn't so much the thunder that woke me up, as much as the water that was dripping on my head. The ceiling over the bed had a massive leak and water was running onto the bed. Before long, the owner knocked on my door and entered with a number of buckets to place on the floor to catch the water, she obviously knew about the leaks. We moved the bed and put the buckets in place and then she left, leaving me to try and fall asleep again, which I did, despite the constant dripping of water into the buckets.

I was up and out early the next morning. I would make my way from Mbalmayo to Bamenda in the north to meet up with Divine. But first, I needed a new sim card for my phone and stopped in Yaounde, at a petrol station, to ask for help in acquiring one. I also bought something to eat and a cup of coffee for breakfast, while a very friendly bloke went about getting me an MTN sim card. The people in Cameroon are really friendly and helpful. I remembered that, before I entered the country there were some people, on my blog and online ride reports, who voiced their concerns about my traveling through Cameroon on my own. I experienced nothing but openness, care and help from the local people.

From Yaounde, I would make my way up to Bafoussam and then, on to Bamenda. It's a 370 kilometer stretch with good tar roads, which isn't that far, but the ever present police and military control points always caused delays. My GPS was having a hard time routing me to Bamenda and Divine had warned me that I could get mixed up in Bafoussam. As luck would have it, I would get horribly lost and ended up taking the wrong turn off, heading in the completely wrong direction. There are a number of roundabouts running through the city and if you take the wrong exit, you're stuffed. After a couple of kilometers after exiting Bafoussam, my inner compass started telling me that something was wrong and looking at my GPS, I was definitely going in the wrong direction. I turned around, back to Bafoussam, to tackle the roundabouts again. This time I got it right and found my way to Bamenda.

Before making it to the city, I was stopped at yet another military control point. A female and a male officer stood guard at this particular post. They were very friendly, asked me where I'd come from and where I was going. As we were chatting, a truck arrived and an obviously irate driver leaned out of his window, shouting at the guards. The female officer walked up to the truck, with her rifle slung over her shoulder, opened the door and pulled the driver out of the truck. In an instant, a fight erupted. I didn't particularly fancy getting involved or getting shot and so, with passport in hand, I sneaked off. All along the road, there are opportunities to buy fresh produce from local vendors, produce mainly consisting of fresh kills of monkeys and massive rats, meant for eating. I'm not all that into monkey and or rat meat, so I chose not to indulge.

It was late afternoon/early evening when I arrived in Bamenda. The road leading into the city is high up, with the city spread out below. There is a view of the entire city as you come down into the valley. Divine was waiting for me on the road leading into town, on the back of a bike taxi. A lot of people in Africa use bikes as taxis to transport people and cargo around in the cities. I was very happy to finally meet Divine and felt as if we had been friends for many years. I followed Divine to the Clifton Hotel in town, where I rented a room for the night. It was a small and fairly basic hotel, but at least they had hot water and I could take a decent shower. Afterwards, we met up for dinner, which consisted of chicken, vegetables, peppers and grilled banana, all mixed together. Very tasty.

The next morning, I slept in a bit, until around 11am. I took the day off to prepare myself for the next day when I'd be crossing into Nigeria, one of the countries in Africa most notorious for kidnappings and violence. To say I was nervous would be an understatement. 'Border days' as I call them, were always extra stressful, as you never knew what you'd be in for. Red tape, corrupt officials and dodgy money exchange individuals, trying to steal what they could from people. Divine was so concerned about my safety, that he decided to travel with me, on the back of one of the motorcycle taxis, to the Nigerian border and across the border to Ikom, to make sure I was safe, before he'd return back home to Yaounde. Now that's what I call going above and beyond!

We left the next morning at 0800, Divine, his driver, James, and myself. Our first stop would be in a town called Mamfe, about 60 kilometers from the border. The road up until Mamfe is a good tar road. Although, it took us about two hours to cover the 130 kilometer stretch between Bamenda and Mamfe, as James and Divine could only average a maximum of 60 – 80 kilometers per hour. From Mamfe onwards, it would be a dirt road all the way to the border, I just didn't know what in condition the road would be.

In Mamfe, we met up with some of the community leaders and friends of Divine's at the Youth Center. We even sat in on a community meeting, for a little while. I found it quite interesting as the discussion topic was how the youth had too much free time on their hands during school holidays, and were getting involved in unhealthy activities. The community leaders felt that the youth should spend more time outdoors and getting involved in more intellectual activities.

We said our goodbyes and left Mamfe around 12H30, to make our way to the border. The going was slow as the road is a narrow, dirt road, leading from Mamfe all the way to the border. It's a new road, being worked on by the Chinese and as a result, most of the way is a muddy track with big trucks and construction vehicles on it. It feels like a track that has been carved through the jungle, which makes for beautiful scenery. We even had to ride through a few small waterfalls flowing over the road. With the road being so narrow and so muddy, a lot of the big trucks would become stuck. Divine and James had an advantage here, with their smaller, lighter bike. I had a few dodgy, muddy mountain pass descents, but always managed to make it out the other side in one piece. We had to pass a number of trucks that had become stuck in the mud.

Nearing the border, we passed through a ceremonial procession which consisted of, first, a group of men in their police and military uniforms, followed by a group of community members, then a group of dancing girls in traditional attire and, finally, two men carrying massive wooden masks that measured from the ground to the top of their heads. As I slowly rode through the procession, I suddenly heard one voice chanting,

"White, white, white", and then more voices chimed in and, before we made it through the group, everyone still, chanting: "white, white, white, white." It freaked me out a bit, to be honest. It felt like I was about to be snatched at any moment and tied to a wooden pole over an open fire, like a chicken on a rotisserie, to be sacrificed to their gods.

I managed to avoid being sacrificed to the gods and the three of us made it to the Nigerian border in one piece. First things first, I went about changing some money and then it was on to have all the necessary paperwork stamped. This time, I had the luxury of having someone to actually keep an eye on my bike. James was too scared to cross into Nigeria with us and opted to stay in Ekok, the border town, to wait for Divine's return the next day. Now, if the locals are too afraid to cross the border, how was that supposed to make me feel?!

CHAPTER 8

The Cameroonian side was fairly easy and we crossed the Cross River Bridge to arrive on the Nigerian side of the border, in no time. Here, I was met by a rather unfriendly female Customs Official. From what I could gather, no one is allowed to hang around on the bridge and only people crossing the border are allowed on the bridge. There were a lot of official-looking people, with very big guns, manning each side of the bridge. Although I had been given a 14 day Visa for Nigeria, the lady Officer held the right to change it at any time, which she did. At first, she wanted to give me only 3 days, to which I pleadingly pointed at my heavily loaded bike and asked her if she could make it through Nigeria in 3 days on that bike. She finally gave in and agreed to 7 days. I didn't argue, as I knew 7 days should be enough and, even if I did need to renew my visa, I would do so in Lagos. There's always a way in Africa. TIA. (This Is Africa).

Divine hired another motor taxi and we were off to Ikom, the first town after crossing the Nigerian border. Here, I was to find the GT Bank and ask for Nkem, my contact in Ikom. Nkem showed us to a little hotel where we could stay for the night. I paid for both my and Divine's accommodation and dinner, as I felt I wanted to repay him for his kindness. I felt very nervous being in Nigeria. There was no turning back now and the next day I would have to cover just over 200 kilometers, on my own... in Nigeria! I always figured that if I could make it through Nigeria, I could make it through any country.

Since my time in the Congo, I had been in contact with a motorcycling club in both Calabar and in Lagos. News of my arrival had spread throughout the country and the motorcycling club in Calabar kindly offered me a place to stay for a couple of days. I bade Divine farewell, the next morning, and thanked him for all that he had done for me. There are some amazing, kind and giving people in this world.

Nkem gave me some information on the road condition, heading south and, by and large, it sounded like a fairly good tar road with some potholes here and there. I knew I could probably make it to Calabar within three hours or so, depending on the checkpoints. These checkpoints were one of the main concerns I had about traveling in Nigeria, I've heard so many horror stories about how people would get snatched and go missing, by way of guerrilla forces, at some of these checkpoints/control posts. I did come across a number of checkpoints in the 215 kilometers from Ikom to Calabar and I was not stopped at any of them, at every control post, I would be waved through without questioning. The road was also fairly good with some, as Nkem had said, potholes here and there.

This part of Nigeria had the feel of a mix of jungle and forest. Tall trees lined the road, once again, and I noticed lots of logging trucks making their way to and fro. The area I was in is also home to the Cross River Gorillas (the primates and not the machine gun wielding kind). I had heard somewhere that there is a place where one can view the gorillas, though, upon doing some research, it seemed that there are less than 200 of these gorillas left in the country and the chances of seeing them are pretty slim, as they are spread out over an area of 12000 kilometers. Too bad, I would love to have seen them in real life.

The road traffic in Nigeria is always busy and it doesn't seem like there are any rules. Or there are, but they're treated more like suggestions than actual laws, like back home in Johannesburg. It also doesn't seem like speed limits apply and the rule of thumb would seem to be: 'he who is fastest, wins'. Trucks come at you at neck-break speeds, in the opposite lane, and you either move over or take your chances playing chicken with a ten ton truck.

I made it to Calabar in one piece, though and my contact here was Chief Matthew Olory. Chris and Andrei - the guys I met in Namibia on their bikes - had told me so much about Calabar and I looked forward to spending some time in this tropically weathered town. A friend of mine back home, Ingrid, had spent a lot of time in Nigeria and said Calabar was one of her favorite places in the country.

Chief Olory, who had been an actual chief sometime earlier in his life, had arranged for someone else to meet me as he was out of town on the day I arrived. I was met at the agreed pick up point and taken to a hotel where I would spend the next three nights. I would meet up with Olory the next morning, when he arrived back in town.

Nigeria borders Benin, Chad, Cameroon and Niger. The country comprises of 36 states and Abuja is the capital city. The country is often known as the 'Giant of Africa' owing to its large population and economy. Nigeria is the most populous country in Africa and 7th most populous country in the world, with approximately 186 million inhabitants, which is made up of over 500 ethnic groups, speaking over 500 different languages, although the official language of Nigeria is English.

The next morning, I got to meet up with Chief Olory, when he arrived at my hotel, along with their club's 'Road Captain', Kenny G. We spent most of the day meeting up with other riders and I had my bike washed as well. Later that afternoon, we had lunch at a restaurant next to the Calabar River. There were two things I wanted to see in Calabar, one being the Calabar River and the other being the Slave History Museum. I, unfortunately, didn't get to see the museum but at least had lunch next to the river. It is also here that I met the Nigerian National Motorcycle Club's President, while he was skiing on the river. They call him 'The King', because he's the President of all motorcycle clubs in Nigeria. There are quite a number of clubs in Nigeria, of which I only knew of a few, The Easy Riders in Lagos, The Millennials in Calabar, The Angels in Lagos, The Crazy Riders in Port Harcourt and more clubs further north, as well.

I really enjoyed my stay in Calabar, which I found to be a pretty laid back city. When it came time for me to move on, Olory would ride with me to the junction, where I needed to turn off towards Benin City. My GPS didn't have routes in this area and so, he wrote down directions for me on a piece of paper. The clouds overhead seemed pretty ominous and I really hoped it wouldn't rain too much. Someone once said to me,

"When it rains, the criminals don't come out to play". So, rain was something of a double edged sword for me. On the one hand, it meant slippery roads and on the other hand, it meant I wouldn't have to worry about being pestered on the road. Or, 'worry less', I guess.

From Calabar, I would make my way through Ikot Ekpene, Aba, Owerri, Onitsha, Asaba and finally, on to Benin City.

To this day, when I see or hear the name 'Owerri', I get cold shivers down my spine. It is one town I will never forget, for as long as I live.

When I entered the town it was pouring cats and dogs. The town has two lanes leading in and out of town. In the middle of the town, there is an island of garbage piled some 3 meters high. On the sides of the road, thousands of little stalls, covered with umbrellas, where food, clothing, car parts, building material, you name it, is being sold. People walk in droves and pass through the traffic that is mainly made up of big cargo trucks, hundreds of yellow tuk-tuks... and me! The tuk-tuks push their way through the traffic and the passing pedestrians pointed at me, saying something in a strange language and some would even poke me or push the bike. I felt really nervous and cranked up the volume on my phone, on which I was listening to music in my helmet, which is something I rarely do, but, on this day it really helped me to kind of disappear into my own little bubble, while all this chaos transpired around me. At the main junction in town, a female Police Officer stood with a baton, beating it down on cars or any body parts protruding from the cars, that tried to jump the queue or, when someone 'stepped out of line', so to speak. When it was my turn to advance, I did so with caution as I didn't particularly feel like being beaten with a baton on this day.

I miraculously made it through this town unscathed and felt the need to pull over for a breather. I made sure I was well outside of town before I stopped for a rest. Soon after I pulled over, I noticed a car drive past me and turn around, heading back towards me. I didn't know what to do and figured that if it was people wanting to kidnap me, then so be it. There wasn't anywhere I could go, really.

It turned out to be a reporter from NTA (Nigeria Television Authority). She had seen me next to the road and thought,

"There's a story!"

She asked if she could do an interview with me and, there and then, pulled out a camera. The interview was featured on that evening's news. Well, it was a far cry better from being kidnapped, that's for sure. She was also kind enough to help give me directions to the Asaba Road, which I probably would have missed, if not for her, thanks to the seemingly endless number of detours.

From Owerri, the road improved a great deal and I was able to get onto the 'Express Road', which is like a highway. I could get up to speeds of over 120 kilometers/hour for the first time since leaving Angola! Asaba is a town just after Onitsha. There is a long bridge that divides these two towns and crosses the Niger River here, on the A232. I had been instructed to cross the bridge and then wait on the other side and to phone the contacts I had been given in Benin City. So I did just that.

While I was standing there, waiting on the bridge, a car pulled over a few meters from me and two young men got out and approached me. They greeted me in German. I mean, white girl in the middle of Nigeria on her own... has to be German right? When I told them that I was not from Germany, they kept guessing, naming just about every European country. When I finally grew bored of the game, I let them out of their misery and told them that I am from South Africa. With that they each grabbed me and hugged me, exclaiming how much they love South Africa and calling me their 'sister'.

They brought me something to eat and drink in town and helped me get to a petrol station. They tried very hard to get me to stay for the night and even offered to pay for the hotel. I could tell they were sincere, but I, unfortunately, had a group of bikers waiting for me in Benin City and had to get going.

I met up with one of the riders waiting for me just before Benin City. He took me to the Uyi Grand Hotel, where I got to meet 4 more riders from Lagos and 2 riders from Abuja, who had come to ride with me to Lagos. I was very happy knowing that I wouldn't have to ride in Lagos on my own and, as an added bonus, I got to meet up with Mohammed Ducati. Andrei and Cris, in Namibia, had given me a shirt to give to him, now, I was finally able to do so. That t-shirt went from Romania to Namibia and back to Nigeria. Pretty well travelled t-shirt.

We only left for Lagos around 12pm the next day. We were a group of six riders, though I would stick with a rider named Busayo. He was kind enough to slow down to my pace and stay with me, while the other guys sped on ahead, then wait for us until we caught up and sped up ahead again. These guys would be doing over 200 kilometers/hour, easily, in pouring rain, while I stuck to just over 120 kilometers/hour. I didn't feel safe going any faster and did want to overload my already overloaded bike! It rained pretty much all the way to Lagos and we met up with more riders on the way, who would accompany us to the hotel where I would stay for my first night in the city. When we arrived at the hotel, a Chief of Police, had also arrived to welcome me to the city. It made my arrival feel pretty... official.

I spent five very enjoyable days in Lagos. For my first night in the city, one of the members of the Easy Riders Club sponsored my stay in a hotel in the Ikeja area, on the outskirts of Lagos. For the rest of my time in the city, a group of riders pooled together to sponsor my stay in another hotel, in the penthouse no less! They certainly made sure that I was comfortable and well looked after.

I arrived in Lagos on Tuesday, 12th June, 2012. My Visa expired the next day and I had to make a plan to have it extended. Another member of the club, Christopher Odigie, helped by putting me in touch with a friend of his who could help give me an extension on my Visa. I knew it wouldn't be an issue, which is why I never worried about it. Being an African, you know that there is always a way to get things sorted out. Chris took me in his car to meet up with his friend in town. We stopped in a little alley and a man got into the back of the car. I had already been prepped to hand over my passport with a photo and a whopping US$120 in it. The man in the back of the car took my passport, stuck a month-long extension Visa in it with my photo, took the US$120 and that was that. Visa sorted. Only cost me double what my original Visa cost me!

I spent the rest of my time with riders from the club and also met a female rider, Gemina, from an all-female motorcycle club called The Angels. Although at the time, they only had 4 members in the club, judging by the enthusiasm that I witnessed from a lot of women who wanted to ride, I had no doubt that they would see significant growth in the near future. Today, they have over 600 followers.

I travelled with Chris to Lagos Island and met more riders. I could see the high-rise buildings of Lagos Island as we crossed the bridge between Lagos Mainland and Lagos Island. With 21 million people, Lagos is a very densely populated city. What I did find extremely amusing was that Lagos holds a reputation, all over the world, for being extremely dangerous, yet, when I told people in Lagos that I was from Johannesburg they would say,

"Wow, isn't that like a really dangerous city there?"

I rode all over Ikeja with members from the club and got to see most of the area. I was also lucky enough to attend a birthday party of a friend of the club and was also interviewed by a journalist for the local paper. A few times, the people would be really surprised that I ate the same food as they did, similar to South African 'pap en vleis', (grits and meat), only a lot spicier. That's the one thing I can say for Nigerian food... they like it spicy! The guys would jokingly say,

"This isn't white people's food", and I would explain to them that, back home, we have similar food. I don't think they ever really believed me.

I would always try my hand at the local food. Besides, this is why one goes on a journey like this, to experience the people, local cultures, food, art and all the rest of it. I thought I was going to have a really hard time getting through Nigeria and ironically, at the end of the day, it turned out to be one of the easiest crossings I had made up, without any hassles or problems, only smiles and a great deal of hospitality. Except for Owerri. Damn that place to hell!

From Lagos, I would make my way to Cotonou, the largest city and economic capital of Benin. Five of the club's members would accompany me to the border and Mohammed Ducati would cross the border with me, as he had some business to take care of in Benin. A win-win all round.

It's about 110 kilometers from Lagos to the border with Benin. On the morning that we left, it was, once again, pouring with rain. With the congested traffic, the rain meant having to be extra careful. We had not even made it out of town, when one of the riders had a crash in the rain. Not a major crash, but serious enough to warrant him having to go to hospital for a potentially broken arm. It just reminded me of how vulnerable you are on any form of two wheels and you always need your wits about you.

Once at the border, I would say farewell to my companions, except for Mohammed, who would cross the border with me. As to be expected, Mohammed had some 'friends' at the border where he would cross over without needing any paperwork or even a passport. I, however, would have to cross the conventional way. Besides, I needed a stamp in my passport and Carnet de Passage anyway, so I preferred the conventional way.

At first, the border looked like a mud bath, with all the rain they'd been receiving, which meant some fun and games for me on my heavily loaded bike. I was stamped out of Nigeria without any hassles. Getting my passport stamped into Benin was another story though. I had my passport stamped at the Customs Office, which went without a hitch, until I asked the Officer behind the counter where I could find the Douane Office, to have my Carnet de Passage stamped. He told me that I need to give him CFA35 000 (Central African Francs, amounting to about US$ 60). I know that he was just trying to make money out of me and so I refused to pay him anything and asked him to please show me to the Douane Office. He told me that there, I will be told the same thing, which I know they won't of course. He eventually grew bored when he saw that I was not about to give in and finally showed me to the Douane Office, a little hut located not far from where I was standing.

Upon entering the hut, I saw five Officers, four of them glued to the television, watching a football match and the other one was playing on Facebook on a computer. At the back, the 'Chief' lay asleep on his arms on a desk. I unfortunately needed to wake him up (does this sound familiar?) to have my Carnet completed and stamped. After about 10 minutes of flipping through the pages, although every page contained exactly the same information, it became clear that he had no idea of how to fill it in. I filled it in for him and just showed him where to place a stamp and his signature, which he did before returning to his nap. When I left the hut, the Customs Officer shouted at me that I still owed him CFA35 000, to which I just laughed and walked away to my bike.

As I was about to get on my bike, I saw three bikes heading towards me. They are riders from Cotonou, who had come to meet me at the border and ride with me to the city. Hooray! Mohammed was waiting for us a few hundred meters ahead. In the time it took me to cross the border, he had gone to prayer, had a coffee and changed money. We stopped for a group photo and then carried on towards Cotonou. Before I could leave the border town, it would give me a parting gift by way of an old, drunk man with a long, grey beard who would beat both me and my bike, with a stick, as we maneuvered our way through the mud and the border traffic. I was so taken aback that I didn't quite know how to react and just rode off in shock.

In Cotonou, I would be staying at the President, 'Djamiou', of the local motorcycling club's house (read mansion). On this same day, Djamiou also had a friend arriving from Libreville, who he hadn't seen for thirty years. I found this strangely ironic, as my friend, Muriel, in Libreville, had given me the number of a friend of hers in Cotonou, should I need help, and now, I was in Cotonou and this guy had a friend arriving from Libreville. Well, maybe it's just me, but I thought it was funny.

I did phone Sylvie, the contact Muriel had given me and we met up at the airport. I wanted to at least say hello to her. We were about 20 riders at this point, waiting to surprise Djamiou's friend, and then we'd all go out for dinner and drinks. Djamiou had 8 bikes in his garage and when he showed them to me, before we left for the airport he said,

"You're welcome to ride any or all of them." I had never been on a street bike and chose his Honda CB 1000 as my ride for our night in town. Everyone else was on speed bikes and I figured, at least this way I'd be able to keep up for a change.

Back at Djamiou's mansion, he showed me his very impressive, fully kitted, music studio. We spent the rest of the night fooling around with some of his instruments and everyone pitched in to play something. We had a lot of fun with loads of laughter and music, late into the night.

Benin is voodoo country. Although more than 50% of the population are Christian, voodoo is seen as completely normal practice and is recognized as an official religion in Benin. Some 40% of the population practices voodoo. It doesn't have the same negative connotations, like in the west, here it is more than a belief system. It is a complete way of life, including culture, philosophy, language, art, dance, music and medicine. It doesn't include sticking needles into a doll to inflict pain onto someone else, as you may have seen in some Western films. The religion consists of a supreme being, Mahou, and hundreds of divinities or voodoos.

Djamiou took me for a ride-out to Porto Novo, the capital, so I could get to see a bit more of the country. The city seemed pretty laid back and far less populated than any city in Nigeria. The people seemed relaxed and very friendly. From Porto Novo, we headed up north for a bit, to see more of the countryside. It reminded me of Gabon and Cameroon, with little villages on the sides of the road and more tropical vegetation, though not quite as dense as these.

Next up, it was time to deal with Visas again. I needed Visas for Togo, Ghana and Cote D'Ivoire. (Ivory Coast). I knew that a common Tourist Visa exists, that allows you entry into all the French-speaking Western African countries (Benin, Togo, Burkina Faso, Mali and Cote D'Ivoire), called a 'Visa Entente'. Djamiou took me to see a friend of his at Immigration, as maybe he could give me more information. This friend of his told me that only citizens from these listed countries could apply for an Entente Visa. For me to be able to obtain one (remember, anything is possible in Africa), I would have to apply for a Visa for Benin, in order to be able to apply for the Entente Visa. None of it really made sense to me, but the bottom line came down to US$60 and 24 hours, which seemed fair to me and so I paid the money and received my Entente Visa, valid for 2 months, the very next day!

I still needed to sort out my Visa for Ghana. Djamiou phoned a friend of his, Fufu, who phoned a friend of his in Togo, who phoned a friend of his at the Ghana border, and told the friend in Togo to tell Fufu to tell Djamiou, that I could get my Visa at the border. So, with this good news, I could get on my way again, heading towards Togo and Ghana!

Benin and Togo are such small countries that I left Benin and crossed into Togo, rode through the country and then crossed into Ghana to make my way to Accra, the capital. Three countries and two border crossings in one day! Djamiou and four other riders would accompany me to the border with Togo and, from thereon, I would be on my own again. It's only a total of 340 kilometers from Cotonou in Benin to Accra in Ghana. The road from Cotonou, all the way to Ghana is a good tar road. Once we got to the border, I thanked my new friends for all their help and hospitality, and then it only took me one hour to ride through Togo to the Ghanaian border. Fufu had given me his friend at the border's number, in case I needed help.

Gabon – muddy road

Gabon – en route to Libreville

Gabon – fuel station

Gabon – crossing the equator!

Gabon – twisty roads!

Gabon - Libreville

Gabon – with friends in Libreville   *Gabon – leaving Libreville*

Crossing the border into Cameroon   *Cameroon –in Bamenda with Divine*

Cameroon – en route to Nigeria   *Cameroon – nearing Nigeria*

Nigeria – with the group in Calabar

Nigeria – with Chief Olory just outside Calabar

Nigeria – onlookers admiring my steed

Nigeria – with the Easy Riders in Lagos

Nigeria - Lagos

Benin – with the guys in Cotonou

Entering Ghana in the rain

Ivory Coast – Elephants Bikers

Ivory Coast – bangles from different countries

Ivory Coast – visiting the Basilica in Yamoussoukro

Ivory Coast – visiting the Basilica in Yamoussoukro

Mali – directions to the mine drawn on a piece of paper

Mali – on route to Senegal border

Mali – maintenance on DAX

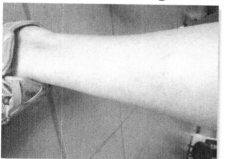

Mali – mosquito bites!!

Mali – with Derick

CHAPTER 9

Ghana is renowned for its friendly people (and their soccer team) and I got a taste of that friendliness when I arrived at the border. Once at the border, I phoned Fufu's friend, who told me that he'd be there within 20 minutes to help me. In the meantime, I was swamped with people offering their service, as Fixer, to help me cross the border. I said thank you, but no thank you to all of them and pushed my way out of the crowd to wait for Fufu's friend on the side of the road. After about half an hour, he still hadn't arrived and I figured I had no choice but to try and negotiate a Visa for myself.

I crossed the border and got my passport stamped out of Togo. On the Ghana side, I explained my position to the Customs Officers who seemed really friendly and helpful. They told me that I had two choices. 1. They could give me a 48 hour Transit Visa for US$35 or, 2. They could give me an Emergency Visa, valid for 2 weeks, for US$120. Guess which one I opted for? Although I kind of wish I had spent a bit more time in Ghana, I chose option 1. Fufu's friend also arrived at the border as I was just about done. A friendly fellow with a big smile, he handed me a small piece of paper with a number on it and told me to phone this person when I arrived in Accra and he would help me find a place to stay!

The roads in Ghana are great, which made for easy going. It's about 190 kilometers from the border with Togo to the capital of Accra. Every 20 or so kilometres, you pass through a little village and every village has a Police Control Point and I would get stopped at every single one of them. At most of them, I would be asked the usual questions and to see my papers and I would then go, with friendly smiles all round. Only one Police Officer spoiled it for me a bit when he stopped me at one of these posts and asked me for my Driver's License, which is the first time I had been asked to produce my license since I started the trip. I was happy to show it to him, but then he kept it up and said,

"Give me some Cedis", the local currency. I just smiled and told him that I didn't have any Cedis. He then said, "Ok, give me some CFA then." I told him that I was sorry but I had no money on me. This was a lie, of course, as I always had at least US$100 on me, at any given time, but I simply refused to pay a bribe. I could play the waiting game with any Officials who ever wanted to detain me for a bribe. You see, the trick is to not get upset or impatient, the moment you lose your cool, you've given away your game and then you're screwed. Besides, I had all the time in the world and even more patience. I could outwait any of them. So I just chilled out with my bike until the Officer grew tired of his own game and handed me back my driver's license. I thanked him with a smile, while putting it away, and was then on my merry way again.

Just before sunset, I stopped on the outskirts of town and phoned my contact, Abam, who told me to wait right where I was and he would come and find me. In the meantime, I was approached by a number of people, curious as to who I was and what I was doing in Accra on such a big bike, on my own. Very friendly people though. I never felt threatened, while in Ghana at all!

Soon Abam arrived and showed me to his house, not too far away. He said that I could leave my bike and belongings at his house as he wanted to make sure it was safe until the next day. Somehow, I just knew that I could trust this man to keep his word and felt perfectly safe to leave my most prized possession in his care. From there, he took me to check out a hotel nearby, where I could stay for the night. He explained that he would've happily let me stay with his family but that they had relatives visiting and unfortunately didn't have space. I completely understood of course and followed him to the Apple Hotel. Renting a room here meant having a bed, a television, a ceiling fan and bathroom with shower and toilet, all at only US$30! I was very happy to pay this as I felt tired and really wanted a shower. Although it's not that long a distance, crossing two borders and having to deal with dozens of checkpoints, up until Accra, can take quite a bit of energy. I went back with Abam and took only what I needed from my bike for the night. I still had food from that morning and Abam brought me a 2 liter of Coca-Cola and some sparkling water. Like I've said before, people's generosity, in general, will never cease to amaze me!

I wouldn't be spending any extra time in Ghana, as I only had the 48 hour Transit Visa. Once in Accra, I really wished that I had rather gone for the Emergency Visa, there was so much I would've loved to explore and see in Ghana and with such friendly people, I would have loved to explore more of the countryside! Alas, I had to carry on the next day to make it to the Ivory Coast before nightfall.

I went up to Abam's house the next morning to fetch my bike and thanked him for his help before I got on my way again. From there, I would have to follow the compass on my GPS and directions from the locals, as the maps on my GPS had no information about this area. I wasn't too worried about it as, one way or another, I knew I'd make it to my destination.

Getting out of Accra is also very easy as there is a great big highway leading out of town in the direction of Cote D'Ivoire. I stopped on route to look at a big dam to my right which, I would later learn, is the Weija Reservoir. It's about 560 kilometers from Accra to Abidjan and I needed to get to the border before nightfall. I knew it would be a long day, but I underestimated just how long it would take me. There are loads of checkpoints on route, which I actually welcomed, as I would ask the Officers at the checkpoint whether I was still on the right track to the border. Meanwhile, back home,

Hanret was sending me messages with town names to try and follow towards the border.

Tropical greenery lined the road all the way to the border, except when negotiating my way through the little towns and villages. The road condition was pretty good for most of the way, with a few more potholes making their appearance again the further northwest I ventured. I started seeing signs indicating that I was now riding next to a rain forest and national park. They turned out to be Ankasa Game Reserve and Nini-Suhien National Park. The rain wouldn't let up and so I would take a break every now and again on the side of the road, trying to get under a tree and out of the rain for a while.

I passed a long line of cargo trucks leading up to the border. Then, the normal chaos that Western African borders bring with them ensued. Hordes of people were moving back and forth over the border. First, the Customs Office, to have my passport stamped and then on to the Douane Office to have my Carnet stamped. I didn't have my Carnet stamped when I entered Ghana, so I had to dodge the Douane office on the Ghana side and have my Carnet stamped into the Ivory Coast. Here, I met a friendly Customs Official, who took it upon himself to help me have my paperwork stamped. The other Officers weren't as friendly and shot a million questions my way, in rapid fire. Where are you from? What are you doing here? Where are you going? What's in your luggage? Where's your Driver's Permit? If not for my new friend, I'm sure it would've taken me hours to get through the border.

Once I'd passed through, I phoned a contact that Vanessa, back in Libreville, had given me. She informed him of my trip and he offered for me a place to stay while in Abidjan. Jackie Thelen is originally from France and a well-known figure in the motorcycling circles in Ivory Coast. He used to race Enduros and heads up the Elephants Bikers Club in Abidjan these days. It's a motorcycle club with cruiser bikes mainly, Harley Davidsons and the like.

It was already dark by the time I made it through the border and although I always tried not to ride at night, it just turned out to be inevitable at times. My GPS still didn't show any information on where I was heading, but the friendly Customs Officer at the border told me to just stay on the main road and that would lead me straight into Abidjan.

It was already past 8 in the evening when I reached Abidjan. I stopped at the first landmark I could see so I could phone Jackie, to tell him I had arrived, I figured the big Shell petrol station, before entering town, would be a good place to wait. My French is not amazing but I thought I'd, at least, be able to explain to him where I was waiting, "a Travers la Shell". I tried to explain to him, but he was just not understanding me. I couldn't understand why not. I mean, how hard can it be to understand "Shell"? A stranger appeared, out of nowhere, hanging around and looking at my bike.

Jackie asked if there was anyone close to me and I said yes, there's this man standing next to me. He asked me to give my phone to the man so he could explain to him where I was, which I did, without really thinking. The man did explain to him where I was, then took a step backwards, turned and ran off with my phone into the bushes next to the road. I knew there was no way I would catch him and could only shout,

"Thanks a lot, asshole", as he disappeared into the night.

I felt so angry, more at myself than anything else. I mean, how stupid can you be? I should've known it a bad idea to just hand my phone over to a stranger! I could've just put it on speaker phone. Anyway, no use crying over spilt milk. I lit a cigarette and stood waiting for Jackie to come fetch me.

Jackie arrived with his friend, Bruno Villers, about 15 minutes later, and I followed them to Jackie's house, situated on Boulevard de Marseille, a stone's throw from the lagoon. Here, I was met with half a dozen of his friends and also members of the Elephants Bikers Club. I told them about what had happened and Bruno, also from France and a man with a wicked sense of humor, burst out laughing and said,

"Welcome to Abidjan". Or 'Akwaba', as the locals would say.

Even so, they were all very kind and understanding. Bruno offered me his phone so I could at least phone home and tell Hanret that my phone had been stolen and not to worry if they couldn't get hold of me. I felt really annoyed. Not just about the phone, but because, just about all my photos from Nigeria to the Ivory Coast were on that phone, as well as all my voice notes, all the way from Angola. To the guy who stole my phone: may the fleas of a thousand camels infest your crotch and may your arms be too short to scratch!

To make me feel better, the group took me out for dinner, Jackie, along with Bruno and his wife, Clothilde, Sonny, Ivan and other members of the club. We had a wonderful evening, despite my misfortune, and these people were out to show me a good time. We went out clubbing after dinner and after that, I don't remember much. I drank way too much and slept almost the whole of the next day, nursing my gigantic hangover.

The next day, Ivan very graciously gave me a spare phone of his. The club guys took me to Grand Bassam for the day, situated 45 kilometers East of Abidjan, it is an old, French colonial city faded in glory, with some buildings that look like they belong in a ghost story, thanks to an Al-Qaeda attack on the city in March, 2016. It used to be the French colonial capital back in the 1890's. Today, it's more of a tourist destination, named a Unesco World Heritage site in 2012. Its seaside streets are lined with stalls with goods for sale. Masks, statues, paintings, clothing and all kinds of souvenirs, it's a bit like an open-air flea market. We went to a really nice seaside restaurant and relaxed for most of the day.

To me, Abidjan is a vibrant city with such a great mix of cultures. I spent a total of 16 days in Abidjan, mainly trying to figure out how to proceed. This was right at the time when extremist Islamic groups were tearing down ancient temples in Timbuktu in Mali. I was in contact with a geologist friend of mine in Liberia, who sternly advised me against traveling through Liberia, due to torrential rain that had all but destroyed the roads in Liberia and also because of military unrest between the two countries (Liberia and Ivory Coast). Guinea was a no-no as the border had been closed, also due to military unrest. My other option was to ship myself and my bike to Senegal and carry on from there. This felt like cheating and like I'd be missing out on such a big part of the trip.

I took my time in weighing up my options and, in the meantime, I enjoyed Abidjan. Like any other big city, it is bursting at the seams with people from all over the world. Lots of French, Lebanese and Chinese people, especially. Across from Jackie's house, there is a Lebanese restaurant that overlooks the 'Lagune Ebrie'. Here you can sit and drink strong Turkish coffee and smoke shisha pipe, while overlooking the lagoon. I ate at so many different restaurants: local, Chinese, Lebanese, Vietnamese and French. I really enjoyed my time in Abidjan.

I decided, finally, that my best bet would be to ride north and then through Mali. I didn't feel too comfortable about chancing it through Liberia or Guinea and decided Mali was the least of the three evils. I would keep to the south of the country and away from the north, where the radicals were wreaking havoc. At the time that I was in the Ivory Coast, a South African tourist was kidnapped in Timbuktu. I did not want to add a +1 to that statistic, so I figured I would get into Mali and ride all day long to try and make it through the country in 1 or 2 days.

I needed a visa for Mali and would apply for one while in Abidjan. Some weird stuff can be seen in Abidjan, like, on the way into the city to go to the Embassy of Mali, I saw a camel walking in the streets. A camel! And then, as I was walking to enter the Embassy, a man squatted down, right in front of me in the street, and went about defecating right there and then. I nearly tripped over the guy! Another phenomenon is mentally disturbed people who walk around naked in the streets. Locals believe you should respect these people and leave them be.

While waiting for my visa for Mali, I took a trip with a group of Chinese friends to Yamoussoukro to visit the Basilica of Our Lady of Peace. It is listed as the largest church in the world in the Guinness Book of Records. This would give me the opportunity to see what the condition of the road is like as I'd be heading out on this same road on my way to Mali. The road wasn't too bad but had a lot of potholes. Yamoussoukro is about a 3 hour drive from Abidjan and our first stop was to visit the crocodiles that live in the lake that surrounds the presidential palace. Afterwards, we went for some lunch, where I had a bite of the worst Spaghetti Bolognese that I've ever had in my life. I mean, how do mess that up? So instead, I tried out some of my Chinese friends' food and ended up munching on some frogs legs (which turned out to be pretty good, actually) and a taste of pig's brain. The latter was very rich and I could only stomach a small bite, so I stuck with the frogs legs.

The Basilica is an impressive sight and something definitely worth seeing! The President of Côte D'Ivoire, Félix Houphouët-Boigny, wanted to memorialize himself with the construction of what he called, the greatest church in the world. He is even pictured beside Jesus in one of the stained-glass panels. It is the largest church in the world and the design was inspired by the Basilica of Saint Peter in the Vatican City. It's both strange and wonderful to find such a magnificent structure, almost in the middle of nowhere. The place is huge and, if not for some groups of tourists, from what I could see, it would be completely empty. Africa may be a lot of things, but it will never come close to being boring. That's for sure.

Back in Abidjan, I still needed to finalize my Visa for Mali. Jackie arranged for his driver to take me to the Mali Embassy and this time, I was shown to an office where a woman sat behind a desk. She asked me for CFA20 000 (US$38) and handed me my passport with a 30 day Visa in it, for Mali. No questions, no hassles, 5 minutes in and out of the building. What a pleasure! As a farewell present, my new friends, Sonny and Ivan Bouquet, gave me a spa treatment at a local Chinese spa, that consisted of a massage and acupuncture treatment. Nothing like a massage to make you feel relaxed! Afterwards, Sonny took me to a local market to look for some gifts. I wanted to find a bracelet that would signify Cote D'Ivoire as I had been collecting bracelets from all the countries I had visited, kind of like a ride report that I carry on my arm. I bought a bracelet made of elephant hair. Now, a lot of these bracelets are made from plastic and then you get duped into paying lots of money for something that it is not. There's an easy way for anyone who cares to know, to test this, just burn the tip of one of the strands slightly. I promise you, from the smell, you'll be able to tell whether it's hair!

On my final day in Abidjan, the Elephants Bikers Club arranged a farewell party for me at a very nice restaurant, where we were showered with food and drinks. Such an amazingly giving and fun group of people. I would miss them, after spending 16 wonderful days in Abidjan with them. I will always carry many fond memories of the Ivory Coast with me. Except for the flea-infested thief who stole my phone.

On Monday, 9th of July, 2012, I set out from Abidjan towards Mali. The idea was to make it from Abidjan, in Ivory Coast, to Dakar, in Senegal, in 4 days. 2500 kilometers through three countries in four days! The reason for the rush? I didn't want to tempt fate by becoming just another statistic of someone captured somewhere in Africa and thought it better not to linger. So day one saw me travel from Abidjan to 'Ferke' or Ferkessoudouko, as it is formally known, some 580 kilometers (360 miles) away.

Ivan accompanied me to just outside of town and, from thereon, I knew my way to Yamoussoukro. The road between Abidjan and Yamoussoukro is a good tar road. There is a big Police Control Point just beyond the city, when heading north. I was stopped at the check point and had a bit of a chat to the Police Officers, while they checked my passport. They didn't quite like the GoPro camera on my helmet. A lot of people in Africa get quite paranoid about cameras and one of the Officers kept pointing at the camera, asking whether it was a camera. I told them that it was indeed a camera but that it was off and that they didn't need to worry about it, when it was in fact, on. Cheeky, I know. I'm not really good with authority and so I'll always challenge it whenever I can. It's how I was made.

From Yamoussoukro onwards, the road started deteriorating more and more the further north I moved. The closer I was getting to Ferke, the bigger the potholes seemed to become. In some stretches, the road would be replaced by a massive mud pool with shards of what must have been part of the road before, sticking out here and there, lying in wait to give me my first puncture. My progress slowed way down, thanks to the dodgy road conditions, but I was still confident that I'd make it to my destination before nightfall. The sun would only go down at around 19h00 in the evening anyway, so I still had some time.

The surroundings, heading up north, are still lush and green sub-tropical landscape. I didn't come across much in the way of traffic, after I had left Yamoussoukro. In fact, I didn't see a single vehicle all the way to Ferke! I started getting worried that I might be on the wrong road, going the wrong way. My GPS was still not showing any information in this area, I had to trust that following the compass on it would get me where I needed to be. Maybe I was just on a road less travelled. Whichever way, I was enjoying the solitude and just being out in the sticks on my own for a bit, even if the road was horrendous.

Arriving in town, I went in search of a hotel and found one right on the outskirts of the center of town called 'Hotel le Chateaux'. Prices per room ranged between CFA 10 000 (US$19) and CFA 50 000 (US$94), I opted for something in between. A room with a bed, a television, air conditioning and a bathroom with toilet and shower, with hot water! Yay! I was so tired after such a long day that I didn't even bother going out to find dinner. I scratched around in my roll bag and found a tin of corned meat and a tin of mixed vegetables that I'd been carrying with me, all the way from back home. They weren't past their expiration dates and if you haven't eaten all day, it makes for a hearty meal. I went straight to bed and set my alarm for 06h00 the next morning.

I ignored my alarm the next morning and completely overslept. I got up at 08h00 and quickly packed up my things, loaded the bike and thanked the friendly staff, before heading out. I stopped at a Total petrol station in town to fill up and bought myself a cold drink and a chocolate bar for the road. My GPS still wasn't showing any information about where I was but I had consulted my paper maps the previous evening. Leaving Ferke, I would come across a split in the road, further north. Turning right here, would take me to Burkina Faso and, taking the split to the left, would bring me to the border with Mali. I felt a bit relieved when I arrived at the border in Mali, at least I had been going in the right direction. What really helped as well was that, as soon as I took the split to the left, the road instantly turned into a perfect tar road!

I had accidentally missed the Customs and Duane altogether on the Cote D'Ivoire side. It was an honest mistake and one I only realized when I heard a ruckus and whistling going on behind me. When I looked back, I could see hordes of people gesticulating for me to come back. The Border Officials were friendly, but also very concerned about my plans to ride through Mali on my own. Remember that thing about everyone being suspicious of their neighbours? They were obviously concerned and wanted to make sure that I knew what I was letting myself in for. The senior Officer wanted to know if I knew where I was going and I told him that I have a GPS and paper maps, so no need to worry. He then asked me whether I knew about the unrest in Timbuktu. News of the radical groups had obviously made it down south so I assured him that I wasn't planning on going anywhere near Timbuktu. It was a crying shame, as any adventure traveller's dream, is to see Timbuktu. Alas, it would just not be possible this time round. Before I left, the Officer turned to me and said,

"Go fast. It is dangerous."

On the Malian side of the border, I was offered a seat under a tree along with some of the Customs Officials. They shared a bag of peanuts with me while interrogating me on where I was going and why. I still had another 450 (280 miles) odd kilometers to do before I would reach Bamako and the clock was ticking. They finally seemed appeased by my answers and let me go. The condition of the road started improving after crossing the border, which made for more speedy progress as well. Traffic also started increasing on route to Bamako as well. The surroundings were still similar to that of the Ivory Coast, topographically, though more and more villages started lining the road and, with that, thinning of the vegetation.

I knew nothing about Bamako at the time, other than it being the capital of Mali, so I had no idea of what to expect. Apart from the perfect tar road I was traveling on towards Sikasso, I couldn't help but notice just how quiet it was. I mean, in the rest of Western Africa, there are people everywhere. It doesn't matter whether you stop in what you think to be the middle of nowhere, people will suddenly start to just... appear. I noticed people working in fields next to the road, mainly corn fields and vegetable plantations, I'd guess. Though, whenever I'd stop for a break, it would be so quiet and I felt a tangible calmness in the air. Even when people would pass me where I'd be standing next to my bike, they would seem almost shy, which is in stark contrast to what I'd experienced up until then! It will never cease to amaze me how drastically a place can change, just by crossing an invisible dividing line.

The tranquillity only lasted until I reached the outskirts of Bamako, which was only at 20h00! I had underestimated how long it would take me to get to the city and border-crossing days always made for delays. From as far as 10 kilometers away, I could see droves of vehicles slowly making their way into the city. I had been given the contact number of a friend of some of my new friends in Abidjan. The traffic was chaotic everywhere. Luckily my GPS finally had information on the area and I could navigate my way around. I looked for a landmark, from where I could stop and phone Valerie. As you enter Bamako, there is a big roundabout with a large statue in the middle, named La Tour d'Afrique. I found a spot within the roundabout in order to pull over and phone.

It took Valerie and Paul about an hour to get to me and, during that time, a young man on a scooter had pulled up next to me and, in perfect English, asked me where I was from. His name was Ali and he was working as a tour guide in Timbuktu. He explained to me that he had to flee the North, with his family, because of the violence and unrest in the North. He showed me pictures of all the tourists he had shown around Timbuktu. I felt sorry for Ali and his family, having to flee the north. Why this kind of negativity and violence has to exist in the world, I will never understand. Well, I guess I do understand, it's the human element, isn't it? As innovative and brilliant as the human race can be, it can be equally as destructive and malevolent.

Valerie and Paul finally arrived and I thanked Ali for keeping me company and wished him well. I would be staying at the Hotel le Campagnard for the night, right in the heart of the city. The plan was to stay for one night and then head for the border at Kayes, the next day. At 05h00, when I woke up from the calls to prayer sounding from the surrounding mosques, I promptly turned over and went back to sleep again. I had been in too much of a rush and being in Mali now, it felt like it would be okay to spend more days exploring the country. I didn't feel like there was an imminent threat and, as they say,

"Everything happens for a reason".

Later on during the morning, I went down to the bar to get a cup of coffee, when Paul, who had led me to the hotel the previous evening, also arrived. He introduced me to some of the people around the bar and a man, sitting next to me, asked me about my journey. While chatting to him, three more people arrived and sat down behind me, at the bar. I recognized their accents the second they started talking and, the moment I got a gap, I turned around to enquire where in South Africa they were from.

In my little hotel in the middle of Bamako, I met up with Francois and Janita from Bloemfontein, South Africa. They happened to work on a mine located on the border between Mali and Senegal. They work three months on and one month off and, as it happened, they were on their way home for their one month break. With them was Pat, a French-born burly, blonde Aussie guy. I know, that's a confusing string of words, but try and imagine what French sounds like in an Australian accent! That's even more confusing! Trust me on this!

Confusing accent aside, Pat is a really great guy. It seemed like he knew just about everyone and their dog in Bamako and, after telling him a bit of my story and that I was heading to Senegal where I'd apply for my visas for Mauritania and Morocco, he called a friend and made an appointment for me at the Moroccan Embassy. Then, he put me in a cab and off I went. A few minutes later, I arrived at the Embassy and the security guard outside asked me,

"Es tu Sud Africaine?" (Are you South African?) I was then showed inside, where a woman handed me an application form to complete and hand back to her, along with two photographs and CFA 20 000 (US$38). I felt so excited about the possibility of having these two Visas sorted out in Bamako, it would mean less hassle for me further on in the journey.

In the end, it was not meant to be as the woman returned with my passport, photographs and money and said that they would, sadly, not be able to process my Visa. From what I could understand, with my limited French, the Embassy could not give me a visa for Mauritania and Morocco in Bamako as I needed to get them in my country of origin. This was not, of course, really an option for me and so I decided I'd just apply for said Visas again in Senegal. By the time I arrived back at my hotel, everyone had gone. I walked around a bit and then spent the rest of the afternoon checking emails and messages on social media.

I spent the rest of the week in Bamako, for no other reason than that I liked it. I would explore some of the city during the day, walking around and eating out. In front of the hotel, four men sat making and selling jewellery and all sorts of souvenirs. Every day, they would try their hardest to get me to buy something and, in the end, I did buy a bracelet to add to my collection. In the evening, I'd meet Pat in the bar at the hotel. He told me not to worry about the Moroccan Embassy and told me to leave my passport with him for a while. Not having my passport on my person, at all times, was a very scary prospect. I didn't like the idea but decided to trust Pat in the end. Before they left to go back home, Francois and Janita had given me the phone number of Derick du Plessis, who also worked on the Mine. They told me they had spoken to him and that I would be welcome at Gounkoto Mine. It turned out that Derick had ridden with his father from Mali to England the previous year, so I knew he'd understand my mission.

So, instead of heading for Kayes, I would head to the Gounkoto Mine, on the border between Mali, Senegal and not that far from the border with Guinea. Pat told me about a brand new road that had just opened and led to the Mine. He said that I'd have no problems on the road as no one yet knows about the road and there would be zero traffic on it. When I told my friends in Saly, Senegal, that I was going to travel along this new road, they advised me against it and told me that he road is in terrible condition and, with the recent heavy rains, it would take me weeks to get to them. I decided to trust Pat in the end and he drew me a map on a paper napkin. It felt like I was going on a treasure hunt!

Armed with my napkin map, a tank full of fuel and a thirst for adventure, I set off on Saturday, 14th July, towards the Senegalese border. Getting out of town takes a bit of manoeuvring through heavy traffic but, once out of town, Pat was correct, there is a beautiful, brand- spanking-new tar road that leads to the border. It was fantastic! No traffic, no potholes, just me and the open road. Amazing! Almost as amazing as the beautiful Mali landscape of long grass, tall trees, lush greenery. The Mali countryside is gorgeous, it reminded me a bit of the Eastern Transvaal/Limpopo Lowveld back home.

I could see clouds building up in the direction in which I was heading. A storm was coming and I didn't know how far I still had to go. Luck would be on my side and I'd get to the mine just before the storm hit. I was greeted by Derick, at the entrance to the mine, and he led me to their compound. A tanned young man with dark hair, Derick was very friendly and welcoming. There is a lot of security around the Mine and you can't get in without authorization. Once at the compound, I also met Derick's co-worker, Chrisjan, a blond, middle-aged man, who had been working with Derick for some time. They immediately made me feel at home by offering me a cold beer and some biltong* from back home (*delicacy in South Africa, similar to beef jerky). My timing seemed to be perfect as another South African couple, Faans and Colette, who also work for the Mine, were celebrating children's birthdays, so I was invited to the party and joined in enjoying the wonderful food and birthday cake! At the time, Jancke was 10, Inge 8 and little Faans, 2. I had a great time with them and appreciated everyone's generous spirits.

Although I had planned on being in Mali for only two days, I had now already been in the country for almost two weeks. The South African guys invited me to stay for as long as I wanted and I spent time with them during the day, seeing how they go about their work and spending some time with the local geologist, who would take me around camp and show me geological stuff. During this time, we had loads of barbeques and spent days riding bikes around the area. I met loads of South Africans and Australians who worked for the Mine and even got to meet the CEO, Mark Bristow, of Randgold Resources, when he flew in to oversee a few matters at the mine and we got talking about my trip and some of his previous adventures. It turned out that he is also an avid adventure biker and had ridden most of Africa with his sons. Mark very generously offered for me to stay at their guesthouse in Dakar and we even shared a 'boot beer' out of a gumboot.

I stayed at the Mine for over two weeks, while waiting for my Visas to be sorted out. There was still the possibility that I might not be able to obtain visas for Mauritania and Morocco while in Mali, and might have to try again in Senegal. But, Pat the miracle worker, pulled through for me and somehow got both my Visas sorted. What is even more is that, when he sent my passport with a driver to the Mine for delivery, the money I had given him for the Visas was still in my passport! I had just obtained two Visas, that, initially, I was told, I had to go back to South Africa to obtain, at no cost!

Once I had my Visas, it was time to start moving on again. It was rainy season and massive storms and torrents of rain moved in from Guinea's direction, on a daily basis. This just confirmed to me that I had made the right decision of going through Mali. With all that rain coming from the coastline through Liberia, Sierra Leone and Guinea, who knows what would have happened to me if I had tried to ride through those countries? Well, this is what I kept telling myself so I wouldn't feel any worse about missing out on seeing these countries.

The other wonderful thing about discovering a new road that few people know of, is crossing the nearby border that few people use. I would set off the next day from the mine and make my way to the border early in the morning. Derick would accompany me to the border to see me off. I was up at 04h00 the next morning to pack up and load the bike. The boys were up early as well and we enjoyed our last coffee together before Derick and I set off. A local fixer and friend, Abdoulaye, took my passport to the border, a mere 10 kilometers away, and had everything sorted for me by the time I got there, passport and Carnet stamped and I was ready to go. I said goodbye to Derick and crossed the border, which consisted of two large oil drums with a boom resting on it.

Abdoulaye rode with me up until the first town in Senegal, Kedougou, then filled up my bike at his expense and wished me good luck for the journey that lay ahead of me. This new road that we had been traveling on, was built in December 2011 and is known as the 'Millennium Highway'. It extends pretty much all the way until the Niokolo-Koba National Park in Senegal. The surroundings are beautiful, wild and untouched. For the first time in a long time, I got to see animals other than donkeys, cows, goats and the like. Riding through the national park, I spotted warthogs, monkeys and meerkats running across the road.

After exiting the park, the landscape changed quite drastically. The land started flattening out and fairly quickly started dropping in elevation towards Tambacounda. On my GPS, I could see the saltpans that stretch all the way from Kaolack to the coast being indicated on my left. The landscape was flat, as far as I could see, and piles of salt lay on the sides of the road. With very little in the way of protection, the wind also started picking up, pushing against me and the bike from the seaside.

From where I had been staying at the Mine in Mali, to Saly, where I was heading in Senegal, is about 750 kilometers. I made good time and arrived at Mbour, the city just south of Saly at about 18h30. I would be meeting up with Laurent and Sahar Desmarets, a couple who had offered to take me in when I arrived in Senegal. The guys back in Abidjan had given me Laurent's details and had told them about me. When Jackie and the gang spoke about Laurent, they referred to him as 'Lolo' and told me he's like a big loving bear.

His reputation as a gentle giant preceded him and I could see why, once I met up with them. He's a tall man with a beard and a deep, burly voice but, when he smiles, I could sense his soft, caring nature. A real teddy bear. Sahar is just as friendly and open and welcoming. The two of them waited for me at the Shell petrol station, just outside of town, and then led me back to their home, where I would be spending the next two nights.

I truly loved spending time in Saly. Situated right next to the ocean, it has a laid-back vibe and loads of touristic restaurants and markets. Sahar was kind enough to show me around town and I told her that I was looking for a bracelet and explained to her that I bought bracelets, as souvenirs from each country. She took me to a local jeweller, a man dressed in blue Tuareg attire, who makes bespoke silver jewellery, with very little in the way of tools. Sahar explained to the man what I was looking for and he told her that he would make me a special bracelet that I could fetch the next day. We carried on shopping and bought some fresh fruit and vegetables from a local market. Walking through the streets of Saly reminded me a bit of Grand Bassam in Ivory Coast, arty and laid back, it has more of a holiday destination feel to it.

I enjoyed my time with Laurent and Sahar, they are such down-to-earth people who really made me feel right at home, made me feel like they really wanted me to stay with them. Even though I always knew that the people who invited me to stay with them, wouldn't have done so if they didn't want me there, I also always felt like I didn't want to be a burden to anyone.

The next day, Sahar and I went to fetch my bracelet. I loved what he had made for me - a thin silver band with markings in the middle, to represent the dunes of the Sahara Desert. I could see that it was a very high quality product and I still wear the bracelet today. It is one of my favourite souvenirs from my journey, because it was made especially for me.

I spent the last night with Laurent and Sahar and another South African they had invited for dinner, as they thought I might like to chat to a fellow countryman a bit. I was sad to have to leave my hosts and newfound friends, but I wanted to get the next border crossing over and done with. The Rosso border is a renowned crossing between Senegal and Mauritania, known as 'Hell on Earth' by many an overland traveller. My next and last stop before crossing the border would be in the city of Dakar. A momentous occasion that would see me enter the town of Dakar on my Dakar. Of course, it also helped knowing that I already had a place to stay when I arrived in the city.

I had a lazy start the next day and only left Saly in the afternoon. I said goodbye to Laurent and Sahar and, although we had only known one another for a few days, I knew I had a couple of lifelong friends who would welcome me back into their home at the drop of a hat.

It's amazing how, when you travel and you're not exposed to the news as much, you get to see and experience so much good in the world. I guess it's all about what we choose to focus on, isn't it? Easier said than done sometimes, I know, but life had taught me that it's not our circumstances that make us, it's our choices and our actions. We may not choose the things that happen to us, but we sure can choose how we react to them.

Dakar was as big and busy as I had expected. The city is probably best known for previously being the finish line for the famous Paris to Dakar Rally. I rode lazily and arrived as the sun was setting. The traffic was horrendous but at least the roads were good. Remember, Mark Bristow had arranged for me to stay at their guesthouse in town and so his fixers in town, David and Moustapha, led me through the traffic and to where I'd be spending the night. Mark had asked them to assist me and so they gave me the number of another David who would meet me at the Rosso border crossing and help me across. It was Ramadan and so the men had to leave to go to prayer and then dinner. They had some food sent to the house for me and I spent some time that night cleaning and lubricating the chain on my motorcycle.

The nearby situated Lac Rose used to be the official finish line for the infamous Dakar Rally that started in 1979, 10 000 kilometers from the start line in Paris, France. Cyril Neveu was the winner that year on his

Yamaha XT500. That was back when the Dakar was still a rugged adventure, it's just not quite the same anymore these days, although I still love watching the Dakar Rally, it's not what it was when it was still held in Africa.

Dakar is the capital of Senegal and also the westernmost point on the African mainland. I had now made it from the southernmost point in Africa to the westernmost point in Africa. Dakar is the French name given to this modern-day Western African city, also known as Ndaxaru (www.blackpast.org) and the nearby Gorée Island, the center of Atlantic slave trade in the late 19th and early 20th century.

I've probably said this before but, border days were my worst and always made me extra nervous. I would always spend the night before a border crossing making sure that I had tied everything on extra tight to the bike, to deter any long fingers. I would place my documentation in the order in which I would need it and just prepare myself as best I could. So, the next morning I set off for Rosso before sunrise to try and get there as early as possible. It's a 360 kilometer (223 miles) ride to Hell on Earth. I was so anxious and my anxiety grew with every passing kilometer. I had read so many horror reports from overlanders who had previously passed through this border.

Senegal, when I think of it, is the country of horses and baobab trees. Horses stand on the side of the roads and in the fields and I started noticing the Baobab trees again from Kaolack onwards, spread far and wide across the countryside. I love these magnificent giants! Did you know that Baobab trees store large volumes of water in their trunks? That's why elephants and eland chew the bark during dry seasons. So if you ever found yourself dehydrated out in the sticks... there's a source of hydration for you, which is something that crossed my mind as I could see my surroundings now changing to more desert-like conditions. The vegetation was starting to thin out and I could see the Sahara already starting to creep in.

I was so anxious about reaching Rosso that I stopped about 10 kilometers outside of the border town to give myself a pep talk and to suck it up. I then counted to 10, got on the bike and didn't stop until I reached the border gate. There were hordes of people that I had to make my way through before reaching the actual border. As soon as I stopped, at least a dozen men swooped in around me, talking to me in a mixture of English, French and Arabic. I felt completely overwhelmed but tried my best to stay calm and keep my cool. I tried to shoo them away and said I was looking for David. I could feel hands with long fingers trying to find their way into my pockets. I knew everything on the back of my bike would be safe, but unclipped my tank bag to take it with me as I knew it would go missing here. A man approached me and claimed to be David. Moustapha had told me to phone him when I found David so he could speak to him first, to make sure I wasn't being duped. It was indeed the man that I was supposed to meet and he immediately helped me start the process of having all my paperwork stamped. He then told me to ride through the gates to the port and there they would load my bike onto the ferry that moves to and from Mauritania a dozen times a day. It takes the ferry only 10 minutes to cross the Senegal River to the other side, though there was a bit of a delay.

Tuareg men, with no less than probably 100 camels, arrived at the port as well. The camels were being transported to the other side of the border, but there were too many of them to be transported in one go, so they had to load a bunch, take them across and then come back for the next load. Rosso isn't the only border crossing, of course, there is another border crossing closer to the coastline at Diama. At certain times of the year, this crossing gets flooded which makes it impossible to negotiate. The only reason I chose to cross rather at Rosso, is because I had a fixer, organized by Randgold, this made me feel like it would be the better option.

Eventually, when it became clear that it was going to take too long before they would be able to load my bike, David had a word with the ferry captain and they loaded my bike on board, along with the next load of camels. I love camels with their big eyes and long eye lashes. They're quite magnificent animals to be able to survive such harsh conditions. When we made it across the river to the other side, the camels were offloaded first and then it was my turn to disembark. What I didn't take into consideration was the ample amount of camel poo that was now covering the deck so, as I rode down the ramp and through the water to get onto the bank, the front wheel of my bike slid out and caused me to faceplant into the water in spectacular fashion.

I felt both annoyed and amused at my blunder. I didn't hurt anything but one of the pannier boxes on the back of my bike took a bit of a hit and was sporting a new dent. Some of the men standing on shore helped me to pick up the bike and then I walked the bike the 20 odd meters to the Mauritanian border post. There, I was told to leave my bike and follow David into the building. It was midday and, with that, prayer time. This meant nothing could be done until the men had finished prayer. I went back outside and found a spot on some stairs, in the shade, from where to watch my bike. It was a very hot day.

By the time the men had finished with prayer, it was already 17h00 and I knew there was no way I'd be able to make it to the next town before dark, which was still 200 kilometers (124 miles) away. David arranged for me to stay at Hotel Maritour, one of only two hotels at the border. He showed me to my room and said that he'd bring me food, in the evening, after prayer. I was very grateful for the air conditioner in my room that meant escaping the sweltering temperature outside. I had a shower and even found an English channel on the television in my room.

I fell asleep and only woke up when there was a knock at my door. I looked at the time, it was already 21h00. I knew it must be David bringing me some food so I unlocked and opened the door to see David standing in the doorway, holding a tray with a plate of food and something to drink. I was extremely grateful for the food as I was starving! David put the tray on the table close to the door, then turned around and locked the door behind him. That's when I knew something was very wrong!

A thousand thoughts went through my mind in a matter of seconds. Do I try and make a run for it? Do I try and get the pepper spray out my tank bag that was lying in the cupboard. Before I knew it, it was too late and he was on top of me, forcing me down onto the bed with his hands around my neck, trying to kiss me. Unfortunately for him, he was quite a scrawny guy and I've always been naturally.... plump and physically strong. Even as a little girl, my brother and our friend, Pieter, would play rugby against me and they never managed to pull me to the ground. He tried to kiss me and I pulled away. He then got more aggressive and pushed me onto the bed with his hands around my neck. I managed to break free and fought him off. I pushed him off me and shouted at him to get out. He suddenly became all apologetic saying,

"C'est pas moi, c'est mon Coeur" (It's not me, it's my Heart). I can assure you, it wasn't his heart, but another organ further south. Again, I shouted at him to get out and he finally left. I locked the door and sat at the foot of the bed, shaking with adrenaline and anger.

The next morning I was up with the birds. All I wanted to do was get out of there. When I looked at myself that morning in the mirror, I had extensive bruising on my neck but, other than that, I was fine. Just angry and bitter. I wanted nothing to do with Mauritania. All I wanted to do was to get out of the country. I packed my things and loaded the bike and quietly pushed my bike onto the road and off I went, heading north. I never looked back.

Derick had warned me about the seemingly infinite number of Control Points on the main road leading through Mauritania. Every 20 kilometers (13 miles,) or so, I would reach a Control Point. There is a stop sign about 20 meters from the actual Control Point, where it is required to stop at the sign and wait to be attended to by the Officer. When I arrived at my first checkpoint, I stopped at the stop sign and then carried on to the Officer standing next to the road. I figured, as there was no traffic or any other vehicles waiting, that I could proceed. Big mistake! I was scolded and told that I should wait at the stop sign until called. Oh well, so we learn. The next thing you need at these Control Points is your 'fiche', which is basically a copy of your passport, with details written on it such as your Visa number, your occupation and your motorbike's registration number. I prepared about 20 copies before I left Senegal, which came in handy.

As Mauritania is entered, you are surrounded by proper desert sand dunes but, progressing through the country, the scenery changes to more rocky-type, arid surroundings. The only animals I saw on the side of, or crossing the roads, were camels (of course) and donkeys and dogs, every now and again. There are also a lot of dead animals on the side of the road, from which, I would catch a whiff of decaying flesh, every now and again. Outside of the two major cities, there are little huts spread throughout the countryside. After having gone through no less than 15 Control Points in the space of 200 kilometers, I stopped in the capital, Nouakchott, at a Shell petrol station, to fill up and also to ask about availability of fuel between Nouakchott and Nouadhibou. I was assured that I would not be able to find any fuel on this stretch of road, and so I filled my two 7-liter fuel cells as well. This is what they were for, for carrying extra fuel, when needed.

A bit of useless information here but intended for the sake of perspective. The Sahara Desert is larger than Australia. Approximately 90% of Mauritania is situated in the Sahara, which is why it is no surprise then that the greatest percentage of the population lives closer to the coastline where there is more precipitation. The official language is Arabic and other spoken languages include French, Berber and a number of local languages. The country is plagued by many Human Rights issues, including slavery. Even in today's modern times, about 4% of the population remains enslaved, which came as a surprise to me when I learned that the Mauritanian society is matriarchal!

There was very little in the way of traffic on the road between Nouakchott and Noudhibou. The N2 National Highway is a tar road in really good condition. I stopped every now and again to take a walk in the dunes. For as long as I could remember, I had always wanted to see the Sahara Desert. Most of the road is made of light grey, shell-grit and the rest black tar. It is as hot as hell and I even had the pleasure of riding through a sandstorm. A mild one, I'd say, but still enough to limit my vision to no more than 20 meters in front of me and a side wind that kept pushing me closer to the edge of the road. I was even stopped at a Control Point in this storm and the Officer on duty had to hold my bike while I fished out my fiche. There was no way of hearing one another in the storm but I knew that was what he wanted and then I was free to continue.

I found a petrol station, about halfway between the two cities, and it did have fuel. I filled up my bike and, as an added bonus, it even had a little shop from where I bought an ice-cold soda! Another sandstorm was heading my way, as I headed towards Nouadhibou. I loved watching the sand moving over the road, never resting on the road, but rather dancing a wavy pattern across the road.

Moustapha, in Dakar, had given me the name of a place where I could stay in Nouadhibou, 'Hotel Tiriz'. Nouadhibou is situated on a small peninsula, shared by Mauritania and Western Sahara. The eastern side belongs to Mauritania while the western side belongs to Western Sahara. Once in town, I tried searching for the hotel, but couldn't find it. Eventually, after an hour of riding around in circles I came up with a different plan. I stopped in the busy main intersection, got off my bike and took my helmet off. Within seconds, I was approached by two men who kindly showed me the right direction. Five minutes later, I was booking myself a room at the hotel, where the owner kindly helped manoeuver my bike down a small alley on the side of the building, to where it would be safe. The staff at the hotel were very friendly and helpful and even brought me some food, for which I was very grateful. This time, I took the food at the door and didn't invite anyone in, just in case. As the saying goes

"Once bitten, twice shy".

The next morning, I had a bit of a lie in and only left around 09h00. The hotel staff helped to carry my heavy bags up and down four flights of stairs. I had some breakfast and then hit the road again, Jack, for another 'border day'. It's a 50-odd kilometer ride to the Mauritanian border post. There, it's the usual routine, having my passport and Carnet stamped. All went fairly easy and without hassles. After I had had all my paperwork stamped, I rode through a gate and found myself in a 'no man's land', a 3 kilometer stretch of land that belongs to no country. Instead of a road, I was confronted with numerous tracks through the desert and the odd sign, instructing me to stay on the road to avoid any landmines which posed a bit of a problem, seeing that there are no roads!!

The best way to this cross no man's land is to follow someone who is familiar with the tracks. Local people, crossing back and forth, or cargo trucks heading north. This was my strategy and I waited for a truck to come along and then followed them to the border with Western Sahara. The tracks also basically consist of thick sand and rocks, which makes the crossing just that little more challenging on a motorcycle. Although I made it to the other side of the border unscathed, I accidently rode past Customs.

A group of robed men, sitting on the side of the road, were calling after me, waving their arms. I realized my mistake and turned back. No harm done. I walked to the Customs Office to have my passport stamped and was met by a friendly Customs Official who tried to guess my nationality by naming just about every Western European country. We had a bit of a chat and he even added me as a friend on Facebook, while in the process of stamping my passport. After having my passport stamped, the rest of the process became a bit of a run-around. I walked to the Duane Office to have my Carnet stamped, but they gave me a blue form and told me to go to the Police, across the road, in order for my bags to be searched. I felt a bit nervous as I knew I was carrying a number of knives, which is supposedly a no-no in Northern African countries, especially. As the

Officer checked my baggage, I tried to distract him, when he got closer to where I was keeping a knife in my tank bag, by asking him about how many other bikes pass through the border in a year. He luckily didn't see the knife and, after having my bags searched, he stamped my blue form and I returned to the Duane Office.

"Do you have insurance?" "No, I don't".

They then showed me to a building, just beyond the border, and told me that I need to purchase insurance. I walked to the building and paid 900 Dirham, valid for one month. I then returned to the Duane Office, where they stamped my blue form again. I asked them to please stamp my Carnet de Passage as well and the Duane Officer ended up stamping both my Entry and Exit Slips. It was so hot and I just wanted to get going, so I figured I would sort the Carnet out later. At least, I had the Entry Slip stamped.

With all the right stamps in all the right places, I made my way to the border. There is a long queue of cars and trucks but I bypassed the queue and rode to the front. The Police Officer, manning the boom gate, asked me for my passport, which I handed over to him. He paged through my passport and acted as if not he was able to find my Entry stamp. I knew this was just an attempt at displaying the bit of power and authority that he possessed. I get off my bike and followed him, as he walked and quibbled with the drivers of the cars and trucks in the queue. After about 20 minutes of wasting my time, he finally seemed satisfied with having put me in my place and handed my passport to a younger Officer, who just handed it back to me and told me that I was free to go.

My throat felt as dry as the Sahara surrounding, so I stopped at a small hotel on the left hand side, just beyond the border. There was a little shop next to the hotel where I bought myself 2 liters of water, a bottle of Sprite and a bottle of Coca-Cola. I put the drinks away and rode off. I stopped, after a couple of kilometres, and downed the bottle of Coke and half of the water. I was then in Western Sahara, which a lot of Moroccan people don't like that this area is referred to as Western Sahara and rather prefer it to be called Morocco. It is a sparsely populated area and has been the subject of a territorial dispute between Morocco and the indigenous Sahawari people, led by Polisario, since 1975. South Africa actually supports the Polisario Front and has done, for years.

To me, it was just another breath-taking part of the magnificent Sahara Desert. Next stop – Dakhla! (Pronounced 'Dahkh-lah', like you're trying to get rid of a hairball in the back of your throat). Dahkla is situated about 380 kilometers from the border, on a road that carries virtually no traffic. Every time I would stop to take a break, the sudden silence would be deafening and caused a ringing in my ears. Sand, sand and more sand lies for as far as the eye can see! I came across some camels, that would be grazing next to the road (on what I have no idea), or lazily crossing the road.

Dakhla is a world-renowned kitesurfing spot. People flock to this location, from all over the world, to kitesurf among the dolphins and flamingoes on the 45 kilometer-long, flat lagoon, sheltered by the Dakhla Peninsula. As I started nearing the town, I could spot kite surfers from a distance. There are camps, set up just outside of town for surfers. What I really loved about reaching Dakhla is the old-world feel I got when I reached the town and saw the old city wall still in place, as the entrance to the town. I booked myself into the Sahara Regency Hotel, as a treat for the night, and watched the crowds gathering in the street later that evening. During Ramadan, there is almost no traffic on the roads during the day, when people are fasting. At night, the towns come alive, as families roam the streets searching for something sweet after having enjoyed dinner together. As a sign of respect, I fasted during the day as well, except for drinking fluids, of course.

A question, posed to me regularly, is,

"What do you think about when you're out there, in the middle of nowhere, on your own?" Honestly, I think of everything and nothing. I don't know how much noise the average person has in his/her head, but mine can be pretty noisy. Being a woman, I guess even more so. I think about where I've been and where I'm heading. I think about my past and future. I think about where I stayed the previous night and where I will stay the next. I think about the people I have met and wonder about the people who are yet to cross my path. I worry about my safety and, at the same time, I trust myself enough to be able to get myself out of sticky situations. I'm scared, all the time, but I carry on regardless, because I don't want to have any regrets when I reach the end of my life.

The next morning, I left Dakhla for Laayoune (Pronounced 'Lie-oon'), situated about 540 kilometers away. As I left town, I spotted a train to my left, running north. There were a number of men standing on the train, with their robes flapping in the wind, as a caravan of camels were lazily grazing near the road. It's like a scene out of Lawrence of Arabia and, for the first time in a long time, I felt cold. Hugging the coastline brought, with it, a fresh wind blowing in from the ocean, so early in the morning. It's like a massive natural air-conditioner.

The ever-present Control Posts persist though. I was stopped at each and every one! I was never asked to remove my helmet, but was met with astonishment every time I handed over my passport.

"Vous etes une femme?" You're a woman? I would nod and answer the usual questions. Where have you come from? Where are you going? Where will you be staying? Just before reaching Laayone, I was stopped at the umpteenth Control Post. This one seemed different though as they wouldn't let me through. They kept me there for more than half an hour, asking the same questions over and over. Where are you heading? Where are you staying? And what is your profession? Always a tricky question, as 'adventurer' doesn't seem to suffice as a profession. This time though, I actually knew where I'd be staying, as a friend of mine in Rabat, Larbi Sbai, had arranged for me to stay with his cousin, Abid Sbai', in his hotel in Laayoune, called the Parador Hotel.

I was, eventually, allowed to proceed, without any explanation as to why they had detained me. I've learned to not argue or ask questions and just carry on. But then, the strangest thing happened. An oncoming car pulled over and the men in the car tried to flag me down. I felt very uneasy as I didn't know what was going on. It is not far from the Control Post and I figured it might be more Customs or Police Officials, so I pulled over. The car pulled up next to me and the driver asked me whether I was heading to the Parador Hotel. This was all very sketchy to me and I cautiously answered yes. They explained that they were from the hotel and that the Police at the Control Post had been asked to alert the hotel when I was on my way. Now it all made sense! They led me to the hotel and there, I met with another surprise, in the form of a big welcoming committee. The owner, Abid, some of his friends and hotel staff, along with a local television crew, stood waiting to welcome me to Laayoune! I was a bit shell-shocked, but had little time to process everything as the television crew immediately started to interview me. I was then taken on a small tour of the town with the television crew filming me, as we went along. We then returned to the hotel where I was given the presidential suite. On a side table, inside the room, was a plate with all kinds of Moroccan sweet delicacies, which I just about inhaled.

I had some maintenance to do on the bike and found myself surrounded by a crowd of men, as I cleaned and tensioned the bike's chain. It must have been a strange sight in those parts, I'm sure. I even met a group of guys from Ghana who were in Morocco for work and, of course, wanted to know whether I had travelled through their home country. Later on, over dinner, I spent a wonderful evening with a group of Sbai's friends. After dinner, I was taken on a tour of the town at night. A local family welcomed me into their home and offered me some tea, the sweet, mint-flavored Moroccan tea that I had come to love. They gave me even more sweets - Baklava, Qatayef and my favorite, Chebakia, a sesame cookie that is fried and then covered in honey! Delicious! Later on, back at the hotel, a group had gathered to watch my interview from earlier on, when I had arrived. It was already airing on the news on national television!

From Laayoune, I would head to Agadir, another coastal town but the first in 'official' Moroccan territory. It's a 600 kilometer stretch between Laayoune and Agadir, which, to me, sounded like a romantic holiday destination. About 200 kilometers into the day, I stopped on the side of the road for a break and a stroll in the sand next to the road. I suddenly thought about my satellite phone and how I had had little need for it on my trip, thus far. It was a good thing but, at the same time, I was also paying for the very expensive airtime that would expire soon, so I decided I'd make some calls to see how my friends back home were doing.

I felt excited about phoning South African friends but, also realized that receiving a call from my satellite phone, might freak some of them out. I phoned Hanret and immediately assured her that everything was okay and we had a chat about how Morocco had been so far. While talking on the phone, another motorcycle appeared on the road, also heading north. When he saw my bike and me standing on the side of the road, on the phone, he pulled over, as he probably thought I had run into some trouble. He asked me whether I was ok and I told him I was fine so he got off his bike and lit up a cigarette.

His name was Federico Bertolini, from Lucca, Italy. He was on his way home and also heading to Agadir for the day. I felt a bit jaded about riding with someone, after my experience riding with Bob! Even so, I decided to give Federico the benefit of the doubt that he was not a dick and led the way to Agadir.

The scenery started to change as we got closer to Agadir. It went from Sahara to more mountainous surroundings. Traffic also started to increase on the road, as we neared the city. More trucks were making their appearance, as we wound our way through a number of mountain passes. Before we agreed to ride together to Agadir, Federico and I had exchanged very little in the way of dialogue. I was later able to deduce that he is a psychologist and that he had ridden down to Senegal on his motorcycle, before turning around to head home. His vacation time was up and so he had to get back home. He's married and lives in a small flat, with his wife, in Italy. I asked why she hadn't joined him on his trip and he just said she didn't want to. He turned out to be a gentle guy and would buy us each a cold drink when we stopped to fill up with fuel.

We finally arrived in Agadir and started searching for the Hotel Royal. Federico seemed to have found it on his GPS and, before long, we stopped in front of the hotel. The owner was a friend of Sbai's, in Laayoune. He had phoned ahead and asked his friend if I could stay at his hotel. Although Federico had planned on staying at another hotel that night, he negotiated a good rate with the owner of Hotel Royal and we both unloaded our bikes to settle into our rooms. Later on, the owner had dinner brought to me. The hotel didn't really serve food as it was Ramadan, but made food especially for me.

After dinner, I went in search of my new friend. He wasn't in his room and I couldn't find him anywhere, so figured he had probably gone out to find food, so I turned in for the night. The next morning, I was up early and loaded my bike, to get ready for the ride to Rabat. Federico wasn't planning to go as far as Rabat that day and so I waited around a bit, hoping to wish him Godspeed for his journey back home. After waiting around for about an hour, I couldn't wait any longer and left him a note on his bike, before hitting the road.

I made my way past Marrakech, through the mountains, past Casablanca and on to Rabat. It's about 550 kilometers between Agadir and Rabat on the main road, the N7. I didn't stop over to spend some time in Marrakech and today, I regret that. In my opinion and, from what I had heard, the town was just such a tourist trap, and I don't necessarily like touristy areas. Although, it is one place that I really want to go back to visit, I had the opportunity then and I should have taken it. Nevertheless, I was happy to see my friend, Larbi, when I arrived in Rabat. He waited for me on the outskirts of town and led me to their family beach house, where I would spend a few days, just relaxing. After Ramadan, I moved into the Sbai family home and was welcomed by Larbi's lovely family, as one of their own. They spoiled me a number of times by taking me to their very popular restaurant in town called, 'El Barrio Latino'.

I loved spending time in Rabat and made loads of friends. What I didn't realize, at the time, is how big an influence recreational drugs have on the Morocco. When I crossed the border from Mauritania to Morocco, it was the first time that I noticed sniffer dogs present at a border. There is a massive problem with drugs being imported into Morocco from South America, hence the sniffer dogs. I came face to face with my first experience with cocaine, one night while out with my new-found friends, who I had met at the Barrio Latino. They wanted to take me on a night-out in town and show me a good time. While in the car on our way to a club, the passenger pulled out a baggie of cocaine and everyone in the car snorted a line. They asked whether I had ever tried it, which I hadn't. They then asked me whether I wanted to give it a try and I figured, well, why not, I'm all for trying things at least once. Except for heroine!

All I can say is, cocaine is the worst drug I have ever tried and the only other drug I've ever tried is marijuana. (Who hasn't right?) I woke up the next day with the worst headache and feeling absolutely trashed. That was the first and only time I have ever tried any other drug and would highly recommend staying away from it! I have just never liked any kind of drugs, except for cigarettes, which is probably actually one of the worst and most addictive kinds of drugs, after alcohol.

Drugs aside, Rabat has a more laid back feel to it and I found it very easy to find my way around. The days on which I didn't take my bike, I'd take a taxi into town. I had a number of issues to attend to, such as sorting out an extension on my Moroccan Visa and applying for a Schengen Visa for Europe, so I could take a ferry to Spain and then another ferry to Algeria, to carry on. The border between Morocco and Algeria has been closed since 1994 and there's no way of crossing by land. Well, there probably is, if I really wanted to risk it, but I didn't.

I visited the Spanish Embassy and they were insistent that I needed to apply for a Schengen Visa in my country of residence. I was told exactly the same upon visiting the French and Italian Embassies. This meant that I would have to fly back home to South Africa, apply for both Schengen and Moroccan Visas again, and fly back. An expensive and time-consuming solution to a simple problem. I revisited the Embassies numerous times to try and persuade them to help me out with a Schengen Visa but, after a couple of weeks, it became clear that I had no choice, I'd have to return home to get a Visa for Europe. The plan then was to fly back home, get the necessary Visas, then return to Morocco and take a ferry to Spain. From there, I would then take another ferry to Algeria and continue from there. It wasn't as I had planned, but I had little choice in the matter.

Before I could return home, I had to place my motorcycle under Customs Seal in Morocco. This meant having to pay a visit to Moroccan Customs in Rabat, filling in a mountain of paperwork and having ten sets of fingerprints taken, to be able to leave my bike behind in Rabat, while I flew back home to sort out my Visas. Under normal circumstances, I would have had to leave my bike with Customs but, because I had a friend who knows people, I was allowed to leave my bike at the Sbai residence for the duration of my time away.

Returning home was a bitter-sweet event. I wanted this to happen at the end of my tour, but things don't always work out the way we plan. Besides, it could've been worse. While back home, I decided to apply for as many Visas as I could for the countries I still had to travel through, this would save me having to go through this same exercise again. I applied for a Schengen Visa for Europe and Visas for Tunisia, Egypt, Sudan and Ethiopia. As a South African passport holder, I didn't need a Visa for Kenya onwards, so my Visa requirements would end with Ethiopia. Hallelujah!

It took a number of weeks to acquire all the Visas I needed and I used the time back home to visit friends and plan the rest of my trip. Visas weren't my only problem as the 'Arab Spring' rose just as I left Morocco. Northern Africa was in disarray and I wasn't sure about whether I'd be allowed to travel through Tunisia, Libya or Egypt. There was nothing I could do about it and so I decided to focus on just getting my Visas and I would decide on a way forward, once reunited with my motorcycle.

Just as I received the last Visa for which I had applied, for Ethiopia, I decided to join a friend in scouting a route for one of his adventure tours near the border with Mozambique. This is such a beautiful area for riding that I thought to myself, why not? I still had my souped-up Kawasaki KLR back home and used that to get around. We had lots of fun scouting gravel roads and playing around on our bikes, although it would soon become clear that the Universe had other plans for me.

One morning, we decided to run out to a nearby shop to buy some goodies. I had never been on the back of a bike, except when I was a little girl and given a ride on the back of my uncle's bike around the block, but that doesn't count. For reasons I cannot remember, we decided to take just his bike to the shop. I jumped on the back and in classic 'I'm just quickly running out to the shop' style, I wasn't wearing my riding boots. I figured, I'm on the back, right, so why do I need to be wearing my riding boots?

It would, very soon, become apparent why. As we reached the gate of the farm we were staying on, the bike started sliding sideways in a bit of mud. We ended up going down and I put my foot down, right between the rear panniers of the bike and the ground, in classic novice-pillion style. As the bike came down on me, I felt and heard my ankle break. I knew it was broken, without a doubt and, to add insult to injury, I started panicking when my buddy couldn't get the bike up immediately and tried pulling my foot out from under the bike. I ended up severing the ligaments in my ankle. I can be the dumbest smart person I know sometimes.

We were on an air-cooled BMW R1200GS Adventure and it was a bit heavy to just pick up, when sliding around in the mud. A local farmer saw the bike lying on its side as he drove past and stopped to offer his help. It was only when he got to the bike that he spotted me. Once they got the bike up, I was able to move my leg and told them that I needed to get to a hospital because my ankle was broken. My friend tried to stay positive and told me that maybe it was just a bad sprain. Nope, I felt something crack and I knew something was broken.

The very friendly and helpful farmer offered to drive me into town to the local clinic, where I could have x-rays done. Once the x-rays had been done, it was clear that the Fibula had been broken, right at the bottom. At the clinic, I was told that I would need surgery and that I'd need to get to one of the bigger hospitals to have that done. The closest hospital was about an hour away but I decided that, since I needed to travel anyway, I would rather have the surgery done back home. I phoned my friend Hanret and told her what had happened and, the superstar that she is, she immediately phoned the local hospital and got an appointment for me with an Orthopaedic Surgeon. She also called my good friend, Shayne Robinson, who was commandeered to fetch me, so we could load the bike and head back to Johannesburg. Shayne, being the awesome friend that he is, drove five hours to come and fetch me and we then headed back home, until it started getting dark and we stayed over at a little motel, before covering the last bit back home the next morning.

At the clinic, I couldn't any strong painkillers and they didn't even have a proper splint. I had some Ibuprofen and basically fashioned a splint out of a piece of cardboard and a bandage. I was in agony and just wanted to get home. The next morning, Shayne dropped me off at home and Hanret drove me straight to the hospital. Once there, the Surgeon had a look at my x-rays, my ankle was severely swollen by this time and he said that he couldn't operate until the swelling had gone down, I would have to wait for two days before having the surgery done. He wanted to admit me to hospital, but I promised to be good, if he'd let me stay at home, and keep my leg iced and elevated to get the swelling to go down. Suffice it to say, Hanret went out and bought the best ice packs ever – frozen peas!

Breaking my ankle hurt, but the pain I experienced, right after the surgery, was absolutely excruciating! I guess, one can understand that, when you have screws drilled into your bone! I had a cast, on which I had to stay, for six weeks and I was sent home with better pain medication this time. Hanret had a big couch moved into her living room and I basically lived on that couch for six weeks. I would wake up, take my pain medication, go back to sleep and repeat. When the cast could eventually come off, it was time for physiotherapy. Only when my physiotherapist gave me the green light, would I be able to return to Morocco to carry on my journey.

The hilarious irony of the whole situation was that I had travelled all the way, from the top of Africa, back home, to break my ankle. My international insurance covered me everywhere in the world, except in South Africa! So, I ended up having to sell the Kawasaki to pay for my surgery and therapy. That was my 'back-up' money and I was now left with a gap in my funding for the trip. When the Kawasaki broke, it cost me an arm and a leg to fix and now I had to sell it. I felt absolutely horrified about having to ask my sponsor, the Angolan Government, for more money. They were very understanding and provided me with the money I needed to carry on, I have no way of ever thanking them for all their generosity!

Once my leg healed, I was able to return to Morocco, but not before having to apply for all my Visas, all over again. Breaking my ankle put a delay on my return to Morocco which meant that, by the time I was ready to return, my itinerary was completely out of whack. Hooray! Not! I applied for all the Visas again, up until Ethiopia, while working on my physical therapy and getting my leg strong again. Before long, I was able to return to Morocco again to continue my journey.

A good friend of mine and an amazing gentleman, Madani Said, fetched me from the airport in Rabat. This time I would be staying with a cousin of his, while sorting out the paperwork to get my bike back from Customs. This also proved to be more than just a straightforward task, as I had now been gone for more than six months and, what I had not been told before I left was, that my bike would be allowed to remain with Customs for a total of six months and thereafter, I would have to pay a fine if I wanted my bike back! What's the saying: It never rains but pours, right?

When asked how much I would have to pay to get my bike back, I was told that I'd need to pay a fine of US$ 1200! At first I thought it was a joke but when the Customs Official's facial expression didn't change, I realized he wasn't joking. I simply refused and asked to speak to Head of Customs and was, of course, refused. Momo (Mohamed), Madani's cousin, went out of his way to look after me. He can only speak French and this actually helped me improve my French, as well. He would travel with me, back and forth to the Customs Head Office in Hay Riad and the Customs Office in downtown Rabat, to try and help sort out the situation. Between Madani and Momo, they wrote a long letter in French, explaining my situation. After three days of back and forth communication, the Customs Office penalty came down from US$1200 to US$700. It was still a lot of money, but better than paying almost double that. It was only later on that I found out that Madani had actually convinced the local motorcycling federation to pay the other US$600.

At night, Momo and I would go out to eat at this little Italian restaurant, as it was Ramadan time again. I loved watching the city come alive at night! If you weren't having dinner with your family, you'd be eating dinner in a restaurant, where a traditional meal would be served, consisting of vegetable minestrone soup, some dates and Moroccan honey cookies (Chebakia). A bread roll accompanied the meal, with some kind of meat, sometimes fish, other times chicken or lamb. A glass of freshly squeezed orange juice, a yoghurt and a hard-boiled egg. I loved meal times during Ramadan!

I also loved watching the city come alive at night as men would sit outside restaurants on the sidewalks, drinking coffee and smoking cigarettes. Children would be playing all over town, with their parents in tow, and dozens of men would be hanging out around the Mosques, before prayer time. There's an energy, during Ramadan that I cannot quite describe. A feeling of peace and contentment would usually fill me as I would sit and watch people go about their business, while sipping a cappuccino and smoking a cigarette.

I was now free to fetch my bike and get back on the road. From Rabat, I would make my way to Tangier, a mere 250 kilometers away, and then hop onto a ferry to Spain from there. I had already bought my ticket and could now rest assured that I could continue with my journey around Africa. But first, my bike needed a service, new tires, a new set of sprockets and a chain. I had brought a set of heavy duty sprockets and a heavy duty chain with me from South Africa and a company, called Bike Gear, situated in Port Elizabeth, South Africa, sponsored my set of new tires, Heidenau K60 Scouts. Speed Moto, in Casablanca, gave my bike a service and fitted the new parts for me. I needed to also replace the battery - because she had been standing for so long - and then, we were good to go!

Madani and a friend of his, Patrick, decided to join me to Tangier. Madani, on his Ducati Scrambler and Patrick, on Madani's Harley Davidson. Before I left, Momo even polished my riding boots for me. I was sad to have to bid him and his family farewell, but also excited about carrying on with my journey. We left just after 1h00 on a Sunday, heading north and it felt fantastic being back on the bike! What felt really weird, was feeling the plate in my ankle as the vibrations from the bike would pass through my body. I felt very aware of my ankle and it felt quite vulnerable on the bike, although I figured that feeling would pass soon, as I got used to being on the bike again.

Halfway to Tangier, we stopped at a small café on the side of the road, as I had an interview with a radio station back home. SAFM would air regular updates on my journey and wanted to know what it was like being back in Morocco and how I felt about facing all the unrest in Northern Africa, as I would now make my way to Tunisia. The truth was, that I was scared and had thoughts of abduction and hostage situations going through my mind. But, I wasn't about to let my fears, or the fears of others, get the best of me and would, of course, soldier on! I had originally planned to travel to Algeria by ferry, after Spain, though this wasn't possible as my Visa application to Algeria was denied, due to the fact that the Algerian government felt it unsafe for a woman to be traveling through the country, on her own, at the time. This left me with no choice but to head for Tunisia, after touching down in Europe.

CHAPTER 10

In Tangier, I met up with a guy named Hachim, who I had met on couchsurfing.com. He offered for me to spend the night on his couch and I was very grateful for it. He met me in town and led me to his apartment, which was on the fourth floor, right on the beach, overlooking the ocean. After showing me around, he pretty much left me to my own devices and I spent the afternoon sitting on the balcony, with my legs dangling over the side, squinting my eyes to try and see Spain in the distance. That, and watching a very conspicuous pink limousine parked in the street below, dealing cocaine well into the night.

The next morning, I had to make my way to the Tangier Med Port to have myself and the bike loaded onto the ferry. What I didn't realize at the time was, that Tangier Med and Tangier Ville are two different ports. I was staying right around the corner from Tangier Ville and so had to ride to Tangier Med, about 40 kilometers away. No big deal. When I arrived at the port, after obtaining my ticket, I then had to wait to board the ferry. Once they started boarding, I had to go through a Police Checkpoint, then Customs and another two Police Checkpoints after that. After everything had been checked and stamped, I rode my bike onto the ferry and the crew secured her in place.

The ferry ride to Spain only lasts one to two hours, depending on which shipping line you go with. I got off in Algeciras and it took all of five minutes to have my paperwork stamped and enter Spain. From there, I made my way to Malaga along the coast and finally ended off in Motril, a mere 240 kilometers from Algeciras, where I would be staying with new friends, Jose and his beautiful wife, Maria. Jose had read about my journey, on Facebook, through a fellow female adventure rider, Alicia Sornosa, who posted about my journey on her page. Alicia is fairly well-known among Spanish adventure riders, as she is the first Spanish woman to have ridden around the world solo! Needless to say, the post got a lot of attention and, before I knew it, I was receiving countless offers for places to stay, along the way.

Jose and his family have the most amazing little house, on top of a mountain, with spectacular views over Motril. We spent the evening drinking, eating, chatting and laughing. Spaniards sure know how to enjoy life! They made me feel right at home and the next morning we had breakfast in town, while Jose helped me to acquire a local sim card for my cellphone. Afterwards, he rode with me up until the city limits and set me on my way to Valencia, where I would be meeting up with Carlos and Alicia Solis.

It was a bit of a stretch, with a distance of about 600 kilometers from Motril to Valencia. Most bikers would say that's not that bad, and it isn't but, when you have to cover such a distance, day after day, for days on end, it gets to you. I had a bit of a schedule to maintain as I had already booked my ticket on a ferry, from Italy to Tunisia and had friends in Spain, France and Italy who I wanted to see. From Motril towards Alicante, there are a lot of greenhouses and plantations next to the road. For miles and miles, there are greenhouses lined up, next to the road, pretty much as far as the eye can see. All the way, you have mountains on your left and the Mediterranean on your right. Spain is such a beautiful country! The closer you get to Valencia, the greener it gets. Pink flowered shrubs line the middle of the road all the way and you ride through so many tunnels! This was like a whole new world for me, Africa was what I knew, Europe was something completely different. All of a sudden, things just work and everything feels so much cleaner and organized, compared to Africa's chaos and carelessness. I had to get used to filling up my own bike at petrol stations, as throughout most of Africa, there are petrol attendants, whose job it is to fill up your vehicle or bike.

That evening, Carlos and Alicia took me out for Sangria and Paella at a local restaurant in town and we had a wonderful evening. I adore Spanish food! Everything is just so... flavourful and good! I loved the old architecture in the cities, it's something that Africa doesn't have. Sure, we have pyramids and old temples, but Europe just has such a rich history! Valencia is known as the city of Arts and Sciences and is one of Spain's oldest cities and the country's third largest city.

I had a wonderful time while in Valencia and Carlos and Alecia even accompanied me halfway to Madrid, where I would meet up and stay with Alicia Sornosa.

I stationed myself in Madrid for a few days to catch up with blog writing, photograph uploads and doing laundry, things that become really important when you're on the road. Alicia, very graciously, let me stay with her for as long as I needed and, through her, I met a whole lot of other adventure riders. At night, we would walk or ride about town, sampling Tapas and beers, while reminiscing about our adventures. Alicia has ridden from the most northern point in Northern America, to the most southern point in South America, through Australia and through Africa, from Egypt to Kenya. By the time this book is published, she will have ridden through Africa a second time, from Egypt to Cape Town.

I absolutely love Madrid! The culture, the architecture, the vibe, the food. ALL of it! I might even go as far as to say that it is my favourite city in Europe, so far. When it came time to leave, Alicia and a number of friends decided to ride with me until just before Terrassa, which is about 30 kilometers (18 and a half miles) from Barcelona, and a total 600 odd kilometres (372 miles) from Madrid. I didn't go through Barcelona, just because my friends in Madrid convinced me that it would be easier for me to pass through Catalonian Terrassa than through the busy, bustling Barcelona. Then, about halfway from Madrid to Terrassa, the chain on my bike decided it had, had enough, even though it was a new, heavy duty chain that I had fitted in Morocco!

Stranded next to the road, I was really glad to have some friends with me. Everyone immediately jumped on their phones, making calls to anybody they knew nearby. It was then decided that Emilio, one of the guys, would ride back to the nearest town where it probably would have been easier to tow the bike, but none of us had a towrope and it's basically illegal.

In Spain, it's not out of the ordinary to have beer early in the day. The Spaniards are a bit like the Germans, in that beer can be seen as food. (Or maybe, I shouldn't compare the two nations with each other, I don't know how either nation feels about it). So, while Emilio went off to buy a new chain, Polo, Alicia and I settled down at the little restaurant next to the petrol station and ordered Spanish Omelette (called an omelette in Spain) and, of course, some beers. When Emilio returned, he arrived with a BMW mechanic in tow! When he finished fitting the new chain, we all had more beers, before carrying on towards Terrassa. The little mishap caused quite a delay and the rest of the group turned back to Madrid after about another 100 kilometers (62 miles). I only made it to Terrassa around 21h00 that evening and would stay at yet another friend of Alicia's, named Domingo. I was knackered and hit the sack after Domingo prepared a plate of his father's home-grown tomatoes and some locally-sourced cheese.

From Terrassa, I would make my way to Montpellier, in France, where I would spend two wonderful days with Charles and Michele Formosa. I had made contact with a motorcycling club in Tunisia and one of their main members suggested I stay with their friends, Charlie and Michele, when I got to Montpellier. The turned out to be two of the most wonderful, friendly and hospitable people I've ever met! I fell in love with the couple and they showed me around town, helped me by taking me to the station to buy a ticket for a ferry from Italy to Tunisia, took me to an open-air music festival and fed me the most decadent French food! I love everything French, a bit like my friend, Hanret, back home, who is a complete Francophile!

It was in Montpellier that I made the decision to carry on to Tunisia. The other option was to carry on through Europe from France through Italy, Greece and Turkey. I could then try and put my bike on a ship to Egypt and carry on from there. The problem was, that with all the unrest in Northern Africa, more and more shipping lines cancelled their routes to these countries, so I had no guarantee that I would be able to get my bike on a ship. Another option was to ship from Italy to Israel and then enter Egypt from Israel. Again, there were so many reports that tourists wouldn't be allowed to cross the Sinai Peninsula. In the end, I decided that it would feel like I had 'cheated' if I didn't go through Tunisia, Libya and Egypt, as I would have missed out on a big chunk of Africa. Algeria was out of my hands and I could try and appeal to get a Visa, but I knew deep-down that it would be to no avail. I also knew very well that I was taking a massive risk, despite many friends and followers who tried to dissuade me from trying to travel through Libya. My gut told me to go for it and if there's one thing life has taught me, it's to always trust your instincts! Always!

I bought my ticket for a ferry from Civitavecchia, near Rome in Italy, to Tunis, the capital of Tunisia. The ferry would leave in four days' time, so I decided that I would head straight for Italy. I would spend one night in Genova with friends from South Africa. I had met up with the 'Cape Town to Dublin on Vespa' boys in Johannesburg, at a farewell party, when they left. They travelled up the eastern side of Africa while I travelled up the western side, and now, we'd meet up again on the opposite side of the world. I was very excited to be meeting up with them again.

I decided to stick to the main roads as I didn't have a lot of time to make it to Civitavecchia. I had two main impressions when I reached Genova. First, I have never ridden through as many tunnels, in succession, as in Italy. I counted 101 tunnels, from the moment I crossed the border from France, until I reached Genova. Second, Genova is one of the most confusing cities I've ever had the pleasure of navigating through. I was in contact with the boys and they were being hosted by the Vespa Club of Genova, somewhere near the port. I navigated my way to the port and was told to look for a boat with a huge 'tweety bird' on it. After about half an hour of riding back and forth through crazy traffic, I finally found Tweety and, with that, the Vespa boys. The club guys were kind enough to offer me a place to stay for the night as well. It was really awesome to see the Vespa guys again and I loved how they now actually looked like overlanders. Their Vespas looked like they'd been on an epic adventure, all dirty and dusty and full of stickers and patches from places they had visited. We all went out for pizza and spent the night sharing stories about our adventures travelling through Africa.

The next day, I, unfortunately, had to wish the boys farewell. My friend, who I had met on the side of the road in Morocco, had been following me on social media and knew that I was in Italy. He offered me a place to stay with him and his wife in Lucca. I would spend my last few days in Italy, crashing on Federico and Bruna's sofa, while catching up on all that had happened since I last saw Federico in Morocco, being spoilt with amazing food and being shown around the beautiful old town of Lucca. I think I've said it before, but in case I haven't, I really love the architecture of the old buildings in Europe. They give me a sense of wonderment as I try and imagine what it must have been like to have lived in Europe, centuries ago.

Federico and Bruna looked after me like family and we would spend the evenings on their patio, enjoying delicious Italian food with equally delicious Italian wine and talking adventure! During the day, they would be out working. I would sleep in and use the rest of the day to do some maintenance on the bike and catch up on doing my laundry. I decided to give my riding gear a bit of a wash as well but forgot to take my passport out of the inside pocket of the jacket. My heart nearly stopped when I realized I had washed my passport. It did have some water damage but luckily nothing too serious. I hung it out to dry along with the rest of my clothes as I was planning to leave the next day, to catch my ferry to Tunisia.

The plan was to leave early in the morning and travel via Pisa, to snap the obligatory photo of the Leaning Tower of Pisa! Getting there was easy, but finding the tower and parking proved to be a bit of a nightmare. I spotted a couple on a Yamaha Super Tenere and stopped next to them to ask whether they were also heading to the tower. It turned out that they were a couple from the UK, on holiday on the bike, and they were indeed also searching for parking to go and see the tower. We stuck together and finally found parking near the entrance. Time was against me as I had already spent more than an hour riding around, in search of the tower entrance and parking. I needed to be in Civitavecchia by lunchtime and it was still a three-hour ride to the port. I literally walked up to the tower, snapped a picture, and back out again. I wished the couple a wonderful holiday and then it was back on the bike to catch the ferry.

I would have liked to have spent more time in Europe as I felt a bit rushed and I know I missed out on so many amazing places and things to see and do, but this journey wasn't about exploring Europe, but rather about traveling around Africa. I entered Europe, as I was forced to do so and loved every second of it. But now, it was time to get back to Africa, to continue my journey around the mother continent. Upon arriving at the port, I parked my bike in the queue of vehicles, waiting to be loaded on the ferry, and made my way to the ticketing office to have my ticket validated. After a four hour wait, we were finally allowed to board the ship and I was showed to the bottom deck where I parked DAX next to some other bikes that were tied down with straps, and I then went up to find my designated seat. My bike was the only one that would go to Tunis, as the rest would disembark in Palermo. I felt unprepared for the trip, as this was my first time on a ferry that would take more than 15 minutes. It would take us 24 hours to travel to Tunisia and all the other passengers seemed to have sleeping bags and pillows with them. I didn't even think about bringing anything with me. People lay down their sleeping bags and blankets, in the aisles, to get some sleep for the night. I used my riding jacket as a blanket and my Camelbak for a pillow. When I woke up, I was wet and freezing. I didn't realize that I was lying on my hydration pack's mouthpiece and so just about all the water had slowly leaked out through the night and left me lying in a puddle of water!

It was early morning and I decided to find some food and a spot in the sun, somewhere outside on the deck, trying to imagine what it would be like traveling through Tunisia and especially Libya. I knew I would have to face some challenges along the way, but I'd come so far, there was no way I could give up. I somehow just knew that it would all be okay and that I'd be safe, something that is really hard to explain to people. I had sent an email to the South African Embassy in Libya to inform them of my plans to travel through the country. The Embassy had replied with a stern warning and requested me to not try and enter Libya under any circumstances. Some people would call me irresponsible, and maybe even stupid, for not heeding their warning, but a girl has to do what a girl has to do.

The ferry arrived in Tunis around 21h00 in the evening. Although I would never have expected it of my new friends in Tunisia, they were waiting outside for me to disembark. I finally made it out on my bike around 23h00, after slow processing through Customs. Even though it was late, I felt wide awake, invigorated and happy to be back on African soil! A little welcoming party was waiting for me, Sahbi, Nawfel, Anis, Mehdi, Ramla and another Mehdi had come to give me a warm welcome to Tunisia! I felt so grateful and blessed to have people who, without really knowing me, cared enough to come out this late at night to make me feel welcome. After introductions, it was time to find something to eat and drink as I hadn't really had much to eat or drink during the day. After dinner, we'd have to travel about 60 kilometers to where I'd be staying with Sahbi and his family in Nabeul. Sahbi and his family were very welcoming and even invited me to have dinner with their family during Ramadan. Tunisian hospitality is definitely something to write about! Everywhere I went, people were very friendly and welcoming and I felt completely safe.

During my stay, I visited Hammamet with its beautiful beaches and, at night, the guys took me riding around town on the bikes and for coffee at the medina, Jasmine Hammamet. From Sahbi's, I moved to stay with Nawfel, his wife Lamia and their beautiful little daughter, Nadia, in Tunis for a while, while I tried to sort out a Visa for Libya. Nawfel rode with me to Bizerte, about 60 kilometers north of Tunis to visit Cap Blanc, the most northern point of the African continent. This was officially the halfway mark for me, I had made it from the southernmost tip of the African continent, all the way to the northernmost tip of the continent. It was a joyous and emotional occasion for me and I knew that if I could make it halfway, I could make it all the way!

Nawfel and his family were very kind to me, just like everyone else I met, they helped me with whatever I needed. When I serviced my bike, Nawfel helped me by giving me oil. He sourced a new lightbulb for my brake lights, as it wasn't working anymore. They took me to Carthage to see the Carthagian Ruins of Phoenicians, who populated the area before the Romans took over the city. I love that one can literally feel the history when you visit these places. I try to imagine what it must have looked like in ancient times, it fascinates me.

Sahbi helped me a lot with getting a Visa sorted for Libya. The problem was - amongst many other problems – was that Libya was no longer issuing Visitors/Tourist Visas, due to the war and civil unrest. Sahbi helped me have my passport translated into Arabic and spoke to the motorcycling club in Tripoli, with which I had made contact, they could only speak Arabic. It looked like I would be refused entry into Libya and I had to consider a Plan B. The only option I would have was to return to mainland Europe and then make my way around, via Greece, Turkey, etc. I decided to think about it, while taking a trip to the southwest region with my friend, Anis, to see the Star Wars sets near Naftah, seeing that I'm a huge Star Wars fan!

Before embarking on the trip, I spent a night with Anis and his family and had the privilege of joining them to Le Bardo, just west of Tunis, where protests were underway. There was a lot of protesting going on throughout Northern Africa and, although I didn't really understand what the protests were about that evening, I joined my friends in supporting their cause and protested with them, flying the Tunisian flag high. It was actually quite a bit of fun and a very jolly event, I felt excited to be part of such a historical event. The next morning, Anis and I hit the road towards Tozeur, he, on his Honda Transalp and me, on my trusty Dakar, of course. It's about a 450 kilometer ride from Tunis to

Tozeur and we made it to the town at around 16h00. From there, we made our way to Naftah and made it to the Star Wars set just before sunset. Another dream come true! I was so excited and happy! I wished they had actual characters walking around. They could make it into a kind of Disney Land, but a Star Wars Land instead! There was a little market where souvenirs can be bought which was, unfortunately, closed. Everything looked just like Tatooine in Star Wars: Episode 1.

The next day, we hit the road to do some fun, off-road riding to the lesser known 'Rommel-Piste', near Gafsa. It is a road that was built by Erwin Rommel, also known as the 'Desert Fox', who was perhaps the most famous German Field Marshal of World War II. It is a windy and fairly challenging ride up and over a mountain, from which the view is stunning. From what I understood, the road was built to carry supplies over the mountain during the war. It was a cool 52 degrees Celsius that day and, after conquering the mountain, we made our way to visit Tamaqzah Oasis. Tunisia used to have a thriving tourist industry and, in all these little oases, there are markets, where all kinds of souvenirs can be bought. With the civil unrest throughout Northern Africa, Tunisia too was feeling the effect, brought on by people being more cautious about travelling to their previously favourite holiday destinations.

From Gafsa, we made our way to Kasserine and then on to El Kef. We visited many sites on our little tour of

Tunisia and I really enjoyed it. By the time we returned to Tunis, I had received news that I would be able to get a Visa for Libya, at the border. The only way this was possible was by personal invite by the Minister of Tourism in Libya. The Motorcycling Federation of Libya had contacted the Minister for help, told her my story and she was generous enough to allow me to enter the country, by invitation. This was fantastic news and I felt very happy and nervous at the same time. I knew that my time in Libya could make or break my journey... and me.

Nawfel and another rider friend, Soufiane, decided that they would make the journey to the Libyan border with me to ensure my safety. Well, at least until the border. Sahbi, a former colonel in the Tunisian army, tried his very best to dissuade me from entering Libya. He believed that I would be kidnapped and ultimately killed in Libya. I told him that everything would be okay and although he really wanted to come with us, duty called and he had to stay behind. From Tunis we headed to Sfax, then Gabes and on to Matmata for lunch. From Matmata, we stopped off in Toujene to visit local carpet makers and were kindly offered tea and freshly made flatbread with olive oil. From there, we visited Ksar Hadada, another famous Star Wars site and, from Ksar Hadada, we headed to Tataouine, where we would stay for the night.

The next day, we left Tataouine and visited the town of Chenini and then the abandoned city of Douiret, a town built up on top of the hills, by nomadic folk, years ago. These cities were used as main storage facilities for food and supplies and the reason they're built so high up in the hills, is to give them a vantage point, to see when enemies approach to attack the village. It's always interesting to learn why things are the way they are. From there, we carried on to Djerba Island, where we stopped to visit a local potter's shop. The potter's son gave us a demonstration of the processes in pottery making. A talented young boy who would no doubt follow in his father's footsteps, to one day own the pottery shop. We then stopped off in Guellala for wonderful freshly grilled fish for lunch. We stayed at the Hotel Riadh in Homt Souk for the night.

We would head for the Libyan border at Ras Ajdir the next morning. I was growing more and more nervous, as we got closer to the border. From there, the guys would head back to Tunis and I would have to carry on, on my own. It was difficult for me to say farewell to my new friends, and Tunisia and her people will always have a special place in my heart. I said goodbye to Nawfel and Soufiane and thanked them for making the journey with me. I then headed towards the border - with my heart in my throat - and no idea of what to expect. At the border, I was refused entry and told that no visitors or non-Tunisians or Libyans would be allowed beyond the border. This posed a bit of a problem and I felt confused as I had been told that I would be allowed into the country. Well, there are never any guarantees, are there?

Nawfel and Soufiane were waiting and they would leave once they saw me cross the border. I returned and asked Nawfel if he would please speak to my contacts in Libya to explain the situation over the phone. I phoned them from my phone and Nawfe spoke to them in Arabic to explain the situation. We were told to wait while they made contact with the Officers at the border. After about twenty minutes, my phone rang and Nawfel spoke to them again. They told him that everything had been sorted and that I should continue to the border and would be let through this time. So, it seemed like this was now finally our farewell, after which I continued to the border. This time I was, indeed, let through and, once I stood on the other side, I looked back and waved to my Tunisian friends, feeling slightly panicked. There was no turning back now!

Not a single person at the border could speak English and I found myself being ushered from one desk to the next, with my passport being passed from one Officer to another. I was eventually given a Visa, which cost me 100 Libyan Dinar (about US$75) and then I got my stamp, allowing me into Libya. It had been arranged, with one of the riders from Tripoli, to meet me at the border and ride into the city with me. I had no idea whether he'd be waiting on the other side, or not, and was very happy and surprised to find not just Ahmed, but a group of about twenty riders, who had come to welcome me into Libya. To say that I felt hugely relieved, would be an understatement! The guys all shook my hand and welcomed me to their country, photographs were taken and then we were on our way to Tripoli. About halfway between the border and Tripoli, the capital, I received another welcome, by way of a man sitting on the back of an open truck who fired a few rounds into the air, using his AK47 as a way of 'saluting' the group of bikers. Immediately, everyone's eyes shot back at me to see how I'd react. It's not the first time I'd witnessed an AK47 going off, so it didn't really faze me. It was also obvious that the guy was just saying.... 'hi'. I gave a thumbs up to the other bikers to show that I was fine and we carried on.

Our first stop, before reaching the capital, would be to visit the 2000 year-old ancient Roman ruins in Sabratha. There are a few English-speaking guys in the group and they gave me an informative tour of the ruins. Back at the bikes, one of the riders approached me with his cell phone in hand and told me that he worked for one of the Embassies, which one I cannot remember, and that he had the South African Ambassador on the line. I was a bit shocked and slowly took the phone from him. Sure enough, the man on the other side of the line identified himself as the Ambassador of the South African Embassy in Tripoli. He asked me what I was doing in Libya and whether I had received their emails in response to mine, advising me NOT to enter Libya. He sounded a bit angry and I can understand why. I tried to calmly reassure him that everything was taken care of and that I would be fine. He pleaded with me to turn around and told me that it would cause them a lot of trouble if I got into trouble along the way. He assured me that I would get kidnapped if I continued. I knew that there was no way I would be able to assure him that I'd be safe and told him that I accepted sole responsibility for my actions and thanked him for caring enough to try and persuade me to turn back. He was not happy. I couldn't blame him.

After our visit to Sabratha, we carried on as a group to Tripoli. Once in the city, I was booked into Hotel Thobacts on Omar Al Mokhtar Street. The Ministry of Tourism had been so very generous as to arrange for me to stay at the hotel for four days, at no cost to me. My plan was to travel through Libya as fast as I possibly could. I just wanted to stay in Tripoli for one day, but that was obviously not going to happen as I had very little say in the matter. It was a very nice hotel and my hosts were very kind but, for some reason I felt like a trapped, wild animal.

The next day, I got to meet loads of riders in and around Tripoli, as well as some extremely talented stunt riders! There are so many amazing stunt riders in Tripoli. Nobody seems to have day jobs and the guys spend their days either at the beach or riding stunt bikes. All without any rider gear or helmets.

The Minister of Tourism, Ms. Ikram Bash Imam, graciously received me at the Ministry of Tourism and wanted to welcome me to Libya, officially. She was very kind and offered me help, whenever I might need it whilst in Libya. I had to dress appropriately, out of respect, covering my head, shoulders and arms. I needed to do so, whenever I went outside in Libya. I have no doubt that if it hadn't been for Minister Imam, I would never have been allowed into Libya. She instructed the riders with me to accompany me all the way to the Egyptian border, to ensure my safety. This made me feel a whole lot better about taking on the road to Benghazi and beyond!

While in Tripoli, I also had the opportunity to meet with the head of the Libyan Motorcycling Federation, Mr. Masaud Jerbi. I was taken for dinner, one evening, and it was an opportunity to thank them for all their help in raising awareness about my journey and for helping me gain safe passage into Libya. As if they hadn't done enough already, they surprised me with a US$1000 donation towards my cause. I was blown away by their generosity that seemed to have no end. They even organized for my bike to be serviced and given a once over by a local mechanic, at no cost!

My time in Tripoli was bittersweet. On the one hand, I had the privilege of meeting all these amazingly generous and welcoming people and, on the other hand, I had to hide in a car when being driven through dodgy areas and had to lie and listen to bombs, going off somewhere close to the hotel I was staying in. It is a country of contrasts and I, admittedly, didn't want to hang around for any longer than was necessary. I always felt uneasy inside. At night when the guys would take me out for dinner, we would ride our bikes to a local restaurant to get take-aways and, as soon as I'd take my helmet off, I would be met with angry eyes from dozens of men, glaring at me, as if to say,

"Who do you think you are to be out here with the men?" Something just didn't feel right and I was very aware of it, all the time.

It was also in Tripoli that I experienced the most ironic moment of my life, to date. It was my second night in the capital when Achmed, who had been appointed to look after me, took me for a ride about town in his green, open Jeep. He could only speak limited English but I had no issue understanding what he wanted, when he pulled into a place where some of his friends were, opened the center console in the car and gestured for me to take out whatever was inside. The console had obviously been modified and, inside, I found a number of hand guns, from which I picked one up, handed to him and he, in turn, handed it to his friends. On our way back to the hotel, driving on the highway, he put a cassette (yes, a cassette and not a CD) in the cassette player of the car and on came Tracy Chapman's 'Talking about a Revolution'. I was stupefied by the irony of the situation and very amused, at the same time.

I spent four days in Tripoli and, in those four days, I also got to meet up with a friend from South Africa. I first met Phillip Zaayman, and his wife, Janine, back in

Namibia in 2011, when I was still cycling, they had stopped next to me on the side of the road for a chat, on their way to a wedding in Namibia. Phillip was working in Tripoli at the time and so we had arranged to meet up one day. He, too, expressed his concern over my travelling through Libya alone but I assured him that I'd have company though and that there was nothing to worry about.

When it finally came time to move on, I had two Honda Gold Wings accompany me with four men. From Tripoli, we would make our way to Misrata, via al-Khums, to see the world-famous Leptis Magna ruins, a spectacular layout of ancient ruins and, probably, one of the most impressive collections of Roman ruins in the world. From there, we made our way to Misrata, where I had the privilege of attending a Libyan wedding. I was checked into a hotel in town, while the guys stayed elsewhere, with friends. They came to fetch me to attend the wedding celebrations, which basically consisted of all the groom's friends, on their bikes and quads, doing stunts around the groom, and live rounds from AK47's being fired into the air in celebration. Thereafter, the whole group of bikers followed the groom to another location, where the groom was placed on a sofa, along with his male family members. All the men attending the wedding then went up to the groom to congratulate him and get sprayed with cologne. I also went to congratulate the groom, which is very unorthodox, which I did not know. I was taken to the ladies' tent, next to the men's tent, to congratulate the bride. The men are not allowed in the ladies tent and vice versa. I'm the only person that got to visit both tents and, out of respect, I shall not reveal what went on in the women's tent as it is highly secret. What I will say is that I preferred hanging out with the guys, after witnessing what went on in the women's tent next door.

Seeing as just about every man in Libya owns at least one rifle or hand gun, I became used to shots being fired around me, all the time. As long as they weren't aiming at me, it didn't bother me too much. What did bother me though, was that the guys informed me that they would be returning to Tripoli the next morning and I'd have to carry on, on my own, to Ajdabiya, a city about 600 kilometers away. I couldn't believe that they were abandoning me! I pleaded with them to please not let me have to travel on my own, as it was almost a certainty that I would get kidnapped, or worse, if I travelled on my own through Libya. They seemed pretty nonchalant about it all though and left me to fend for myself. I didn't have much of a choice and pulled myself together to come up with a plan.

I figured that I would fill up my bike and my extra fuel containers, this way I wouldn't have to stop at a petrol station on the way and could fill my bike's tank myself, on the side of the road somewhere. I wouldn't stop, except for filling up, and keep riding until I made it to Ajdabiya. Hopefully. You see, the problem with traveling through Libya, is that there are so many armed Control Points and, if you travel on this road, as a woman, you have to travel with your husband. You also have to prove that the man is your husband. If you cannot do so, you get thrown into jail, kidnapped or even killed. I was a woman, alone, a foreigner, non-Muslim, on a bike and couldn't speak Arabic. I took a deep breath and hoped for the best.

I made it through the first checkpoint unscathed, I wasn't even stopped, thank goodness. My luck only lasted until I reached my second checkpoint. A man in uniform, holding an assault rifle, instructed me to remove my helmet. He spoke in Arabic of course, so I couldn't understand him, but it wasn't hard to guess from his gesturing. My heart was beating at a thousand beats per minute and I was so scared. The moment I removed my helmet, the man jumped back and started shouting at me in Arabic. The other men, standing around, came running towards us as the man kept shouting at me. I thought to myself,

"This is it, Jo. You're dead. They're going to throw you in a jail and rape you repeatedly and finally kill you". I pulled out my cell phone and phoned Achmed and then handed the phone to the Officer, who was still shouting. After a few minutes of him talking to Achmed, he handed me back my phone and said only four words,

"Go! And no stop!"

I left as fast as I could and hoped that there weren't too many checkpoints ahead. I managed to make it through three more, without being stopped, until I made it to Sirte. Achmed had given me the contact number of a man in Sirte who could speak English. He, at least, informed the man that I would be passing by Sirte and he kindly invited me to see the town. When I arrived in Sirte, he met me at the edge of town and led me to his home where a table stood, with a white tablecloth and a glass of milk and dates, to welcome me. The man spoke perfect English and offered to give me a tour of the town. It was the saddest day on my tour, we passed by houses that were shot and bombed to pieces. He explained to me how he had lost most of his family and friends, how babies died because their parents couldn't go out to find them milk or food, on account of the war. Almost every building in Sirte carried the mark of war. Bullet holes in the walls of some houses and blown up walls in others. I felt really sorry for all the innocent people who had lost their lives. Pain and sorrow haunts that town and many others in Libya and even through all the pain and hurt and loss, the people welcome you with open arms.

I filled up in Sirte, using my fuel supply, and then carried on to Ajdabiya. As far as my lucky streak went, I lasted as far as passing through the checkpoints, without being stopped. The road was a pretty good tarmac road, all the way and, during the last 100 kilometers from Ajdabiya, a pickup truck pulled up next to me, on the road. Two men inside, the passenger, next to the driver, hung out the window, shouting at me,

"Where are you from?" I didn't answer and just kept going. Then he said,

"Do you know where you are? Do you know how dangerous it is here?" All in perfect English. Still, I did not respond.

"Stop and we'll load your bike on the back and take you where you want. It's not safe to ride here". I just kept going, hoping that they would grow tired and leave me alone, eventually. Which they did.

When I finally arrived in Ajdabiya, I felt relieved and emotionally drained from the day's stress. My contact there, Nabil, met me at an arranged meeting point and then took me to the hotel, where I would be staying for the night. I asked him if we could stop at a shop, on route, as I needed to buy some water. While in the shop, I bought some cold drinks and snacks for the road. When I got to the till, the man, who I presumed to be the owner, started packing chocolate bars and bags of chips in my bag. I wasn't quite sure what to make of it, but when I wanted to pay for the goods the man refused and said,

"Welcome to Libya".

Senegal – en route to Saly

Senegal – shell road

Senegal – Saly

Senegal – shopping with Sahar

Senegal – jeweller in Saly

The bangle made for me

Senegal / Mauritania border

Mauritania / Senegal border

Entering the Sahara

Mauritania – on the road

Mauritania – camels on the road

Mauritania – sandstorm

Morocco – Dakhla

Morocco

Morocco – swimming camels

Morocco – with Momo

Morocco – with Madani (left)

Running into Federico

Spain – with Jose in Motril

Spain – with Carlos and Alicia

Spain – in Madrid with Alicia and Polo

France – with Charly and Michelle

Italy – with Federico & Bruna

Tunisia – near Algerian border

Tunisia – with Anis (middle) & Sahbi (right). Playing guitar on the beach

Tunisia – with Nawfel at Bizerte near the northernmost point in Africa

Tunisia – Carthage

Tunisian pottery

Tunisia – Star Wars set

Tunisia – Star Wars set

Tunisia – Tozeur

Tunisia

Tunisia

Tunisia

Tunisia

Tunisia

Tunisia – with Soufiane & Nawfel

Tunisia

Libya – Sabratah

Libya – Sabratah

Libya – Khoms

Libya - Sirte

Libya – Ahmed on far left

Libya – welcome in Tripoli

Libya – on the road

Libya – Leptis Magna

Libya – Leptis Magna

Libya – Leptis Magna

Libya – Leptis Magna (toilets)

Libya – Leptis Magna

Libya – Leptis Magna

Libya – Leptis Magna

Libya – the guys who rode with me to Tubruq (Nabil in the back)

CHAPTER 11

I stayed in the Amal Africa Hotel, for the night and, the next day, Nabil, along with four other bikers, would travel to Benghazi with me. It was at this time that we received word that the border with Egypt had been closed, after civil unrest broke out at the border, and shots were fired from both sides. It was unclear as to how long the border would be closed, and in the meantime, I would be stuck in Libya. I stayed at the Hotel Juliana, while in Benghazi and, what I remember best about my time there, was how there would be fireworks and gunshots going off every night at the hotel, in celebration of someone's wedding. There are a lot of weddings on a daily basis in Libya, it seemed. We spent three nights in Benghazi, before carrying on to Tubruq, mainly because of the issue at the border. A fellow adventure rider in Alexandria, Omar, was advising me on the situation in Egypt, on a daily basis, via social media. The news advised that the border would open for a short time period, only in two days' time so, that's when we made our move and carried on to Tubruq. We took a quiet road through the desert, so as not to draw too much attention and, it was on this road, that I had another experience that brings a smile to my face, whenever I think of it. We had stopped at a petrol station, to fill our bikes up with fuel, when a short, elderly man came and stood next to me. He was talking to the men who were travelling with me, who obviously explained to him who I was and what I was doing there. More elderly men came and joined this man, who took my hands in his and repeated, a dozen times: "Ahlan wa Sahlan, Marhaban, Ahlan wa Sahlan, Ahlan wa Sahlan", which basically means: welcome.

Before arriving in Tubruq, we met up with another group of riders who had ridden from the city to meet us on the road. When we arrived in the city, the guys led us to the town square, where a television crew and a group of locals were waiting to welcome us with food and drinks. A grand welcome, in my last town in Libya. I stayed in a little hotel just off the square and would remain there until we received word that the border had been opened. My room overlooked the town and the nearby Mosque. I don't know why, but I always feel deeply nostalgic whenever I hear the Adhan (Azan) – Call to prayer.

I had a small negative encounter in this hotel. One of the boys working in the hotel came to my room one morning, under the pretence of wanting to know whether I wanted breakfast served in my room. I had just woken up and told him that I'd have breakfast in the dining room a bit later on. He then pushed the door open and stepped towards me to try and kiss me. I stepped back and he pushed me against the wall and asked,

"Are you afraid of me?" I was awake now and pushed back hard, hard enough to push him right out of the room. I shouted at him to leave me alone and to go away. He was suddenly very apologetic and begged me not to tell anyone and gave me a chocolate to try and bribe me to not tell anyone, which I found both insulting and amusing.

At first, I didn't consider mentioning it, as I didn't believe it to be that big a deal. I've been through worse and I bet that the boy was just taking a chance. Later on, during the day, I was at the beach with my group of rider friends when Nabil, the guy who had been looking after me, asked me if something was wrong. I guess I wasn't quite myself and told him about the incident, earlier on in the hotel. He told me not to tell anyone about what happened and to remain quiet. I figured it was because I was a woman and women don't have many rights in Libya and just left it at that. We received news that the border would be opening the next day, for one day only. This was my chance to cross into Egypt and so, it was agreed that we would leave early the next morning, for the border.

Morning came and I stood outside, waiting for the guys, all packed and ready to hit the road. When the guys arrived, the leader of the motorcycling club in Tubruq asked me if the boy who had tried to assault me the previous day was in the hotel. This man is a highly orthodox Muslim and wouldn't even look at me. I was also not allowed to shake his hand when I first met him. I confirmed that the boy was actually in the reception of the hotel. Nabil told me to stand back and a group of about seven angry, Libyan bikers stomped into the hotel. The next moment, I heard a lot of screaming going on and then they dragged the boy outside and made him apologize to me several times. He received the beating of his life that day. I felt bad at first, but then Nabil told me,

"The boy needs to learn respect". I was just glad to have them on my side.

At the border, the guys were super helpful in helping me obtain a local sim card for Egypt and in changing my Libyan Dinar for Egyptian Pounds. I thanked them for all their help and got in the line to cross the border to Egypt, through the Salloum border post, also known as "The other hell on Earth". There were thousands of people at the border and I happened to land up right next to a trigger-happy Customs Officer, who insisted on firing off a few rounds on his rifle, every few minutes. I'm not sure what the hold-up was, but I spent about an hour on the Libyan side of the border, before I was finally stamped through and allowed to proceed to the Egyptian side of the border. My Libyan friends waited to see me proceed through to the other side and then waved goodbye to me, before heading back. On the Egyptian side of the border, I came across the first luggage x-ray on my entire trip. As I piled my luggage onto the conveyor belt, to be carried through the x-ray machine, I didn't even stop to think about the knives I was carrying in my bags, especially the really big one that I'd been given back in Libreville in Gabon. As my bags went through the scanner, the Officers looked at the monitor, then looked at me and then back at the monitor. They took my bags off the conveyor and told me to open them. They collected all the knives I had and then instructed me to follow one of the Officers to a nearby building.

Inside the building, I was put in an office with the Egyptian equivalent of their Secret Service. Two very serious-looking men sat at their desks, inspecting the knives that had been placed in front of them. That was problem number one. Problem number two was that neither of them could speak English. The only thing I could think of doing was to send Omar a message to ask him to explain to the Officers what was going on and why I had these knives with me. Omar was a star and rode to the border, from Alexandria, to come and help me. An explanation over the phone was just not good enough and he took matters into his own hands. I was extremely grateful, as everything had come to a grinding halt and I was kept in that room for hours. In the end, Omar was allowed to explain my situation and once the air was cleared, the two men's attitudes changed 180 degrees. All of a sudden, I was offered tea and cookies and a lot of apologies. If it wasn't for Omar, I might be rotting in some Egyptian jail now.

After nine hours at the border, I was finally free to go. It was already late and there was no way that I could travel at night. A 19h00 curfew had been enforced nationwide and nobody was allowed to travel at night. Omar and I stayed at the border town, in a little dodgy guesthouse, it's not like we had much of a choice. The next morning, we left very early, hoping to reach Cairo in time, before the curfew.

We made our way to Marsa Matruh and then on to Marina El Alamein for lunch, before heading into Cairo. There were countless military checkpoints on the roads and I had to unpack all my bags at each and every checkpoint. This caused us quite a delay. It was best to just smile and co-operate. I had been given back my knives at the border but I refused to take them back. I knew that if I had those knives on me, I would run into trouble at every single control point and it just wasn't worth the trouble.

I finally made it to Cairo late in the afternoon. I had been contacted by Mahmoud Mazen, from the Bikers Zone in Cairo, who offered me a place to stay, as well as support from the group for anything I would need. He met up with us just outside of Cairo, where Omar handed me over into his care. Mahmoud and I immediately became great friends and I met the rest of the gang over the following couple of days. The situation in Egypt was very fragile, at the time, and I had to be accompanied by Tourism Police whenever I wanted to move outside of my hotel. Again, word reached the Ministry of Tourism about my journey as I got a lot of media exposure: Girl on her own riding through Egypt at this fragile time with an Arabic tattoo on her forearm that says: "Love is the answer". I became national news and, wherever I went, people seemed to know me. While I was there, the guys from Phenomena and Biker Zone in Cairo, led by Mahmoud, organized a massive group ride to the Pyramids of Giza, along with a number of other events in my honor. I had always dreamed of seeing the pyramids and wished I had more time for these famous structures. I also met the Minister of Tourism in Cairo, who arranged for me to have places to stay at resorts and hotels throughout the rest of my journey south to Sudan. I was even given the honor of receiving a plaque, honoring me as a Goodwill Ambassador for Cross-Cultural Tourism. I felt like they were making far too big a deal of me, but at the same time, if it meant safe passage, I'd go with it. I was honoured, of course, but didn't feel deserving of the honour.

I had a fantastic time while staying in Cairo, I became part of the Biker Zone and Phenomena Team and made so many wonderful friends. I need to give Iysal Khalifa, Hadeer Nasser and Jessie Yehia special mentions as they became like my sisters and I have a special place in my heart for all of them, forever. I was also, unfortunately, starting to run out of funds on my journey and wouldn't be able to make it home, by my calculations. I only needed another US$1000 to make it and the Phenomena team put together a biking event, to raise the money to help me. This was right after the 'Million Man March' in Egypt and, although the country was still at war, these people put their worries aside to help me, a stranger. Again, they went out of their way to make sure I was safe and looked after, like on so many other occasions on my journey.

I spent a total of about three weeks in Cairo and loved the time spent with the local motorcycling community. I hadn't even left and we had already made plans for me to return. By week three, I was negotiating the crazy Cairo traffic, on my own, I had become a local! I got to see the new and the old Cairo and explored the wonderful history of this ancient city. When it came time to leave, I felt sad to have to go and I'm sure I'll return, one day.

From Cairo, I had a group of riders who accompanied me all the way to Hurghada. My stay at the Crystal Bay Resort was sponsored by the Sunrise Grand Select Group, who learned of me during one of the many interviews I did for local news and television shows. I stayed at the very fancy resort for four days and they even organized a quad ride into the desert and snorkelling in the Red Sea! I was treated like royalty and felt like I was in a dream. The very first time I went snorkelling was in the Red Sea, I mean, how lucky can one girl get? I also loved my time in Hurghada and would go back in a heartbeat! Once again, while in Hurghada, I had the pleasure of meeting the local Governor who presented me with a plaque for my efforts in circumnavigating the African continent on my own and spreading a message of peace.

From Hurghada, I was on my own again and made my way down to Luxor, where I was hosted at the beautiful

Maritime Jolie Ville Hotel Resort on King's Island. Luxor has frequently been described as one of the world's greatest open-air museums, as the ruins of the Temples at Karnak and Luxor stand within the modern city. I had the opportunity to see the temples, which are amazing, especially if you love history. You can feel the history when walking among the ruins, it is something really worth putting on one's bucket list of things to do. The one thing that broke my heart though was seeing how the tourism industry in Egypt was suffering. So many vendors tried desperately to get me to buy something from them as business was slow, due to the unrest in the country, and these people were struggling to support their families.

I would make my way to Aswan, from Luxor, my final destination to visit in Egypt. There are two options for traveling between Luxor and Aswan. The main road and the 'desert' road and as far as I know, and I might be mistaken, one needs a Permit to travel on the desert road. The main road is fine, except that it is very busy and has a million speed bumps. It's not that far between these two towns, only 220 odd kilometres, but it took me 5 hours to travel those 220 kilometers, due to the heavy traffic and endless speed bumps, which I thought a little excessive.

Once I arrived in Aswan, I met up with Kamal, THE fixer in Aswan. Many, many overland travellers know Kamal and have made use of his services. Omar had given me his details. Accompanying him was a French man, named Francois. I later found out that Francois had flown his bike into Cairo and planned on riding down to South Africa on his BMW R1200GS. He seemed a fairly decent gu, but, after having the bad experience of riding with someone before, I wasn't jumping at the opportunity to suggest that we ride together.

First point of order was for me to sort out a new Visa for Sudan, as mine had expired. We headed straight to the Embassy and I handed in my application where, I was assured, that I would have my Visa before it was time for me to get onto the ferry to Wadi-Halfa. After sorting out the Visa, Kamal led me to the hotel where I would be staying for the duration of my time in Aswan. Once again, the Mövenpick Resort offered to sponsor my entire stay in Aswan, where I had the most wonderful welcome, with traditional Nubian music and dancers. I even joined in and danced along, as we took the barge across the river to the island on the Nile where the hotel is situated. I was being spoilt rotten! I had my own double storey apartment, complete with lounge and sliding doors that led out onto the banks of the Nile River. Management and staff welcomed me with drinks and snacks in my room and a personalized welcome note. I don't know what I did to deserve all this luxury, but I wasn't going to look a gift horse in the mouth, that's for sure!

My stay at the resort was out of this world, the hotel management and staff really went out of their way to make me feel welcome and again, I met the local Governor who presented me with a medal for my efforts. I may have lost a bunch of knives, but I gained the same weight back in medals and plaques.

I partook in a Felucca tour on the Nile to a traditional Nubian village, where we had drinks overlooking the Nile. I also had a traditional henna tattoo done by one of the local woman, I wanted to experience as much as I could while I still had time in Egypt, and it certainly has a lot to offer.

The next day was D-Day and Francois and I needed to have our bikes loaded onto the barge that would leave ahead of the ferry to Wadi-Halfa. While having our bikes loaded, we met Obai, a Sudanese rider who was on his way to completing a solo ride from Senegal to his hometown, Khartoum. I knew of Obai, as some of my Tunisian friends had met him in Tunisia and told me he was heading in the same direction. I could hardly believe that he had caught up with me, but then I had spent about a month in Egypt and this meant that there were three of us with bikes on the barge, heading in the same direction. Obai suggested that the three of us travel together and we all agreed and, even though I had been sceptical at first, I actually enjoyed the company of both Francois and Obai, they were both fairly relaxed travellers.

Two days later, it was our turn to get on the famous ferry that travels from Aswan to Wadi-Halfa and back, once a week. If you miss the ferry, you have to wait for another week. My Sudanese Visa did come through in time and now, all I had to do was sit back in my first-class cabin and relax for the 24-hour ferry ride to Sudan. A new road between Aswan and Wadi-Halfa had been built and opened, by the time we took the ferry, though they were not yet allowing tourists on the road at that time. I understand the road is open to all travellers today.

What can I say about the ferry between Aswan and Wadi-Halfa? It's an experience, that's for sure! My first-class ticket bought me a cabin with very small bunk beds, a broken air-conditioner and a filthy window. The toilets on board are beyond disgusting! I didn't go to the toilet for 24 hours, I just kept it in as there was no way I could face going to the toilets on board. So, if you ever plan on taking the ferry, don't take in any fluids beforehand! A ferry that was designed to carry, let's say 100 people, gets filled with 500 people and their goods all squashed up together. The food, however, was not that bad though. For dinner we had Foul, a bean dish and bread and salad. Obai teased me, saying that I'm like a typical Egyptian because I love Foul and drink lots of tea, I think that makes me more English than anything else. Francois had also taken a cabin, while Obai decided to hit the deck. I think he had the best spot! After dinner, I hung out on the deck for a while, watching the stars come out, before hitting my bed. I slept on top of my sleeping bag, on the top bunk, even though there were fitted sheets on the beds. I tossed and turned a lot and just couldn't get comfortable. And sometime after midnight, I went outside onto the deck, where hundreds of men and women lay sleeping. I found a little open spot and lay watching the gazillions of stars overhead, while we bobbed down the Nile. In those few minutes, I felt completely immersed in the present and so grateful for this journey called life!

When we made it to Wadi-Halfa the next day, the barge, with our bikes, had already arrived. Disembarking was like being caught up in a feeding frenzy, with hundreds of starving people wanting to get off the ferry. Francois and I were instructed to stay behind, for some reason, I guess, because we were the only foreigners on the ferry. After everyone had disembarked, our Sudanese fixer, Mazar, came on board. He handed us each a form we were required to complete and then instructed us to follow him. Outside, we were led to a little office where we handed in our forms and had our passports and Carnets stamped.

Obai and Mazar went to find out whether we could get out bikes off the barge, on the same day. In the meantime, I found a seat in the outdoor waiting area, under a roof, among a group of men. In no time, I found myself being given peanuts and chatting to the guys about my trip. (Why is it always peanuts)? Sudanese people are super friendly and I felt completely safe!

After about four hours of waiting, it became clear that we would only be able to get our bikes off the barge the next day, so Mazar took us to a local hotel where we could stay for the night. We settled in and I took a long, blissful, hot shower, after which we headed out to find something for dinner. As this was Obai's home turf, he insisted on looking after Francois and I and refused to let us pay for any of our meals! Not only are Sudanese people super friendly, they're also super generous!

There isn't much to see or do in Wadi-Halfa. It's a tiny, dusty, border town with a hotel or two that offer the very basics, and a number of curious shacks and little outdoor restaurants. It makes up for it in personality, friendly people and good food though. We took a tuk-tuk into town and had a wonderful meal at a local restaurant of various fried meat strips with onions and hummus. Everything is made fresh, so it's really yummy. Obai also helped me get a local sim card for my phone before we headed back to our hotel to turn in for an early night.

After breakfast the next morning, which consisted of very sweet doughnut balls and even sweater milky tea (made only with milk and tea), we headed back to the barge to fetch our bikes. Mazar, our fixer, handled everything, we never came into contact with a single Customs or Immigrations Officers. Everything was taken care of, at a price of course. We were free to collect our bikes and a dozen men gathered to help lift the bikes off the barge and down onto the ground. It took some manhandling, but the men were capable, within an hour, we had our bikes and were back at the hotel to pack our stuff to hit the road. Next stop – Dongola!

The main road through Sudan used to be a sandy track, but nowadays there's a new tar road that runs right through the country, from Wadi-Halfa, all the way to the border with Ethiopia. The road has long, lazy corners and is surrounded by miles and miles of desert, as far as the eye can see. Every now and again, you can spot a small settlement on the side of the road where you can always find a small shop or restaurant to buy something to eat and drink. We stopped about halfway to Dongola for lunch and again, the food was freshly made and absolutely delicious!

Obai suggested a hotel for Francois and me to stay in, while he would be staying with some relatives of his in Dongola. We agreed to all freshen up and meet back, outside the hotel, to go for dinner. We were joined by one of Obai's cousins and again, we piled into a tuk-tuk to go into town for the meal. This time it was Obai's cousin who offered to pay for dinner, saying that we were welcome as his guests. We walked back most of the way to the hotel, in order to see a bit more of the town. It's a bit bigger than Wadi-Halfa, but then, it doesn't take much to be bigger than Wadi-Halfa. Everywhere we went, people were super friendly and again, I had this feeling that we were absolutely safe in Sudan. Even with our bikes standing outside in the street, nobody ever went close to them or gave the impression that they might be up to no good. Just good, wholesome people.

The next day was a very big day for Obai, as it was the final day of his journey, riding solo from Senegal to Sudan. We would make our way to Khartoum and there, Francois and my path would split from Obai's. He would obviously stay behind, while we continued further south. In the few days that I got to know Francois, it became obvious that he's a really good guy. A shy Orthopaedic Surgeon from France, he was just out to live a dream of his, of riding from Cairo to Cape Town. I decided to give him the benefit of the doubt and said we could ride together for a bit, if he wanted. I even chatted to his wife over the phone and promised to make sure that he didn't get into any trouble.

Francois and I both shook Obai's hand, before we set out to Khartoum and wished him luck on the last day of his journey. I felt honoured to be a part of his final leg to the finish line and it made me think about what it might feel like when I finally stood where I had departed from, so many months ago. We left Dongola just after sunrise and it was obvious that Obai was eager to get home! It is just over 500 kilometers from Dongola to Khartoum and our average speed picked up quite a bit on this day. We made it to the capital at around 15h00 that day, where a television crew was waiting for Obai on the outskirts of town and followed him to a meeting point, where a large group of people were waiting for him. Family and friends came to welcome him home and even the town's Mayor was there. It was a very joyous occasion and we were very happy for him.

Francois had already booked himself into a hotel, while I met up with a local friend and fellow rider, Mohammed Nasir, who suggested that I stay at the local youth hostel for the night and showed me where it was. It was agreed that we would all meet up for dinner later that night, including Obai. I was surprised that he'd want to join us for dinner as I would have thought he'd want to be with his family. He clearly still considered us his guests and would go out of his way to make our stay comfortable.

I found a Subway sandwich shop across from the youth hostel where I was staying and bought a sandwich for lunch. The owner started chatting to me and I then found out that my Cape Town to Dublin on Vespa's friends, whom I had met up with in Italy, had stayed in the same Youth Hostel and also bought sandwiches from his shop. It's a small world, after all!

We spent two nights in Khartoum as Francois needed to sort out his Visa for Ethiopia and we hoped he'd be able to do so the next day. The local riders tried very hard to convince us to stay longer but Francois had time constrictions on his Visas, going ahead, and needed to get going. To be very honest, I was starting to itch to get home as well. The next day, we hit the road early in the morning and the plan was to find a spot about fifty kilometers from the border to camp wild on the side of the road. The landscape started changing dramatically, the further south we ventured. From desert to thorn trees, dotting the countryside, from camels to donkeys and goats. About sixty kilometers from the Ethiopian border, we came across a Police checkpoint. I asked the Police Officer whether there was a good spot nearby where we could set up camp for the night. He sternly told me that nobody was permitted to camp next to the road. So, we carried on for about another ten kilometres, until we found a suitable spot and set up camp anyway. Out of sight, out of mind.

We had stopped earlier in the day for lunch, next to the road, and bought some extra food that consisted of hard boiled eggs, bread and some deep-fried fish. After pitching our tents, we took out our extra food and sat watching a thunderstorm rolling in, while pondering what Ethiopia might be like.

I was up before the sun the next morning and went about boiling some water for coffee on my super cool MSR Expedition Stove. It was my last day in Sudan and I was happy that I'd spent the night in a tent. I hadn't spent much time in my tent since my cycling days and I was, after all, lugging it with me around the African continent, might as well use it, for a change. I woke Francois up and we had coffee while breaking up camp and packing up our gear. We found a little petrol station, just before the border and filled up our bikes before entering the border town.

At the border, we were directed to a building next to the road. A short descent, down a muddy path, brought us to a group of Customs Officials. We were greeted with friendly smiles and shown inside. No fuss, no hassles. Quick and easy. So quick and easy that I wandered off in search of more coffee at one of the little café's next to the road. After we'd had another cup of coffee, it was off to Immigration to have our luggage checked and our Carnet's stamped. Once again, we were met by friendly faces and efficient service. I was shown to a seat inside the building and the Officer, on the other side of the desk, asked me questions like,

"Where are you from?" "Where are you going to?" "Any electronics to declare?" You see, in Ethiopia, you have to declare all your electronics, like mobile phones, cameras, laptops, GPS's, etc. I don't really know why. The Officer accompanied me to my bike to make sure that the VIN number on my bike matched that of the number on my Carnet de Passage document, then he stamped my Carnet and I was free to proceed.

Once Francois was also done with all his paperwork, we proceeded to Gorgora, next to Lake Tana. We would stay at a well-known little overland spot named the Tim & Kim Village. (www.timkimvillage.com). It's not that far from the border, so we weren't in any rush. Reaching the village is like arriving in paradise, it is a jewel of a place. You make your way up and down a gravel road and then you're most likely to be greeted personally, by either Tim or Kim... or both, as you're welcomed to their beautiful piece of heaven. You can choose between staying in a bungalow or pitching your tent or staying in one of their readily pitched tents. They have great facilities, you are right on Lake Tana as well and as a result, you can enjoy the most spectacular views while kicking back and enjoying a cold one. We did just that and were later introduced to another South African, who joined us for dinner. Seeing as there were now two South Africans, it called for a fire to be lit and a braai (BBQ) to be had. It is a law that wherever two or more South Africans meet, a braai (BBQ) must be had. We spent the rest of the evening in conversation with our hosts and swapping stories of adventures.

The next morning, I was up early enough to watch the sun rise over Lake Tana. After breakfast, we loaded our bikes and headed towards Debre Markos, where we would spend the night, before heading into the capital, Addis-Ababa, where we planned on staying at yet another famous overland spot, Wim's Holland House, also frequented by many an overland traveller.

At first, the plan was to stick to the main road, Route 3, through Ethiopia to Kenya. The road is busy, perpetually and has throngs of people, donkeys, cattle and goats walking to and fro on the side of the road, all at the time, from sunrise to sunset! I have never seen so many people walking back and forth on the side of a road, as in Ethiopia! I couldn't help but wonder what they were doing. Some were obviously herders and loads of women carrying fire wood and large bundles of grass on their heads. That's another thing that is immediately noticeable in Ethiopia, most of the work seems to be done by the women, even tiny, old ladies, in the winter season of their lives, can be seen carrying loads up to three times their size, on their heads. It's a striking site and I can't help but feel that it shouldn't be this way, it should be the young ones doing the hard labour, but then, I don't know enough about their social structures and culture, to be able to judge. I'm sure it's worked for them for centuries, otherwise they wouldn't be doing it, I suppose.

Ethiopia is perhaps one of the most visually striking countries I have ridden through on my journey around the continent. Massive valleys and mountains with green fields as far as the eye can see, it's beautiful. The road to Debre Markos is a good tarmac road. We stopped about halfway for some coffee and the obligatory Injera, Ethiopian flatbread, a sourdough risen flatbread, made of teff flour, it has a spongy texture and a sour taste that, I'd say, is an acquired taste, you either love it or you hate it. And, for those who do not know, coffee is thought to have originated in Ethiopia as well. It's nearly impossible to find a bad cup of coffee in Ethiopia. Well, at least in my experience or maybe I've just been lucky.

Whenever we'd stop on the side of the road, whether for coffee, lunch or just to stretch our legs, groups of children would always surround us. They never asked for money though which really surprised me, as it's unfortunately a bad habit learnt by children, especially in developing countries. In Ethiopia though, I was only ever asked for stationery which made me wish that I had actually carried some with me.

We took our time going through Ethiopia and could therefore really take in the scenery. Majestic mountains that would rise up beside you in all their glory, followed by valleys that would plunge down below to reveal hundreds and hundreds of farmlands below. I know there are areas in Ethiopia where famine in a sad reality, but everywhere I rode, I only saw fertility and richness in soil.

From Debre Markos, we made our way to Addis-Ababa, the capital of Ethiopia. A steep descent leads you into the chaos that is Addis. It was raining the day we arrived and low hanging mist meant limited visibility. I was confident that I'd be able to navigate us to Wim's Holland House in no time, though, after about half an hour of riding in circles around the location without being able to get to it, I had to phone Wim. I found his number on the internet and stopped on the side of the road to call him, for directions. There was a great deal of roadworks going on throughout the city and, what used to be the turn-off to Wim's place, had been demolished so, he tried his best to explain to me how best to get to his place.

As I stood next to the road, consulting my GPS, two young boys stopped next to us on a scooter and asked if we needed help. I didn't trust them from the outset and just kept going over my maps and checking my GPS. They said they knew where Wim's Holland House was and I don't know what made Francois decide it would be a good idea, but he got on his bike and followed the boys. I couldn't believe my eyes and jumped on my bike to follow them. When I caught up with Francois, I tried to gesticulate to him to turn around. My gestures became more frantic when it seemed like he didn't understand. He eventually turned around and we returned to the traffic circle where we were previously standing and trying to figure out where to go. I explained to him that those boys were leading him in the opposite direction and, had he followed them down an alley, he'd probably be left standing with empty hands. As I was explaining this to him, another group of kids showed up, supposedly interested in looking at my GPS. The one boy pushed up against me to look at the GPS and then I felt a little hand find its way into my shoulder bag. I didn't say a word, I just slowly reached down, took hold of the hand, squeezed and twisted. Needless to say the hand retracted and the boys left.

We eventually did find our way through the chaotic roadworks to Wim's place. Once we arrived there, he informed me that the guesthouse was closed, due to a run-in with the government... whatever that means. The restaurant and bar were still open, so I asked him whether we could pitch our tents outside in the yard. It had been raining that whole day and he offered for us to sleep in his house, which was really kind of him. The bar is like a local hangout for overland travellers, from all corners of the world. I met and chatted to so many interesting people that night, some traveling in Land Rovers, some by bicycle and others using public transport. One particular man had some crazy stories to share of how he had been chased by Bedouins, in his car, through the desert in the South of Egypt, how he'd been thrown in jail in Iran and loads of other stories. I sat chatting to Wim for a while and asked him about the best route south and he suggested we not take the main road to Kenya, but rather a back route that is less congested and far more interesting. He scribbled a map and wrote directions for me, on three different scraps of paper and, with that, I turned in for the night, confident that I'd be able to navigate us safely out of Addis, the next morning.

I didn't like Addis very much, it was just like any other major city on the planet, overpopulated and filled with loads of hustlers. We'd only been there for a night and that was enough, I was looking forward to following the backroad with less traffic and less people and I also felt uneasy, from the moment we entered Addis until we left. We would now make our way towards Arba Minch, via Butajira, through Sodo. Francois had read up about a posh-looking lodge next to Lake Abaya and so we decided we'd head in that direction.

This road was far less congested and made me feel more at ease as well, it felt like I could breathe again. We went at an easy pace and stopped off at a little hotel next to the road for breakfast, which was really good! Once we made it to Arba Minch, we went in search of fuel as we were both running really low. The two petrol stations in town had no fuel and we were told that none of the surrounding towns had fuel either. This made me really nervous but, I knew, if it came to it, we would be able to buy fuel from the locals, at an exorbitant rate, but we wouldn't have much choice.

We found a lodge next to the lake with the most wonderful views and negotiated to stay for the night at a rate of US$40 each, which was better than the going price of US$70.

The next morning, we starting looking around to find fuel. The filling stations in town still didn't have fuel and news had it that none of the surrounding towns had either. One of the guides, back at the lodge, said he could help us and led us down to a little village down the road. Halfway there, he told us to wait on the side of the road because,

"They will charge double if they see you are tourists". I thought that was really considerate of him as he could easily have taken advantage of the situation. We waited on the side of the road and entertained the crowd gathering around us, taking pictures and allowing kids to sit on our bikes. About 15 minutes later, a group of men came walking down the road from the village with 2liter Coke bottles filled with fuel. We each put in 10 liters of fuel, which should at least get us to a place where we'd be able to fill up. We thanked them for their help and waved good bye to the crowd as we left.

The tarmac ended and we were on a gravel road for the rest of the way, until we would get to the border with Kenya. It was a good, graded dirt road, so we made really good time. The scenery was gorgeous and we were in no hurry. We took our time and just enjoyed the last bit of Ethiopia before we'd be crossing into Kenya the next day. When we finally did re-join the main tarmac road, we stopped for lunch and refilled at the first available petrol station, at least they had fuel! We decided that we'd find a cheap hotel or guesthouse, just before the border, to stay for the night and then we'd cross the border the next morning to tackle the notorious 'Hell Road'.

We found a little hotel, with a restaurant, next to the road, just before the border and booked two rooms. Francois' bike's rear wheel had lost a number of spokes and this was a bit of a cause for concern. We checked the other spokes on the wheel and there were more that were dangerously loose, so, I helped him to tighten them up and he then went in search of someone who could change his tyres. He had a set of knobby tires that he'd been carrying since Cairo and wanted to have those fitted, for the road ahead. I had a shower and then a cold beer in the bar while he went to have his tires fitted. I found another guy on a BMW R1200GS and started chatting to him, it turned out that his name was Odette and that he was an Israeli travelling around the world. As we chatted, I found out that he had met a couple of friends of mine who were riding through China at that time. It's a small world!

I was getting worried about Francois as he had been away for longer than two hours. Just as I was about to saddle up to go save the Frenchman again, he came riding into the parking lot with new tires fitted and a big smile on his face. I think it gave him a psychological boost for the road ahead. At first, I wanted to do the Lake Turkana route but then I read up a bit more about this route and it turned out that we'd need to carry a lot of our own fuel for days and it is a bit more challenging, so, if anything happened I would be on my own in the middle of nowhere. So 'Hell Road' was the logical way to go.

The next morning, we had breakfast with Odette before packing up and leaving. He would be heading north while we were heading south. We would tackle the notorious 'Hell Road' of Northern Kenya. 'Hell Road' is - or used to be - a 350-odd kilometer stretch of dirt road, of which the majority consisted of badly corrugated conditions and sometimes, no road at all. Though the Chinese have been working on this road and tarring all of it up to the border, most motorcycles, travelling this stretch of road, suffered from overheated rear shock-absorbers because of the incessant shaking on the corrugations. They're so bad, it doesn't matter how fast you go, there's just no escaping the shake.

The other obstacle that one might, very possibly, face on this stretch of road is bandits, mainly from Somalia. This is why I decided not to travel through Somalia, I had been through so much going through Northern Africa, I felt like I had pushed my luck enough. And as usual, I let my gut have the final say – and it was telling me to stay away from Somalia. So that's what's I did.

Crossing through the Kenyan border was easy. As a South African passport holder, I wouldn't need any more visas from here, which made things so much easier. The Customs and Immigrations Officers were very friendly and had us stamped through the border in no time. The scenery changed again, from lush greenery to more arid conditions. I went on ahead and Francois followed. We were making steady progress, but it wasn't meant to last. Only 30 kilometers into Hell Road, the rear shock absorber on my poor, overloaded Dakar overheated and gave in. I felt something strange going on and, when I looked down, I saw oil all over my boots. I stopped immediately and it took only seconds to figure out what the problem was. There was nothing to do about it and I had very little choice other than to slowly make my way to Nairobi where I could hopefully source a new shock absorber. I told Francois that he could go ahead if he wanted to, but he insisted that he was happy to stick with me, even if we did have to go at a painfully slower pace.

What would've taken us a day from the border to Nairobi, would now take us at least three days to cover. The going was slow and tiring, it was like riding a mountain bike at 40 kilometers an hour for hundreds of kilometers. My body was taking a beating as I had no shock absorber, which meant that all the vibrating and hellish shaking went straight through my body. For our first night in Kenya, we would stay in a tiny little village called Turbi/Torbi, only 130 kilometers from the border town of Moyale. We arrived in Turbi early afternoon and called it a day. I only knew about this town because Omar had mentioned it to me, it's literally a one-horse town and, if you blinked, you'd miss it. The people are extremely friendly and helpful though. We entered a building with 'Torbi Hotel' painted on the walls outside, though the building seemed to be abandoned with nothing and no one in sight. Across the road, another building stood, with the name 'Subhana Seven Hills Hotel' painted on a sign outside, so we tried our luck with it.

This time, we were met by three men inside the building. We explained that we were looking for a place to stay for the night and they indicated that this would not be a problem at all, though asked that we give them some time to ready our rooms. They suggested that we relax outside, in the shade, at one of the two tables. We asked whether they could provide us with something to eat for lunch while we waited and lunch consisted of strips of grilled meat with some flat bread. Simple but really tasty.

The rooms were very basic with two single beds in each room with mattresses that had seen better days. No running water. No electricity. No flushing toilets. This didn't really bother me but I could see it was a bit of a culture shock for Francois, who had probably never seen a long-drop in his life. I asked where I could wash myself and was shown to a shack about 30 meters from my room and given a bucket of water, from which to wash myself. I am not a big fan of the long-drop either and would prefer just 'going' in the bush, it feels far more hygienic than non-flushing ablutions, you know.

Each room had a name painted, outside above the door. My room was called 'New York City', which I thought quite comical. I struggled to sleep that night because it was just so hot! After an hour of tossing and turning, I decided to rather go and lie outside, to try to get some sleep. As I opened the door to go outside, I got a terrible fright when I realized there was a man, lying on a mattress, right in front of my door. I suspected he was there for security reasons, but he didn't seem to be the best of guards, as I just stepped over him a number of times to go in and out of my room and to the loo, without waking him once!

The next morning, I was approached by a local Rastafarian who seemed very interested in my collection of bracelets that I was wearing on my arm. He asked me if he could have one of them and I explained to him that I could not give him one as each bracelet carried, with it, memories from all the places I had visited and that many of the bracelets had been given to me by people I met along the way. He stood quietly, seemingly pondering this information for a while and then took off one of the bracelets on his arm and gave it to me. This really brought a smile to my heart.

Turbi to Marsabit is only another 120 kilometers, but it would take us the best part of the day to cover this short distance, thanks to my broken bike. There isn't much in the way of scenery on this stretch of road, which didn't really bother me as I was more focused on the road and trying to find any smooth parts among the seemingly never-ending corrugations, dodging rocks and trying to not fall in the patches of soft sand. Omar had bet me that I would fall, at least once, on Hell Road, so I was, of course, set on winning that bet. Francois would, unfortunately, have lost the bet as he put the bike down once in the sand. But only once! He was doing really well.

About halfway through the day and halfway to Marsabit, we passed a man standing on the side of the road, wearing a military uniform and waving his AK47 rifle at us. It looked like he was trying to get us to stop. I was in front and there was no way I was stopping. This seemed a bit strange to me, so I nervously sped up and kept going, waving as I passed him. I just hoped that he wouldn't jump in his vehicle and start chasing us down. Later on when we stopped for a break, the first thing Francois said, as he took off his helmet and walked towards me, was that he was sure that he was going to get shot and that I was going to just ride away. I just smiled and assured him that I wouldn't leave him behind, he was my travel buddy for this section of the journey and I felt like I needed to look out for him. We luckily never did get chased down.

All along the way, we would pass men working on the road here and there and they would always be very friendly and wave and whistle as we passed them. Once we made it to Marsabit, we checked out a place called Nomad's Trail that I found on my GPS. A clean hotel with secure parking, restaurant and Wifi at an affordable price. Perfect! We booked ourselves in, had a little something to eat for lunch and then we decided that we both needed an afternoon nap. Later on, we went out to explore the town a little bit and found a nice pub, where we ended up having a few cold beers and watching a movie they were screening on their television. I asked about the road's condition further ahead among the locals in the bar. I wanted to know how much dirt there still was left for us to cover. Answers ranged from 20 kilometers to 120 kilometers. It didn't seem like anyone really knew and maybe it had something to do with that number always changing on account of the road being tarred.

The next day, we were both starting to get a bit fed up with having to put up with the incessant corrugated road and about 60 kilometers into our ride, heading to Nanyuki, we were taking a break, when Francois turned to me and said,

"How much further, Jo? This is your Africa, so you should know?" I had no idea of course, but was very happy when we hit the tarmac 30 kilometers later! I'm all for adventure and love riding off-road, but three days of riding without a shock absorber on that road was enough for me.

As soon as we hit the tarmac, the landscape also suddenly began to change again as well. We went from the arid, flat and dry conditions, we had experienced over the last couple of days, to sudden greenery and hills visible in the distance. We would spend the night in Nanyuki, staying over with a friend of a friend of mine and you could see Mount Kenya from their home! On this day, I also crossed the Equator again, on the opposite side of the continent, at an altitude of about 1900 meters, which made for a very joyous occasion, I had made it all the way to the other side of the African continent! From here on, it would be all downhill, back to South Africa! I could sense a feeling of anticipation starting to stick its head out, the anticipation of making it back home to the point from where I had started. I didn't entertain the feeling too much just yet as I still had a long way to go and needed to focus on what was still to come.

From Nanyuki, we would make our way into Nairobi to the famous overlander's spot called 'Jungle Junction' or 'JJ's', run by a German named Chris. They had just moved from their old premises and Odette, the Israeli we met at the border, had been kind enough to give me their new address, which was way at the southern end of Nairobi. We had no choice but to brave the traffic and man, was there traffic! It took us a good two hours to get across town, but it was all worth it once we got to JJ's. The first thing I noticed as we entered through the gate, were at least half a dozen bikes standing on the other side of the property and Land Rovers all over the show. It made me feel excited and like we were in the company of kindred spirits. Then, both of us decided to treat ourselves to booking into rooms rather than having to camp and settled in for the next couple of days, which we spent mainly catching up on our blogs, doing laundry and tending to Francois' bike, as he would be carrying on, on his own, from here, while I stayed behind to fix my DAX. We met people from all walks of life and on all kinds of adventures. A Japanese bloke on a bicycle riding through Africa, a French couple overlanding in their 4x4, a South African birdwatcher, a girl from the Netherlands and a group from South Africa.

I started asking around and researching my options in terms of sourcing a new shock absorber for my bike. Chris said he could help me fit the new shock once it arrived, at a fee of course. But buying a new one was just way too expensive and I couldn't afford it. Lucky for me, fellow adventure riders and good friends of mine from back home, Michnus and Elsabie Oliver, said they had a spare off one of their Dakars and that I could have it, at no cost! They were touring Europe at the time and I just had to handle the shipping of the shock from South Africa. This was fantastic news and they were real life savers! I contacted a courier company in South Africa called TNT and asked whether they could help with the shipping. After hearing my story, they sponsored the shipping of the shock absorber to Nairobi! There are some really amazing and generous people out there!

In the meantime, a girl named Chantel Young had read about my journey on Facebook and contacted me, saying that I'd be more than welcome to stay with them, once in Nairobi. So, I decided to move and stay with them once Francois left to continue on to Cape Town. When D-Day came, I bid Francois farewell and good luck on his journey ahead. His wife would fly out to meet him in Cape Town and together they would tour the area for a while or that was the plan. I told him that I'd try and catch up with them in Cape Town, but it all depended on when I'd receive the new part for my bike. Francois is a good guy and I enjoyed his company for the little while that we rode together. It's very difficult to find someone that you can travel with for an extended period of time, but Francois was a good buddy, with whom I had no problem travelling. After he left, I packed my stuff to move over to Chantal's family's home. When I wanted to check out of the hotel,

I found out that Francois had settled my entire bill, without saying anything before he left, as a way of thanking me for being his 'guide' on the first leg of his journey. Like I said... decent guy.

It turned out that Chantal's parents' house was literally just around the block from Jungle Junction! She had read about my trip on a mutual friends' Facebook page and contacted me and, as Chantal and her whole family is very much into motorsport, and even though this was the first time I had met the Young family, it felt like I'd known them for years. Chantal and her brother, Zane, and I were like best buds instantly and the Young family very generously allowed me to stay with them for as long as it took to receive the new shock absorber. In the meantime, Chantal and I went on a road trip in her car to the Nakuru National Park. We were lucky and saw so many animals ad it felt like all I had seen, for the last year, was camels, donkeys, sheep and goats, so I really enjoyed seeing some other wildlife for a change. We saw loads of Cape Buffalo, Zebra, Giraffe and even some rhino and lions chilling in a tree. The lions, not the rhino.

Back in Nairobi, Chantal and Zane entertained me by taking me go-kart racing, partying at night, archery by day and joining their team and playing a game of Rounders. I also got to tick off another bucket list item by visiting the well-known David Sheldrick Wildlife Trust, a sanctuary that cares for orphaned baby elephants and then reintroduces them into the wild when they are older and ready. Each elephant is introduced to his or her own personal carer and that carer will physically live with that elephant, sleeping next to them at night and caring for them and looking after them during the day. It's a remarkable place. It is no secret that elephants are my all-time favourite animals and so visiting this place was a really special day for me, it is a cause I will always support and if you are ever in the area, I would urge you to visit the sanctuary.

I had so much fun, while in Nairobi, that the couple of weeks that it took for the new part to arrive literally flew by. The whole Young family have been or are involved in rally racing. Chantal herself is a rally car navigator and so, when the shock absorber finally arrived,'6re it was no challenge at all for a bunch of petrol heads like us to figure out how to remove and replace the part. Everyone kind of pitched in and it sure beat having to pay someone else to do it!

The arrival of the part I needed to fix my bike was a bitter-sweet one as well. It meant that I could now carry on with my journey, which was great, but it also meant saying goodbye to my new family, which saddened me. I had grown so fond and so close to these people that when it came to saying goodbye, we all had tears in our eyes. Chantal would accompany me for about an hour's ride, south towards the Tanzanian border. We stopped off at a place called 'Whistling Thorns' for breakfast and then, it was finally time to say farewell to my new sister/friend/travel buddy. It was really hard saying goodbye to one of the coolest people I'd met on my journey. I didn't hang around as I hate goodbyes. I know we'll see one another again someday, I have no doubt.

From here, I would make my way to the Namanga border post where I'd cross into Tanzania. It's only about 170 kilometers from Nairobi to the Namanga border post and, when I finally reached it, I spotted two Land Rover 4x4's with my adventure idol's name on them, Kingsley Holgate! The two Landies (Land Rovers) were packed to the rafters and covered in sponsors' names and logos. I searched for, and waited around a while, but saw no sign of the man himself, unfortunately. After about an hour, I decided to carry on to Arusha, another 110 kilometers from the border, where I would spend the night. Arusha is home to the Arusha National Park and its own Mount Meru that many people come to climb in preparation for climbing the famous Mount Kilimanjaro. In town, there is a sandstone clock tower that is supposed to mark the halfway point between Cairo and Cape Town. The town was alive with so many guesthouses and restaurants, roadside stalls and fresh food markets. There are so many safari companies operating in this area and I didn't want to get caught up in any of the tourist traps, so I stayed just outside of town at a place called Sakina Camp at US$25 for the night. The owner of the establishment was super friendly and helpful and gave me information on where best to go for something to eat and anything else I needed, while helping me carry my bags to my room. I already liked Tanzania!

Rain was forecast for the next couple of days and, although I was really looking forward to seeing Mount Kilimanjaro, it was just not meant to be. It was overcast and raining as I passed by the mountain so I stopped on the side of the road for a little while, hoping to catch even a glimpse of the giant at some point, but the clouds didn't let up, so I carried on. I could feel something inside of me stirring and I felt like I wanted to get home now. I opted to skip Dar es Salaam and would head to a town called Morogoro instead. I didn't feel like having to negotiate my way through another busy city, and so I headed straight south, direction Malawi!

I soon learned that Tanzania is very tourist friendly, with loads of accommodation options available in even the smallest of towns. It was just over 600 kilometers from Arusha to Morogoro and it rained for all of those kilometers! I had left my full-face Uvex Adventure Helmet in Egypt and was riding with an open face endurance helmet, with goggles. Anyone who has ever had to ride in the rain with goggles will tell you how unpleasant it is. The rain drops feel like little darts that hit your face at a thousand miles an hour and it really hurts. I tried to cover my face as best I could with my Buff headwear but it didn't really help that much. It was a long ride to Morogoro and I was happy when I finally made it to town.

I found a little hotel just outside of town and could have a room at US$20 for the night. I was so tired that I ordered some food from the downstairs restaurant and then took it up to my room to eat and then fell asleep soon after.

From Morogoro, I made my way to Mbeya. Another long day in the saddle, clocking just under 640 kilometers for the day. It was still raining intermittently but when the clouds gave way, it shone down on a beautiful landscape. Tanzania would make it onto my top five list of most beautiful countries visited on my journey. On my way to Mbey, I passed through what is known as the 'Baobab Valley', situated between Mikumi and Iringa, on the edge of the Udzungwa Mountains National Park. A stunning area with majestic baobab trees, for as far as the eye can see, it was a very welcome surprise as I hadn't known about the Baobab Valley's existence up until then. I also passed through the Mikumi National Park that is home to loads of wildlife. There were no fences and buffalo, all kinds of antelope and zebras crossed the road on many occasions, while making my way through the park. I was amazed that one is allowed to ride through the park on a motorcycle as it wouldn't be allowed in most national parks in South Africa. I loved every second of it, being so wild and free!

That saying that says you should be extra careful, the closer you get to home, is very true! It was raining nonstop while I was riding through Tanzania, and I was making my up through this beautiful mountain pass, just before Mbeya, when I got a little taste of the tar, literally. The pass winds up high into the mountain with loads of awesome hairpin bends and, as I was nearing the top, I came into the last corner to the right, but never saw the spilled diesel in the road. The bike slid out from under me, the panniers hit the ground and then flipped the bike to high-side me off the other side. I went sliding along the road, feeling a bit confused at what had just happened. I remember hitting the road with my chin first, so thank goodness for protective gear! I had come down hard and needed a second to catch my breath and get my bearings straight. My bike was lying on the other side of the road and I walked over to pick it up so I could get it out of the road, I didn't want anyone hitting it. A man who had been standing right at the top saw the whole ordeal and came running down towards me.

"Are you okay", he wanted to know. I assured him that I was fine and asked him to please help me pick up my bike. He kindly did so and we pushed the bike to the side of the road so I could inspect it for any damage. Both bike and rider were ok. A few scratches and bruises on both of us, but nothing serious. I had a very bad ache in my left shoulder and ribs, down the left-hand side of my body but I didn't suspect anything was broken, maybe just badly bruised. I thanked the Samaritan for helping me out and got back on the bike again to make my way down the other side of the mountain, at a much slower pace.

Just before getting into Mbeya, I started picking up the pace a bit. The left-hand side of my body was killing me and I really just wanted to get to a place where I could have a hot shower and lie on a bed. As luck would have it, I was caught for speeding, literally just before town. Urgh. I was hurting and annoyed and really didn't feel like dealing with this now. I tried to play the sympathy card and explained to the Traffic Officer that I'd just been in a crash and that I was hurting and just trying to get to a hotel. It was my lucky day as the Officer took pity on me and let me go without a fine. Just outside of Mbeya, I found a hotel overlooking a massive roundabout which would lead me to Malawi the next morning. I went about getting some food and then booked myself a room. I had a hot shower, ate the food, popped some anti-inflammatory painkillers and promptly passed out.

I didn't' wake up until the next morning and when I did, getting up took a bit longer than usual. My body was aching all over, especially my left shoulder and it hurt when breathing, so I suspected some bruised ribs, although I was still convinced that it was just bumps and bruises, I figured that I would've known if something was broken. I slowly packed up and loaded the bike. Today was another border day and I would cross into Malawi. The original idea had been to never travel through Malawi but rather to make my way down way south, along the coastline in Tanzania and then to cross into Mozambique from there. But as it seemed that I attracted political unrest wherever I intended to travel to, RENAMO, the Mozambiquan National Resistance Force, had flared up again in Northern Mozambique. RENAMO is a militant group, guilty of numerous war crimes and crimes against humanity as part of their destabilization strategy in the country. I received loads of messages and emails from friends and people who were following my journey, suggesting that I try and give Mozambique a skip altogether. Obviously, this was not an idea of which I felt fond.

And so, I decided to enter Mozamabique through Malawi and then dodge most of the danger going on in Mozambique at that time.

My little Nikon Coolpix camera had broken in the crash, the day before, and so I had to rely on taking photos, with my phone only, for the duration of the remainder of the trip. Next stop: the Songwe border post between Tanzania and Malawi, which is about 110 kilometers from Mbeya. Arriving at the border, I first went about having some money changed. I usually changed money right at the border but, for some unbeknown reason, I chose differently this day. Mistake number one. A man approached me asking me how much I wanted to change. I told him and he returned with a wad of notes. The packs were divided into denominations of ten but, as a way to trick you, they quickly flick through the notes, counting in denominations of hundreds. I wasn't falling for it and argued with him that he had not given me enough. The argument started drawing some attention and, before I knew it, I had about 6 hagglers around me. Mistake number two is that I remained seated on the bike. This left me with little room for movement and, even though I was clutching my wallet for all my life, they still managed to make off with $150! Buggers!

More good news awaited me when I made it to the other side of the border, I was pulled over to have my insurance inspected. When I had bought third party insurance in Tanzania, I was advised that this was COMESA Insurance that would last me all the way to Mozambique. Turns out, it wasn't the insurance I needed and so I was fined and had to buy new insurance back at the border. An awesome day!

Luckily for me, I'd receive a little picker-upper only, a few minutes later, when passing fellow adventure riders on the road. We all immediately pulled over and turned back to say hello and it turned out that I knew these two guys, who were busy making their way north to Egypt on their Honda XL 650's. Jan-Lucas and his son, Bas de Vos, were embarking on an epic father-son journey and they still had so much with which to look forward. They had contacted me, some while ago, saying that they were planning this journey and asked for some information on the road conditions, Visa requirements, etc., for riding up to Egypt. I warned them about the scammers ahead at the border and gave them some contacts for on their journey up north and, in return, they gave me the name of a nice place to stay next to Lake Malawi. After about an hour of chit chat and taking photos, well wishes were exchanged and we were all on our separate ways again. This was a very pleasant surprise.

I would make my way to Nkata Bay, right next to the Lake, and stay at Makoya Village Beach Lodge, right on the water. The place is amazing! The perfect getaway haven for switching off, forgetting about life and just chilling out! I loved and enjoyed this place and could easily envisage just vegging there for a week, but I wanted to move on and get home, I was getting so close now! I was also well aware of the fact that if I rushed this last leg of the journey, I might regret it later on and so I tried to force myself to slow down just a tad.

So, from here, I would make my way down to the southern end of the Lake to stay at the Fat Monkey Lodge in Cape Maclear. Michnus and Elsabie Olivier, who I had recently mentioned had suggested I check this place out. They had travelled Africa before they started exploring Europe and had lots of valuable information and suggestions. You can check out their site at www.pikipikioverland.com

I figured I would pitch my tent this time round, seeing as I hadn't been using it a lot and I couldn't have picked a better time or place to do it!

I spent two blissful days at the Fat Monkey Lodge which, in my opinion, is THE place to go if you want to disappear from the world for a while and do nothing but sunbathing, swimming and eating. There are many amazingly awesome lodges along the lake and I will definitely return someday for a little holiday! While at the Fat Monkey, I met a whole lot of other interesting people busy with their own adventures. There was a Dutch couple in their 4x4, who'd been riding all over Southern Africa for a few months, a bunch of guys from London, who were doing a trip from South Africa up to Tanzania and then, Yves, a French cyclist with a very American accent (he'd spent a few years as a rickshaw rider in New York). He had cycled down the East Coast of Africa and was making his way down to Cape Town, after which, he'd be making his way up the West Coast from there. We immediately hit it off and became camp buddies. I really enjoyed my time relaxing at the Fat Monkey and my rest days were spent lying in, giving DAX a wash and generally just being lazy. Treasured time.

On the morning that I wanted to leave, the electricity for the whole area was out and so I couldn't pay with my Visa card. (First world problems, I know). Nevertheless, I had to pay for my accommodation somehow and was out of Malawian Kwacha. Yves offered to pay for me and then I could repay him when he got to South Africa, but I kindly declined his offer. It didn't want to have to take any of his money and possibly leave him in the lurch. I asked if they would accept US$, as I still had few single notes left. They luckily accepted this and so, I headed into the nearest town to draw some more money and have my bike filled with fuel. I asked around to find out whether there was another petrol station nearby and was told that the next town, with a petrol station and ATM machine, is about 50 kilometers away. I only had about 40 kilometers of fuel left and figured, if I went really slowly, I should be fine.

I made it to the next town and there, they had electricity. The next problem popped up though as I was unable to draw money from the ATM, it seemed like there was something wrong with my card. It HAD to work as I needed to pay for the fuel I had just put in my bike. I started feeling a little panicked and phoned my friend, Hanret, back home to ask if she could please phone my bank to find out what was wrong with my card. They checked it out and said that there was nothing wrong with my card and I had sufficient funds and that I should give it another try. Of course, this time it worked and, with that, I paid for the fuel and could now head for the border with Mozambique. I felt a bit like a doofus.

I still had about 250 kilometers to go, to make it to the border, and then another 370 kilometers, on top of that, to get to Tete in Northern Mozambique, where I'd be spending the night. Best I get a move on! I didn't want to have to ride around at night, especially not with the whole Renamo Resistance unrest that had broken out. I would be crossing the border into Mozambique just beyond a town called Mwanza in Malawi at the Mwanza/Zobue border control, between Malawi and Mozambique. It was a fairly quiet border and I was stamped out of Malawi and into Mozambique in no time. On the Mozambican side, a man approached me and I quickly figured out that he was a fixer, working this border, and he offered to help me have money changed to local currency. I thanked him for his offer but told him that it wouldn't be necessary. When I came out of the office from having my passport and Carnet stamped in Mozambique, the guy was still there, standing next to my bike. He was obviously desperate to get something out of me, so I gave him a Coca-Cola. With that I was now officially in Mozambique and had to ride fast to get to Tete. The first 60 – 80 kilometers of the road were being worked on though, so I had to make my way through endless detours that really slowed me down.

The rest of the road is a pretty good tarmac road though and so now, I could pick up the pace. It was nice and hot throughout the day with no signs of rain. By the time I reached Tete and crossed the Zambezi River into town, over the Tete Bridge, the sun had just begun to set. I had no idea where I was going to stay for the night and stopped at the first motel I could spot on the side of the road. The place was obviously under construction and a man standing outside the building was kind enough to suggest another motel/guesthouse across the road, on the left, directly after exiting the bridge. I found it easily enough and, although the owners couldn't speak any English, there was a South African man in the reception area, when I wanted to check in. He could speak Portuguese and helped me out, I had just about forgotten all my Portuguese by this stage. If you don't use it, you lose it.

The owner showed me to a room and helped me to carry my bags. The room was clean, with a shower and air conditioner. Perfect! After a shower, I went to hunt for some food. The South African guy was still around and offered to help me with whatever I needed. He showed me to a little, local restaurant, next to the river, where we ordered some food and I told him a bit of my story. He was working in Mozambique, a Construction Contractor. It was nice catching up with a fellow countryman and I was well aware of the fact that I was getting so close to home now, I could almost smell it!! (Not that I know what South Africa is supposed to smell like).

The next day, I would make my way from Tete to Chimoio, about 390 kilometers away. I'd spend the night in Chimoio, before braving 'The Red Zone'. I had only learned of the existence of this from the South African guy and then finding information online. It was basically an area of about 260 kilometers long, being attacked by the Renamo forces, so no civilian traffic was allowed on this road, without being accompanied by an armed convoy. Problem was, how would someone like me even guess where this convoy meets or what time they leave and where from? I asked around, once I arrived in Chimoio, but nobody seemed to have any information of value to me. And so, with that, I decided that I'd just gun it the next day and just not stop on this stretch of road! I filled my fuel pouches and would only stop in the event that I needed to refuel. How bad could it be, after all I'd been through, right? I know what you're thinking.

"So, you wouldn't take a risk going through Somalia but would take this risk going through Mozambique?" I know. I have no real explanation for this, other than I was so close to home and all I could think about was,

"Get out of my way, I'm coming home". I had home stretch fever. I'm coining that term!

The next morning, I was up early, packed and ready to hit the road. At first, it was awesome, so quiet, no traffic, no people at all actually! But, after two hundred kilometers of not seeing another soul, it started to feel a bit eerie. Like a ghost road that had been abandoned. After 300 kilometers, I needed to stop for a break to fill up with fuel. Still, no sign of a single soul around. I could just imagine how there were armed rebel soldiers lying in wait in the bushes behind me, feeling super confused and thinking to themselves, "What the hell is this girl doing"? That's what I would be thinking.

After I'd filled up, I got back on the road again. Finally, one of the armed convoys that was making its way up north, passed me. The convoy consisted of a Casper leading the charge, then an army truck with armed soldiers in the back, behind the Casper, with civilian vehicles in between and another army truck filled with soldiers, bringing up the rear. They totally pushed me off the road (thanks guys!) and the soldiers looked at me with total confusion in their eyes. I just carried on and, eventually, made it to the checkpoint before the Rio River, where I was met by another very confused Officer, who kept checking for 'more of me' behind me as I took my helmet off. He asked me why I was alone and why I didn't wait to ride with the convoy from Chimoio. I explained to him that I didn't know where to find the convoy or what time they would leave and so I carried on by myself. He seemed perplexed and told me that a convoy had just been shot to pieces the previous day and that I had just ridden through a very treacherous area. I was fine, so I didn't understand the fuss. I would understand a fuss being made if something had happened, but nothing had happened, so no need for a fuss. All I wanted to do is continue to my next destination.

The Officer told me that I would have to wait for him to radio his superior to get approval for me to carry on the rest of the way on my own. Otherwise. I'd have to wait for the next convoy heading so, but that they would advise me to not stop anywhere next to the road for anything or anyone. I promised I wouldn't stop and was allowed to continue.

Mozambique is also a pretty country. Fairly tropical with loads of greenery and the main road, leading through the country, is a good, tarmac road. People are mostly friendly, though I couldn't help but detect a tinge of underlying aggression in the locals. Like South

Africans. We are quite an aggressive nation, in general. That night, I stayed at the Sunset Lodge, near Inhambane. My friend, Kurt, who had helped me get DAX overland ready, before I set off on my journey, suggested the place. A beautiful place, right on the beach to rest my weary body.

Egypt – with friends from the Biker Zone in Cairo

Egypt – pyramids with Iysal and Hadeer

Egypt – Pyramids of Giza

Egypt – riding in Cairo

Egypt – Cairo welcome by the team from Biker Zone

Egypt – given to me by the Governor in Cairo

Egypt – Luxor

Egypt – Hurghada

Egypt – Aswan (The Nile)

Egypt – Ferry in Aswan

Sudan – Mazar in Wadi Halfa

Sudan – on the main road

Sudan – Obai finishes in Khartoum

Sudan – Camping next to the road

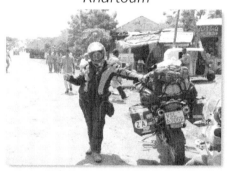

Entering Ethiopia

Ethiopia

Ethiopia

Ethiopia – so many people

345

Kenya – Hell Road

Kenya – Hell Road

Kenya – crossing the equator a second time

Kenya – visiting the David Sheldrick Elephant Sanctuary

Kenya – with Francois at Jungle Junction

Kenya – the very generous and kind Young family

Tanzania – Baobab Valley

Tanzania – on the road

Malawi – meeting Jan-Lucas and Bas de Vos on the road

Malawi – rode through a strange swarm of some kind of bug

Lake Malawi

Lake Malawi

Mozambique

Mozambique

CHAPTER 12

It was here that I started feeling ill. It felt like my body had had enough. The fall in Tanzania and the last couple of days' emotional, mental and physical stress and fatigue had seemed to catch up with me and, that night, my body broke out in an aggressive fever. I spent most of the night struggling to fall asleep, because my body was aching so badly and the fever had me feeling like I was on fire. And then, a thought hit me: MALARIA! Maybe it had finally got me!

The next day I would meet up with a South African friend in Matola, who had contacted me previously and offered me a place to stay when I made it to Maputo, Mozambique's capital. I kept telling myself that I just needed to make it there and then I could have myself tested for Malaria. I felt a bit better in the morning and actually had quite a pleasant ride down to Matola. Apart from being stopped by traffic police every now and again, I never infringed on any traffic laws and so they only stopped me because they could, sometimes, not even saying anything, just waving me down to stop and then they'd let me carry on again. Strange.

Then, about halfway to Matola, another disaster struck when the bolts, holding my bike's sub-frame together, broke. I pulled over on the side of the road and took off all my luggage and the bike's seat, to get to the problem. I was carrying spare bolts, though I didn't have a spare nut that would fit the bolt I needed, to fix the problem. Then, I remembered that I had carried a nut in my handbag, for over a year. It was a perfect fit and now, I finally had use for that nut! I put it all back together again, with a few cable ties as security and then carried on again. I smiled, thinking about how far I had come, mechanically, being able to fix stuff on my bike, it made me feel good.

I met up with fellow rider and South African, Ken Vaughan, just outside of town. He led me into town and to The Courtyard Moz, where I would be spending the evening. When they heard about my story, they very kindly offered for me to stay there at no cost. The generosity of people will always blow me away.

I told Ken that I wasn't feeling well and suspected that I might have malaria and so he took me to a local clinic to have myself tested. Luckily, the test came back negative and I was convinced that it was just pure fatigue. I had been through a lot and never stopped to really digest it maybe. Adrenal fatigue is a real thing and it could've had something to do with it, I don't know.

That evening, I was spoilt to dinner by Ken and his wife and a group of other South Africans, living in Matola. On the menu? PRAWNS, of course! Mozambique is famous for its prawns! I got to eat the best prawns in town and they were delicious!! I sat, regaling the people with some stories from my travels and also had butterflies in my stomach, knowing that this was my last night before I would be back on South African soil! The next day I would re-enter my homeland on my motorcycle, for the first time in a year and a half...

This was it. The final push to the finish line.

The next morning, I felt filled with so many emotions. Ken would ride with me to the South African border, crossing through Swaziland. There, a group of friends and followers were waiting to surprise me on the other side of the border and to welcome me back onto home soil! I was excited and very emotional. We crossed into Swaziland from Mozambique at the Mhlumeni post. It is, to date, the quietest border post I've passed through and, on this morning, it was only myself and Ken at the border, apart from Customs and Immigration Officials. As a result, our passports were stamped and we were through in a matter of seconds and free to continue to Oshoek, where I would cross back into South Africa.

Swaziland is a beautiful little country to ride in and I would've liked to have taken more time to explore the area, but as I said, I was suffering from home stretch syndrome. When we got to the border, I took my time. I didn't go into the Customs and Immigrations Office right away, I wanted to savour the moment. Ken stayed with me until I was ready and then went inside with me to have my paperwork stamped. I thanked Ken for his generosity and hugged him goodbye. He'd head back to Matola, while I carried on to the South African side of the border.

I slowly made my way to the other side and spotted the group of riders at the entrance, on the other side of the border. They cheered and whistled the moment they spotted me and this just really added to my emotional state. I went into the office to have my passport and Carnet de Passage stamped, for the very last time! Back outside, I handed my passport over for final checks and, when the Officer handed it back to me, he looked me in the eye and said

"Welcome home, Jo". I will never forget that moment for as long as I live and couldn't help bursting into tears. I was home! I made it back home! I rode over to the group, eagerly waiting for me to get to them and lots of hugs and photographs ensued. I felt so grateful for this group of people, some friends and some of them, who had never even met me before, who had come to welcome me back home.

This wasn't the end though and there was still some way to go down the coast, to get back to the spot from where I had left.

The celebrations started there and would, pretty much, continue all along the coastline until I reached the finish line. I had worked out an itinerary and posted it on a local riding forum, the Wild Dog. Before I knew it, plans had already been made and settled and I would be met by groups of riders before each town and accompanied down the coast, until we'd meet the next group, who would take over from the previous group and so on and so on. The human chain would continue all the way to the finish line!

My route back down to L'Agulhas would take me through Piet Retief, Durban, Port St Johns, East London, Port Elizabeth, George and, finally, Robertson, where I'd meet up with a group of riders for the annual 'Breede Bash', before being accompanied by a whole entourage of bikers, down to the southernmost tip of Africa.

I became a package, collected from the border and then carefully passed along by the adventure biking community, all the way down to the finish line.

It was beyond wonderful to see so many old friends again and making loads of new ones as I made my way from one town to the next. Every night was turned into a celebration, in anticipation of the grand finale. I met so many people and would have a gathering of dozens of people each night, in each town where I stayed.

There are so many people who went out of their way to make me feel like a winner. There are too many people to mention but some of the key players I would like to mention are:

Allan Tweddle, Anton Engelbrecht and Kean Maxwell Webster from Kwazulu-Natal,

Mike Stone and Jaco van Vuuren in East London,

Gerard Wolmarans and the group in Port Elizabeth

Renee Heyns and Vicky de Clercq, along with the group in George,

Piet and the gang in Worcester,

Jan de Beer and Roelf and Michelle du Preez.

There are so many other people, whose names I've left out and I'm sorry. But you know who you are and, to each and every one of you, I'd like to say a heartfelt thank you for all your love and support.

It was both awesome, and a tad surreal, being back in South Africa, officially. There was so much familiarity after so much exploring of the unknown and the unknown becoming the familiar. It's like waking up from a dream that you've had all your life. The unfamiliar has become what you're most comfortable with, and everything seems upside down.

Those last few days flew by but I savoured every moment of riding into Durban, in the pouring rain, with Allan, Kean, Anton and the guys; the braai they organized at Ryder Motorrad and the talk I gave there, then having them accompany me to Port St Johns, one of my favourite places in South Africa and the place where I had that weird, sensual, full body massage by two girls, remember? Meeting up with Mike and Jaco on route to East London and stopping for milkshakes! Having this massive group of people come together at Gerard's house that night, in Port Elizabeth and having a blast telling them all about my trip and answering a gazillion questions. Meeting up with the group from

George and blowing out candles on a cake in the shape of the African continent with 'Welcome back Jo', that the girls had made for me. Thank you to each and every person who came out to ride with me or meet me at the many gatherings on my journey down to the finish line. I appreciate each and every one of you!

I savoured every single moment leading up to the conclusion of my journey, knowing how long I had dreamt this dream. How long I had pictured the day that I'd finish this mammoth journey I had set out on, as a fragile, scared and insecure girl. I was grateful for all the hardships and challenges faced along the way. The ups and downs. The people who had touched my heart along the way and will forever live in my memories. The places I'd seen, the extraordinary moments I had experienced and the person I had become.

On the final day, I got up early that morning and broke down my tent for the very last time. I had a mashup of emotions running through me, from excitement to happiness, anticipation, sadness, love, joy, gratitude, nostalgia... you name it.

I had no idea what to expect. I had waited so long for this particular moment. I had visualized what it might be like a million times before and suddenly, had no expectations of what it should be like, I felt completely overwhelmed but didn't really show it.

The time finally came to get on with it. A group of riders would accompany me down to L'Agulhas and more people would join along the way. I had been informed that the Agulhas Tourism Office had organized something for me, before I headed down to the marker to, officially, celebrate the end of my journey.

I was instructed by Agulhas Tourism to wait at the Caltex petrol station, situated on the right as you enter Struisbaai. Here, an NSRI (National Sea Rescue Institute) vehicle would meet up with me and the group, to lead us to the lighthouse where representatives of the Aghulhas Tourism Office would be waiting for me. The final moment would then be when I would make my way down to the marker, to stand where I had left from, more than a year ago.

When we pulled in to that petrol station, I started to feel really emotional. It is so difficult to explain what it feels like to have gone through so much and to, actually, finally succeed in finishing what I had started, no matter what. It had been a massive life-changing journey of epic proportions! Before I left, I suffered from severe social phobia, was afraid of just about any social interactions, in so much pain and so many doubts and insecurities. And here I was, 45 000 kilometers later, I had made it!

Once the NSRI vehicle arrived, we followed it to the lighthouse and here, members of the board of Agulhas Tourism waited for me with a certificate to say that I had officially circumnavigated the African continent, to successfully reach the southernmost tip of Africa. As we made our way through town, down to the marker, I started noticing signs outside the local shops and restaurants, with the words,

"WELCOME HOME, JO" and "WELCOME BACK JO", written on them. This was it, the final stretch. In my helmet I was singing Brandi Carlisle's 'The Story' to myself. In my side mirror, I could see this long line of bikes following me. As we neared the spot, I looked back and noticed that the group of bikes had pulled back behind me to allow me to savour this historical and special moment for myself. I was sobbing in my helmet and it was like 29 years' of emotions came rushing through me.

The guys helped me manoeuvre my bike to get it to the final marker and there, I parked my DAX again, from where we had started our magical journey together, 45 000 kilometers, through 28 countries, over 18 months. We finally did it!

I had become the first woman in history to have circumnavigated the entire African continent on a motorcycle, on her own!

The group surrounded me and champagne was being sprayed all over the show. I was still sobbing and trying to process what I had just achieved! Six and a half years since I decided that I wanted to become the first woman to travel around Africa, on my own, I had done it.

I had learned and grown so much along the way and standing there, looking at the people around me, the thing that really overwhelmed me was a gigantic realization.

I wasn't afraid of anything anymore.

It was the best day of my life!

Welcome Home – Swaziland Border

Welcome Home – Durban

Welcome Home – East London

Welcome Home – Port Elizabeth

Welcome Home - George

THE FINALE!

Special Thanks

I didn't make it on my own, though. There were so many people along the way who, literally, saved my life at times and, to them, I would like to say thank you. Thank you, from the bottom of my heart and with all the love I possess. For each and every person who had a part in my journey, you made a difference in my life, no matter how big or small a part you may have had to play, I will forever remember it and be thankful for having had the privilege of meeting you.

As a special thank you: To the Angolan Government for their help and incredible generosity.

To my good friend Hanret. You are amazing. You are my family and I will always be grateful for the mammoth amount of effort you put into helping me live my dream! I am immensely grateful for you and love you dearly.

And Elise, you helped me from the outset and always believed in me! Thank you for being Aunty E and for always being there for me. I love you and cherish our friendship.

Epilogue

Since completing her journey around Africa, Jo has become the first female Brand Ambassador for BMW Motorrad South Africa and, later on, qualified as one of only 4 (at the time) internationally accredited female motorcycle off-road instructors. She pioneered the way to introducing the first-ever female team to an international event, hosted by BMW Motorrad each year, called the GS Trophy and took part in the event as the first ever female Marshal.

Jo now runs her own business called 'Jo Rust Adventures', offering motorcycle off-road training and bespoke adventure motorcycle tours in South Africa. (www.jorustadventures.com)

Jo is also a motivational keynote speaker, who has spoken to a myriad of audiences ranging from schools to big corporate functions and international conventions. You can find more information, or book Jo as a speaker by visiting: www.jorust.com.

As for Jo's fight with depression and anxiety, she was diagnosed with Bipolar II Disorder, in 2017 and is now an advocate for mental health, addressing stress, depression and anxiety in the workplace and in everyday life, through her talks. She plans on studying Psychology and to, ultimately, practice as a Clinical

Psychologist – while retaining a spark of madness as the girl who rode around Africa on her own.

Printed in Great Britain
by Amazon